from

Mrs Thos. P. Bryan

October 19. 1940 –

Plays of Clare Boothe

The Women (1936)

Kiss the Boys Goodbye (1938)

Margin for Error (1939)

EUROPE IN THE SPRING

EUROPE *in the* SPRING

CLARE BOOTHE

ALFRED · A · KNOPF

NEW YORK 1940

 Manufactured in the United States of America. Published simultaneously in Canada by The Ryerson Press.

PUBLISHED SEPTEMBER 16, 1940
FIRST AND SECOND PRINTINGS BEFORE PUBLICATION
THIRD PRINTING, OCTOBER 1940

For H. R. L.

WHO UNDERSTOOD WHY

I WANTED TO GO

SPRING SONG

OR, RETORT COURTEOUS

"When the crocus blossoms," hiss the women in Berlin,
"He will press the button, and the battle will begin.
When the crocus blossoms, up the German knights will go,
And flame and fume and filthiness will terminate the foe." . . .

"When the crocus blossoms, not a neutral will remain;
All the happy Balkans will bless the Führer's reign;
And half the horrid English, repenting of their sin,
Will soon, they say, be welcoming Gauleiter Göring in."

"When the crocus blossoms," hiss the women, "breaks the war."
But can it be that we have heard some hint of this before?
When the first chrysanthemums were burning red and gold,
Something very similar, I fancy, was foretold.

Still, when the cold world wakes again, and sings in sap and sod,
When the very rat salutes the noblest work of God,
Herr Hitler and his cohorts may *send death to me and you—*
For it's just the sort of silly thing that silly man would do.

A. P. H. in *Punch,* London, February 14, 1940

INTRODUCTION

YOU MUST UNDERSTAND I am not a historian nor a philosopher, nor an economist nor a political columnist nor even a professional journalist. I am just a curious American and sometime scribbler (of plays) who happened to be in Europe all this spring, and who lived like everybody else there in the invisible shadow of the Blitzkrieg that has now almost destroyed it.

So in this book you will find no exhaustive historical résumé of the political and diplomatic plots that resulted in surrender, no detailed journalistic study of the effects of German propaganda on Europe's nervous system, no exposé of fifth-columnism, no solid economic blueprint with long ladders of percentages and figures of capitalistic versus totalitarian finance, and certainly no broad philosophical thesis of Spenglerian Decline or World Revolution. This is just a confused, hastily written eye- and ear-witness report, a sad sheaf of notes on a few sad cities inhabited by many sad, confused people in two hopelessly confused nations.

Because I had no intention when I went to Europe of writing a book at all, I kept no exhaustive notes. A few conversations jotted down on the backs of envelopes, some personal letters, and news clippings torn out of papers whimsically and often then thrown away, and a wafer diary in which only appointments were noted were all that I brought from Europe. Therefore it is a little vague as to dates. I remember in Paris after the invasion nobody ever knew what day it was or how many actual hours had elapsed since the last awful thing had happened. Let me see, you said, was that before or after the break-through at Sedan? Or was that the day the Bulge reached Arras? The daily habits which give us our sense of time were all brutally and irrevocably broken. You made no dates for the morrow. You followed no routine, or a skeleton one, had no plans, no plans at all for the future. You ate, you dressed, you walked, you did the chore or deed or duty the moment demanded. But pity, anger, frustration, uncertainty, the extraordinary feeling that tomorrow, tonight, an hour, might bring sudden death to those you loved, or to yourself, blurred all remembrance of place and people and occasion. You lived in a timeless world, punctuated at timeless intervals by sleepless nightmare nights. Only the progress of the battle out there, or the air-raids here, were matters for timing. In this Blitzkrieg world even the familiar faces of friends lost their meaning. Often you couldn't quite remember who had told you what, even an hour before, because the "who" had become so curiously unimportant to you. All faces were like the dim faces which a dying man sees at his bedside when his eyes are fixed on Life alone, or perhaps on Eternity.

This was even a little true before the invasion. Looking back on it now, I see that from March until June I lived not in time and place with people, but in an atmosphere of War, which echoed with strange voices, coming from half-focused faces. No one, or anything he did or said, became vivid or memorable unless he said something or did something that gave the war itself (the only reality) more special meaning. Or perhaps I subconsciously knew that many of the people I saw I should never, never see again, so subconsciously I listened to them and watched them as phantoms. This feeling of being in an unpleasant dream-world accounts for the fact that I am unable in this book to give more than occasionally the names of places, and the dates of time, and who said what to me. It also accounts for the fact that, except as the unusually beautiful weather itself lent a vivid surrealist note to the black goings-on in Europe, and that I had long ago perceived Paris to be beautiful and London splendid, and felt them still to be so, I did not really look at them with my whole eyes, nor consider them with my whole mind. So you will not even find in these pages much literary description.

This book is a mood, a mood of uneasiness and bitterness and pity and doubt that I brought back from Europe.

You will say all that happened in Europe in the spring was too solemn, too significant, and certainly too complicated for you to write about it so formlessly—and so hastily. You are right, of course.

But when I returned to America and saw my country again, and heard it, and felt its mind and temper a little, I said: it is later than you think. I must tell you—tell you badly and hastily, with unconsidered phrase and unedited thought, in tumbled unbalanced prose, sometimes too scanty, sometimes too prolix, often repetitious, making shallow or unfair judgments as I write, sometimes correcting them a paragraph later, only to make more on the next page—still, I must tell you. Because if one phrase, one thought, one little incident, one question raised or answered, can make you think even a little more clearly or a little more anxiously about America, then this queer book will be beyond literary criticism and censure. It will have served its only purpose.

I know you cannot fail to understand much that is in this book, because in political matters, like yours, my comprehension is very much that of an average American, and I have written it from an average point of view in average language. If you had been in Italy and in England and France in March and April and May you probably would have seen many of the same people that I saw, asked many of the same questions I asked, and got most of the same answers that I got. And on the strength of what you saw and heard you probably would have reached the same conclusions I reached.

In early spring they were still, as you will see, quite optimistic. But, being an average American, when the bombs began to fall uncomfortably close to you (as they did to me in Brussels and Paris) you would have thought first of yourself and then of your family, and both thoughts would have counselled your hasty departure from Europe. Whereupon you'd have clutched your dear red American passport firmly to your breast, gathered together your remnants of luggage, and, your curiosity about "what was going to happen in Europe" quite satisfied for the time being, you'd have got back as best you could to your native country, revising rapidly in transit many of your more optimistic conclusions. And once at home in physical security but mental torment, you also would then have begun to ask yourself: *Is the same thing going to happen in America?*

Reading this book over now that it is written, I am heartsore. I can see now that no matter how passionately I may wish it otherwise, much of it reads like "an indictment of democracy." And it makes me sick in my soul, it almost paralyses my mind, even to imply in it that because democracy failed in France, it will therefore probably fail in its last stronghold—America. I don't really believe that any more than you do.

What I do believe is that France and England failed democracy, and that we are in danger of doing likewise. But I also believe there are still brains enough, patriotism enough, idealism enough, objectivity, initiative, unselfishness, youthful guts and tradition enough left in this dear country to throw the lie in Hitler's teeth about that "failure of democracy." And I believe that for our own lives' and souls' sake, and for those of our children, we will soon embark wisely and decently on the policy that will divorce in the future the two words which Hitler married in the blood of Austria, Spain, Czechoslovakia, Poland, Norway, Holland, Belgium, and France, and in the cold terrified sweat of all the "little neutrals": Decadence and Democracy.

So with the passionate conviction that we will not also fail democracy, I can without further apology or preamble paint the picture of lethal inertia, woeful ignorance, blind patriotism, corroding jealousies, mortal miscalculation, and criminal complacency which characterized the background of Hitler's First Spring Blitzkrieg—which is the same background we are all living in today here in America.

Greenwich, Connecticut
July 1940

CONTENTS

EUROPE IN THE SPRING

ONE

Hard questions must have hard answers.

Plutarch's *Lives*

IN NEW YORK, on February 10, I made a decision. I decided to go to Europe and see about the war. Nominally I went as a "journalist," because if you didn't have some "business reason," the State Department just wouldn't let you go. If I had said to the State Department what I said to my family: "Look, for my own peace of mind I've just got to find out whether this war is our business or not, and I believe that Europe's the place to find it out," the State Department would have said:

"My dear woman, the U. S. government doesn't care a hoot about your mind. We passed the Neutrality Act to protect your body, so you stay right where you are. Read Walter Lippmann, read Dorothy Thompson, read Raymond Clapper, read General Johnson—and, for heaven's sake, look at the Gallup poll!"

But that was the real trouble: Lippmann and Thompson and Clapper and Johnson all disagreed violently with one another, and even more violently with the Gallup poll.[1] And besides, because I am an American, what happened to America was certainly going to happen to me (and *something* was going to happen to America as a result of the decisions all Americans took about that war). I felt very strongly that I was well within my rights, as one individual citizen of a free country, in wanting to make up my own mind. It didn't seem to me then (and it doesn't now) that that was a very unusual point of view. But if I had tried to explain that to the State Department, adding that I could afford to go, and that I was perfectly willing to travel at my own risk, they would have said: "Your point is nicely taken, but please be more pragmatic about it: Suppose every American who sincerely and honestly wanted to find out about the war just whipped off to Europe like that, what would happen? Why, there'd be thousands of them over there and sooner or later they'd run into a mess of bombs and get killed, and then everybody in America would grow indignant and say: 'Those lousy Germans, massacring our American citizens!' and the first thing you know we'd be dragged into Europe's war! No matter how interested individual Americans may be in finding out the truth, the nation is much more interested in just keeping out, you see."

Therefore instead of going as an average American in quest of the truth, which is how Americans have gone to Europe's wars for a hundred and thirty-four years, I had

[1] The Gallup poll for February showed that 68 per cent of Americans thought we would stay out of the war because: (1) the United States learned its lesson in the last war; (2) the nation would have everything to lose, nothing to gain. Asked: "If it appears that Germany is defeating England, should the U. S. declare war on Germany?" 71 per cent of the people said "No." *Fortune's* poll showed that of 85 per cent of the people who thought we might get into the war, 38 per cent thought it would be because business interests or the stupid foreign pol-

to go as a "journalist." So I made a contract with a national magazine to write about what I saw in Europe.

But although I was in Italy, France, and England all the months of March, April, and May—until the very day of the invasion of the Lowlands, I never wrote a single word. That was for three reasons: first, I quickly found out I couldn't get past the Italian, French, and English censors the truth as I saw it on any given day; second, the very things I perceived to be "true" one night often seemed lies that only an idiot would swallow "holus bolus" by the following morning, so often did yesterday's hopes become tomorrow's fears, and sunrise certainties, midnight improbabilities. And third (and most important), I wasn't really a journalist: I tried very often, but I just wasn't interested in writing "news." I was really interested in what people I met were saying and feeling. I was interested far less in events themselves than in the effect they had on people's hearts and minds. Above all, I was interested in how *I* felt about how they felt, which is a highly emotional and egoistic approach that would disqualify anybody at once as an "objective journalist." So although I went in all sincerity as a "journalist," that turned out to be just a convenient fiction for the State Department, so that if I got killed, I wouldn't be a *casus belli*, which, as I say, is something that even in my most ambitious moments I never dared dream I might be.

When I decided to go to Europe, I didn't know at all how I really felt about the war. During the autumn and

icy of our government engineered it, 14 per cent because of Allied propaganda, 34 per cent because we hated Hitler. 1.2 per cent thought we must help the democracies. If Germany won, 61 per cent thought she would be a threat to us, 27 per cent thought she wouldn't be, the rest didn't know.

early winter I had had whole days of feeling that it just *might* be our business. War news occupied almost the whole first three or four pages of the daily papers. The columnists to a man were dedicated to its discussion. And nobody I knew talked about anything else: just Hitler and Chamberlain and Finland and the Maginot. Even more than about Roosevelt. I tried very often, but it was impossible to switch the conversation from the war.

Many were the nights in autumn and early winter that I sat up until one or two in the morning arguing with two, four, six, eight friends about the war. Now, a group of friends arguing and interrupting and contradicting and often talking all at once doesn't talk in clear neat paragraphs, developing one point at a time the way columnists and lecturers and platform debaters do. So these conversations were very scrambled and heated, and one person said one thing and another something else, and a third disagreed flatly with both, and a fourth said: "That point is not consistent with your first," and then somebody would say: "Never mind the first point, the real point is what I'm about to say." But considering that everybody contradicted everybody else, the thing that was so remarkable about most of these conversations I had with my friends about the war was that they always wound up with nearly everybody saying: "But of course the war is none of our business." I'd never in my life before heard so many people talk so long about something that was absolutely none of their business. That didn't seem natural. Maybe, I thought, we've become a nation of kibitzers and busybodies hanging over the Atlantic back fence just gabbing on and on about our neighbours' family brawl. But that was a humiliating admission. Or maybe, I thought, we're just being wise: trying intelligently to analyse what we're going to stay out of—though usually people aren't interested in what they're going to stay out of, but only what they're going to get into. But when I said that, everybody retorted: "Why, naturally we're interested. We want to see the Allies win, don't we?" (That's how these scrambled conversations always began.)

"Why do we?" I asked.

"Why?" they all said, patient and patronizing.

"Why, because European democracy is at stake!" I answered. "Isn't that pretty important?"

"Yes," they said, "to them it is, but not to us. We've got a wonderful democracy of our own, which is in a terrible mess. We have to think about that and not about Europe's brawl."

I asked: "Then why don't we stop *talking* about Europe's brawl?"

"Don't be superficial," somebody else always said. "How can anybody talk about anything else, with a terrible war, like that about to break out right here in front of us—a war which might spread all over the world?"

So then I said: "Look, if that is all we can think and talk about, it really might be our business, don't you suppose? And if there is a danger of its spreading all over the world—?"

And somebody always interrupted: "It won't spread here unless we deliberately stick our noses into it."

And I said: "Isn't it just possible it will spread faster if we turn our backs on it?"

Then they all said, very crossly: "What? Do you want us to risk our prosperity, or depression (or whatever the hell it is we've got—but we like it), and the lives of our brave boys, and all that gold we've got buried down in Whatchamaddie, to save Europe for the French Sidewalk Café and the British Week-end? We did that the last time.

What did we get out of it?" (When they put it that way, you had to say no, so you said it.)

"And besides," somebody would go on, "Europe's been having these wars for hundreds of years, and doesn't England always win them?"

I said: "But suppose this time she doesn't?"

A couple of hours later, after everybody counted up all the Nazi barrels of oil and tightened the North Sea blockade and brought about a political and economic collapse in Germany, just by making pencil marks all over the tablecloth, they all agreed: "So *how* can England lose? You must be pro-German!"

"All right," I said, "if you're *sure* the Allies have got it, hands down?"

And they said: "Exactly! The thing for us to do is to keep our own country strong and rich (in spite of the fact that F. D. R.'s practically ruined it) and to guard this last outpost of democracy (which a third term is going to destroy anyway) so that when European democracy goes down the drain-pipe we'll be going great guns over here and can help bankrupted Europe get on its feet again."

"You mean," I asked, "we're going to lend them the money to get started over again?"

"No," somebody always said, "why should we be the suckers again? We'll just set them a fine moral example—or sell them the things they need."

And if I said: "But if they are bankrupted, how can they pay for them unless we lend them the money?" somebody always replied: "Now wait a minute, you don't understand international banking and finance," which was true. So I always said, "Please don't try to explain it to me, I want to go back to 'democracy.' You said the Allies were going to win. Now you say European democracy is going down the drain-pipe."

"Of course," somebody said, "it's going to be a long and bitter and exhausting war, so *no matter who wins, democracy in Europe is finished!*" (It started off just being at stake, but at this point it was always finished.)

"Well," I said, "if European democracy is finished *either* way, what difference does it make to us who wins?"

"Oh, you're an idealist, aren't you?" somebody would always inquire. "Just be realistic for a change. First, if Hitler wins, he'll be harder to do business with, and second, he'll try to mop us up next."

Then I'd ask: "But if he can do business with us, why should he try to mop us up?"

Then somebody else would laugh, and say, "You don't understand the economics or dynamism of Nazism; you can't really do business with those boys long. He's got to try to mop us up!"

"And will he?" I asked.

"Of course not," they all replied, very indignant. "How will he get here?"

"Why, across the ocean," I'd say.

They'd remark: "Well, that's thinking a long way off. But why do you suppose we're building such a big navy?"

"Are we building a big navy?" I'd say.

"Are we? We've appropriated millions for it," somebody always replied very happily.

"Well, I do hope we won't have to use it," I'd say.

"Oh, we won't, if the British win," somebody answered.

"Oh," I said, "are the British fighting so we won't have to?" When you said that, everybody got very ugly indeed.

"Listen," they said, "you just want to get this country

into a foreign war. And we don't want a war with *anybody*. Look at Japan: slaughtering the poor Chinese and insulting us and shoving us all over the Pacific! Do we get tough about that? No! We go right on selling them scrap and oil."

"You mean we are appeasing the Japanese?" I put in.

"Of course not," somebody always said. "We can lick them any time. It's only appeasement if you are playing for time to get armed."

"Well," I would say, "that makes appeasement sound rather reasonable. Perhaps when Chamberlain and Daladier appeased Hitler—"

"Chamberlain and Daladier!" (That always made them mad.) "Appeasement was wrong for them, because they had to make a stand somewhere, and the best place to make a stand is in the other fellow's country. If they had fought for democratic Czechoslovakia, Czechoslovakia would have fought for them."

I said: "Then, why don't we make a stand now, against Japan, and let democratic China fight for us?"

So somebody replied: "You're being idealistic again. The real reason we don't want to fight Japan is that Japan is our third largest customer, and we need our foreign trade like hell just now."

"Who are the other two?" I asked.

"France and England."

"Oh, that's too bad," I answered, "because if Hitler wins or Europe just collapses, will they be able to buy anything from us?"

"Probably not," they said, a little sourly. "But the loss of our foreign trade isn't really going to ruin us. We are a pretty self-sufficient nation."

Then I naturally said, "But if we don't really need our two biggest customers, why do we need so like hell our much smaller trade with Japan?"

"The real reason we appea–go on selling to Japan," they replied, "is that until we see who's going to win in Europe, we can't risk a war in the Pacific."

I said: "I thought you said before that the Allies were *certainly* going to win?"

Then they were very patient indeed. "Now, please understand us, our position is very clear: we are willing to do business with anyone who is willing to do business with us —on a strictly cash-and-carry basis, of course. All we ask is to be decently let alone to work out our own problems."

"But if Hitler wins—" I said.

"You don't listen, do you, when people talk to you? We told you in the beginning, the Allies are going to lick Hitler."

"Oh," I said, "so you did, that's wonderful."

"What's so wonderful about it? The Allies are only defending their own vital interests, and that is exactly what *we're* going to do!"

At this point somebody always said: "You are *all* wrong. The whole war is a phony. Nobody is going to fight over there. The Allies can't because they know a long war is the end of the capitalistic system and democracy in Europe. Hitler won't because he knows he's sure to lose. They're both stalling. You'll see, Hitler will sue for peace by Christmas."

"Will the Allies talk peace with him then?" I asked.

Everybody always said: "They are damn fools if they do. . . ."

Now, although I thought, too, that the Allies were going to win, conversations like this still left me very, very confused because they did not help me to decide whether democracy in Europe and the awful peril it was in really mattered to America or not.

On Saturday, February 24, I sailed for Naples, one of only seventy-five cabin-class passengers. As we stood on deck, and the ship swung into the river, everybody waved to friends on the pier. All around me I heard people calling: "Good-bye!" "*Auf Wiedersehen!*" "*Au revoir*," and "*A rivederci!*" But it was not like any sailing I had ever made before, because nobody on the pier yelled back: "Oh, boy! Give my love to Fouquet's" or "Toodleoo, see you on jolly old Bond Street," and down below on the dock you could see women and men who were really crying very hard. As we nosed into the river from the slip, everyone stood on deck, looking very quietly at the people who waved fluttering white handkerchiefs, herded in a solid safe group under the American flag that floated fair and lazily over the pier of the United States Lines. When the flag was out of sight, the passengers one by one began to drift away from the rail and go to their cabins. They were mostly very serious-looking middle-aged men, and a few women. I remember, there was not a single young arm-in-arm couple. You could see right away that everybody on this ship was travelling for a good reason. Nobody looked gay, because the only time travellers are really gay is when they are travelling for no good reason at all.

There was a tall man with a long lean face, leaning on the rail, next to me. He said:

"Things are going to be a lot different before any of us see that skyline again." You could hear he was from the West somewhere.

"Yes," I said, "they're going to be a lot worse."

The tall man smiled patiently.

"Not just *worse.* I said: different. The world is all of a piece—or it isn't."

He jabbed the stem of his pipe in the direction of the great grey soaring city that was disappearing in the cold February mist. "These are the good old days now," he said. Then he smiled and tipped his hat a little awkwardly and went off to his cabin.

I was just about to go down to my cabin too, and fuss about with my bottles and bags, when I saw rounding the deck toward me a young woman in a very chic hat, with two tall feathers that whipped and tugged at their moorings as though they were in a frantic hurry to fly back to Paris.

This woman turned out to be a friend of mine, Margaret Case, who is an editor of *Vogue.*

"Oh, hello," I said, very, very pleased. "Where are you going?"

"Darling! To the Paris collections," she said, and we pressed cheeks and kissed off in the air so our lipsticks wouldn't smear.

"Oh, are there collections?" I said. "I'm so glad!"

"Yes," she said, carefully unstraightening her hat, "the French spirit—indomitable.[2] Of course, they're mostly for the American buyers now."

Then she told me a terrible story about how a group of American buyers who had landed at Genoa in December (thirty very chic women with the usual amount of excess peace-time luggage) were put off the train at the French border and spent a most insanitary and uncomfortable night on a snow-covered platform in the pitch dark. This

[2] As to this she was right. Some of the French couturières reopened their salons in German-occupied Paris in July, in preparation for showing their winter collections.

episode had for a little while discouraged other New York buyers from going to Europe. "But that," she said, "was at the beginning of the war, when things were bad. Now everything's getting more normal." Still, she felt the war more keenly than practically any American I had met at home. She said:

"Oh, you don't know how the war has hit clothes!" Fashion, she thought, would become a very different thing in America if the French influence disappeared. She thought that would be a real loss to American women, who would then fall into all sorts of garment errors and perhaps become very dowdy and comfortable, like the German or English women, who have never exposed themselves to the spirit of France as Americans have. She thought American fashions owed, if not everything, very nearly everything to France, and that we ought to consider that when we thought about isolationism. I said:

"Do you really think we ought to die to make the world safe for Schiaparelli?"

She twinkled. "Oh, I don't know," she said, "men of all nationalities have been willing to die for women turned out by Schiaparelli." [3]

She was worried about her excess baggage, because of this story about the buyers. She had an enormous number of things that her friends had sent to the boat for her to give their friends in France, because they couldn't be sure they'd get to Europe by the mails. She had a big box of monogrammed paper napkins for Lady M– in Paris, who was determined to keep up her spirit and go right on giving buffet luncheons, but couldn't use her lace cloths any more

[3] When Miss Case left Paris in early April, her ardent interest in clothes had definitely waned. She found herself writing long and passionate articles on those far from fashionable folk, the French refugees.

because they were stored with the silver in the bombproof cellar. Also a bottle of Vicks nose-drops for Mr. P–, six pairs of elastic panty-girdles for La Duchesse D–, a big box of peanut brittle for a man with a passion for peanut brittle in the *Vogue* office, piles of American silk stockings, which are called "French" when we buy them, a big bag of sugar, and two hundred pounds of coffee, for friends in Italy, and a heavy carton of "sweet" Victrola records, which the purser told her would be confiscated at the border. (That took only one thing off her mind.)

"All these things you can't get over there now," she said. "They think it's terribly annoying! They still want to buy them, but the government is just importing things for war."

I said: "I suppose it's also quite annoying to panty-girdle and peanut-brittle boys who want to sell them over there."

We began to walk around the deck, in a listless fashion. Walking ahead of us were a woman and a child. I heard them talking German. The woman was very thin, with bright red spots of colour on her cheeks, and the little girl was very thin, like a funny little bird, and she wore thick glasses. The mother held her hand. They walked slowly. The child was not skipping. Then, as we passed them, I saw the woman was Jewish. I wondered where and to what they could possibly be returning. There was nobody else on deck but a man with a high stiff collar and a beret who walked very heavily with his nose in a fat book. Then we went and had tea in the Palm Court. There were about twenty men, who were reading books, turning the pages very, very slowly, and several women, knitting with dark brown and grey wool. The orchestra played some classical music. It sounded so very sad, I wished they'd stop it. Presently they did, and began to play *In the Morning, No*, very swingy. I saw right away that that jarred on everyone's nerves even more than the classical music. A man with a French-looking moustache got up abruptly and shrugged and slammed his book shut and disappeared. A young American–wearing well-polished shoes and silk socks and looking reasonably happy–looked up and smiled at both of us foolishly. We didn't smile back because this was only the first day on board, so he looked sheepishly at his highly polished shoes and ordered a whisky. In another corner was a long-toothed man with a short scrubby moustache that grew upwards. He turned to a flat-shoed woman he was with and honked through the bridge of his nose: "Let's clear out of here. Too gay, what? Ping-pong?" It was very depressing. We went into the bar, to see if that was any more cheerful. It was a little. In a corner, under a bad mural of *The Winning of the West*, a group of very well-dressed men sat, on leather chairs around a circular oak table, drinking rounds of Scotch and soda. Most of them were talking very loudly not with but at one another, and each as he talked laughed at the last thing he had said, but not at the others.

The *Vogue* editor said: "Those must be the oil men. The stewardess said that there were a lot of important oil men on board. I hope we can meet some of them. They must know what's going to happen in this war. So many people say oil is the answer to everything."

I replied: "If it is, that would be wonderful, because then I would know what I came to find out and could turn right around and take the next boat home from Naples."

There was a broad burst of laughter from one of the oil men, who had said something he thought was hilarious. Then he got up from the table and went over to the slot machine in the corner and took out a big handful of quarters and began to drop them in one by one while the others watched him, spellbound. There was a series of clangs as little pictures of pineapples and cherries and pears and apples showed through the little window of the machine. He deliberately made a face like a village idiot and held his open hand under the money slot expectantly. When all his coins were gone, his hand was still empty. He pretended he had been hit in the solar plexus and staggered against the machine.

"Oh, boy," he said, "what a gyp! What a world! Now you fellows try it!"

Then they all got up, fishing through their pockets, and came over to huddle and weave around the clanging machine. I said to the *Vogue* editor: "I don't think they know the answer to anything." It was very depressing.

We left the bar.

"I'm going to send a radio to my family saying it's a very safe trip so far," I remarked.

We went to the cable room. I wrote my cable, and while the *Vogue* editor was writing hers, I picked up a little pamphlet that was lying on the desk. It was printed by the American Cable Companies and was called *A Summary of World Censorship*. It listed every country in the world. It began with Ægean Islands, Afghanistan, Albania, and went through dozens and dozens of countries, winding up with Union of South Africa, Yemen, Zanzibar, Zululand. "Well," I thought, "it's after all a very big world, and, cheerio, a lot of it isn't fighting." But then I read the cable instructions. I saw there was only one country in the world where there was not at that time censorship of codes or cipher, or language restrictions of some kind. And you were warned in the pamphlet that your cables in many of the countries might never be delivered ("Sent at sender's risk"). To Poland and Czechoslovakia, of course, all cable contacts were cut. It said that only to the United States of America could you send what you wanted and be sure that it would reach the eye it was intended for. I thought: "Everybody says this is the great age of communications, but what's so wonderful about that if you can't use them? If you can't any longer send a cable to a friend (if you had one there) in Cocos Island, Sarawak, or Iran, saying: 'I des miss oo dreful orful, signed Honey child,' without exposing him to the suspicion of being an *agent provocateur* or a spy, then the whole world must somehow be mixed up in the war." I remembered what the tall man at the rail had said a few hours ago: "The world is all of a piece—or it isn't." It was very depressing.

Then we went down to our cabins. The passageways were deserted, except for the gently smiling white-uniformed stewards and stewardesses who padded about delivering a few baskets of fruit and flowers, closing cabin doors behind them softly. It looked and felt a little like the corridors of a hospital. At her door the *Vogue* editor said in a pained, remote voice: "I'm not really dressing for dinner. Just my long black Chanel. I think anything else would be—well, inappropriate."

"I'll wear my old black lace," I said.

In my cabin, while I jammed red roses and orchids into inadequate tasteless vases, I thought: "Well, here we are on a big, handsome American ship, with a big American flag painted on its side, and still everybody is so melancholy or quiet or tense, just as if we might be torpedoed, which is foolish." But I knew what the truth was. Not only were we all going away from safety, going to where bombs just might bop us one unexpectedly, but we were all headed toward a tragic world, which is to say a war world where men have decided to die together because they are unable to find any way to live together.

Except for the fact that everything always shudders and shakes on an ocean liner, the first few days were very calm. The general gloom on board was not dispelled by the constant watery sunlight on the lead-coloured sea, but little by little the passengers began to make friends and to talk to one another, and nothing is really bad when people can still talk. There was the usual Jap on board and the usual Chinaman, who kept strictly to themselves except for when each dined once at the captain's table. There was also a blonde English actress, who was merged by the oil men right away. She stayed enormously popular with them, all the way over, not only because she was divinely pretty and wore spangled dresses (while all the other ladies on board wore their old black laces and Chanels), but because she laughed at them and with them incessantly. There were a number of French people, and Swedes and Italians and a famous English author whom everybody consulted hourly about the course of the war in England, although he himself had been lecturing in South America for almost a year. Naturally, nobody talked about anything but the war to which we were all going.

The *Vogue* editor said: "One of the saddest things to me about war is that it spoils conversation so!"

Because we were at sea, and cut off from the hourly news reports which at home fed this conversation, as gasoline feeds a motor, we all soon had to fall back on pretty wide generalizations about war.

My stewardess summed up all these generalizations in a very few words. She said: "Since September I've seen lots of nationalities go over and lots of nationalities come back and they use an awful lot of words to say that maybe the war was not such a hot idea."

I think what we Americans on board missed most the first few days was not our families, but the morning papers. I know I acutely missed their fat friendly soggy weight on my ankles and knees as I drank my morning coffee in bed. I missed the sense of detachment their very comprehensiveness gives you from the world in which you are living. I mean, when you first pick up an American daily or (particularly) Sunday newspaper, and you see all the thousands and thousands of words and hundreds of pictures there are about everybody else and everybody else's country, you have a very definite feeling that the world's history is all being made just for you to read about, and think about remotely and quietly. The American newspaper is the biggest news-counter in the world, and just because it is so big and impossible to digest all in one sitting, because you must pick and choose from its almost encyclopædic contents, you sometimes forget that the news you often just skim is being suffered somewhere in the world by the people who are making it. There was, of course, a paper of sorts printed on board. It was called the *Ocean Times*. It was one sheet, the size of a piece of typewriter paper, and under the title it said: "World-wide News of the United States." The day I had left New York the American papers were full of the news that President Roosevelt had just let pass the deadline for taking his name off the Illinois preferential primary ballot, and the third-term talk was at its highest pitch. All America was indignant over "Britain's high-handed procedure" in taking American mails at the point of a bayonet and rifling them. Senator Nye referred to our cousins across the sea as "the arrogant British," and the rest of Congress was busy echoing or toning down that description. America was morally bedevilled and politically confused about what to do with three quarters of a million German, Polish, Czech, Italian, and Hungarian refugees who were begging to be admitted to the land of the free, and somebody was despairingly pointing out that although those nations had long since filled their quotas, France, England, Norway, Sweden, and Ireland had used only about thirty per cent of their quotas to date. Secretary Hull had just fought and won a bitter fight in Congress to extend his authority to make reciprocal trade agreements with Europe. Robert Taft and Thomas Dewey were generally conceded to be the only two formidable contenders for the Republican nomination. The betting on the tortoise versus the hare was intense, and a few people had even heard of the whippet Wendell Willkie, who finally got it. There was trouble brewing for America in the Pacific, and for Britain in the West Indies and India. Sumner Welles had just sailed on the *Rex* on his one-man fact-finding commission, peace-proposal talk filled the air, and at the same time interest in Europe's phony war was at its lowest ebb. And there were the theatre and art and literature and society and sport and, above all, *Gone with the Wind* to think about.

The *Ocean Times* on Sunday, February 25, reflected nothing of all this. There were ten or twelve short items date-lined Birmingham, Stockholm, Berlin, Istanbul, Dublin, Oslo, Munich, Helsinki, London, and Moscow, but not one word in it about the United States, not even one mention of Mr. Roosevelt. However novel and pleasant that might have been at home, the first morning on board it depressed me. I thought: "Here we are, only four hundred miles out, on an American ship, and I am reading an American paper, and now suddenly America doesn't even rate a blat in it. Well," I thought, "if you're going to be an isolationist, you ought to be prepared to be isolated." The little paper was all very big bad news: Chamberlain had made a speech saying Hitler had to go or else, and Hitler had made a speech saying England had to go or else—and Turkey had mobilized and had another earthquake, and Sweden had gone off the gold standard, and the white-hooded Finns and the white-hooded Russians were still staining the white snow crimson. And there was no Dick Tracy or Little Orphan Annie or Walter Winchell to take my mind off that, nor even Walter Lippmann to say everything was going to be much worse or much better providing we would do something complicated but nevertheless obvious to any intelligent man. That's when I thought how awfully stark and real and challenging the news might seem to Americans if we didn't have so many able columnists to explain it away for us, in such totally different ways, and then I thought for the first time that the New York Sunday *Times* had often been my Ivory Tower.

I don't remember now what conclusions most of us Americans reached on that trip when we all sat about on deck wagging our jaws with endless eagerness about the war. The events of the next few months obliterated them from my mind completely. And in any case they, like the scrambled conversations of the winter, were all based on the same false premise, that American isolationism was possible. But I do remember everything the lean man said, because he was my first real interventionist. (The lean man turned out also to be an oil man, though he said he was an oil engineer which was a little different. "A good engineer," he said, "is against the slot-machine principle in politics, love, and business.")

He said: "Isolation is the unwelcome compliment America pays the British navy. We Americans are not going to see anything straight until we realize that—until we realize it is *our* war. After that we can debate all we want whether the smart thing for us to do is to fight it."

I said: "That's a very cynical attitude," and he replied:

"The time has not yet come in the history of the world when nations are willing to fight a war they can get someone else to win for them."

I said, because I wanted to get off on democracy right away: "We fought the last war, for an ideal—to make the world safe for democracy—"

He interrupted: "We fought the last war because we insisted on the freedom of the seas, while the Germans insisted on sinking our shipping. And we fought the last war to protect our overseas investments, and because if we hadn't got in when we did, and sent what we sent before we did get in, the Allies would have lost it and we should have lost our dough and the freedom of the seas for ever. . . . The 'Make the world safe for democracy' gag was a fine propaganda angle which gave the great masses of the American people, the hinterlanders and the hillbillies who didn't and couldn't understand what freedom of the seas and foreign trade and investments mean in dollars and cents to a great expanding capitalist nation, a sorely needed moral reason, a crusading idea, for getting into it. Unfortunately," he went on, "the democracy gag was a terrible boomerang. We and the Allies overplayed it. We didn't intend to, and without us they couldn't, even if they'd wanted to, deliver democracy all over the world. But now, because most Americans have forgotten what we really were fighting for, because they now only remember that it was 'for democracy,' which we didn't save anywhere, they are completely soured on Europe. In fact, they were so sour on Europe that the day this war began, the United States of America *voluntarily* gave up the very thing we really fought for and won in the last war: the right of neutrals to trade with foreign nations whether belligerent or not. When we passed the Neutrality Act we presented Adolf Hitler with his first great victory over the Allies; of its own free will America renounced the first and greatest tenet of democratic capitalist nations, the freedom of the seas. By quickly clearing the seas of our shipping, by refusing to give the Allies credit, by cash-and-carry legislation, we have put perhaps a fatal strain on the navies and armies of the very nations we say stand between us and our enemies. I can see Kaiser Bill now scratching his beard at Doorn and saying to the wife: 'Herminc, how in hell did this fellow Adolf pull that off? If I'd been able to do that, baby, I wouldn't be sawing wood here now in Holland.' "

The oil man continued: "But if the Allies can win in spite of the handicaps we have put on them, dandy. We've saved ourselves a blood bath and perhaps a lot of money. If they can't, we've got nobody but ourselves to blame if we are the next to get it in the neck."

I said: "You're really an interventionist."

"Not really," he answered, "because the way things look now, we've got a good gambling chance of getting out of this thing without spilling one drop of American blood in Europe. But what we risk if we lose," he said, "is spilling gallons of it in America. Still, since dead men presumably sleep better by the millions in Arlington than they do by the thousands in Château-Thierry, I am, as I say, all for the gamble."

"But some people say, even if the Allies win, this time it's really the end of democracy in Europe."

He replied: "Please don't let's talk about democracy. That's the great red political herring Hitler dragged across the trail of every nation's vital economic interests. Just start them fighting among themselves about what democracy is, who's got it, and whether it is, after all, worth defending, and then when everybody's sore or exhausted by that scrap, step in and take whatever the damn thing is away. Great idea. Hitler caught onto it, watching Woodrow Wilson floundering around with it, after Versailles."

I said: "But you believe there is such a thing as democracy?"

He replied, grinning: "Well, maybe you'll find cut what it is in Europe. Be sure to let me know, will you?"

These are not the actual words, but this was the gist of what the oil man said. I could see, no matter what he said, that he was an interventionist. What discouraged me about that was that he didn't seem to be interested so much in the preservation of democracy in the world as he was in the freedom of the seas, which I suppose was just another way of saying foreign trade and commerce. I could see right away he was the sort of man nearly everybody at home called a war-monger.

Of course, I asked him about oil, which so many people said was the answer. About that he was very discouraging, too. He said:

"If anybody could tell you exactly how much oil Hitler has stored, how much his war machine will use, and how much he is likely to get in the future, whether by striking new wells or getting access to sea-borne oil, or cutting off the Allies' oil—all of which will largely be decided by the course of the war itself, and how it influences Russia, Rumania, and, more important, the Arabian oil states, Iran, Iraq, Syria, and Saudi Arabia—you would then know the answer. Try to find that out in Europe. It's another thing I'd like to know."

That, as far as I was concerned, settled the oil question, or rather left it wide open, until the very end of the war. I never brought it up again.

And so we talked and talked. . . . For the rest, we played ping-pong or cards, ate excellent food in the handsome but mournful, almost empty saloon, and received the undivided attention of wonderful stewards and stewardesses. Most of the Americans on board were discovering for the first time that American boats were really quite all right. The *Vogue* editor said: "If they sink the *Ile* or the *Queen Mary*, I'm never going any other way."

Sometimes we went to the movies. The only one I remember now was *Young Tom Edison* with Mickey Rooney, and that's because it made you think all the time about the one thing, so far, that Europe's phony war was most notorious for: the black-outs. I thought: "Isn't it extraordinary? The electric light bulb was invented, by an American, only about sixty years ago. And there were millions of them in Europe lighted up every night until September. But now nearly everywhere all over Europe, after sunset, they sit screwed in their sockets like the eyes of a million blind men."

Very early in the morning on March 1 we reached Gibraltar. There the American mails were thrown overboard into little launches and taken to the port to be searched by the British. Watching this infringement of our sovereign rights as a mighty neutral nation, I was also indignant. Then I remembered what the oil man had said about giving up the freedom of the seas, and I thought: "Well, one thing certainly leads to another," and I saw that my indignation was spurious.

"Besides," as Captain Richardson said that night at dinner, "we don't intend to fight the British about it, do we?"

"Oh, no," I said.

He went on, cheerfully: "Then the whole question of searching the mails is just one of those phony issues that help keep a senator's mind from coming to grips with a real one."

As we left the shadow of Gibraltar's impregnable golden rock, rising so steeply and sternly from the sunny land of Spain, the thin match-stick prong of a submarine's periscope crossed our bow silently and disappeared in the direction of the mole.

The *Vogue* editor said: "I don't think there's anything creepier to watch than a periscope. The way it cuts the water like a little knife, and you know all the time that underneath it's attached to a nasty whale thing that can whoop death right smack into the biggest ship afloat."

The English author, who was standing beside us at the rail, said, very pleased: "That's what's called the Command of the Seas. That's why England must win. That's why Italy will probably stay out."

"And as long as you've got it, that's why America will stay out too," the oil man said.

The English author, very surprised, answered: "You're one of the few Americans I've met who's willing to admit we're fighting the war for you."

The oil man declared cheerfully: "That's right. And I

hope to God you do a good job of it."

The *Vogue* editor said: "Oh, I do hope it's not true that they are fighting our war. It does make us seem like such awful heels."

The English author looked very superior and patronizing. "Oh, we don't really hold it against you," he said. "You're just going through what we went through at Munich. You, as you say, will 'snap out of it' in time."

The *Vogue* editor agreed: "Oh, I know we will." Then she said to the oil man: "What do you think of Roosevelt's foreign policy?"

The oil man said: "What is Roosevelt's foreign policy?"

The *Vogue* editor explained: "Why, he hates Mr. Hitler, and likes the Allies."

The oil man said: "That's not a policy. That's a predilection. A real foreign policy is often at total variance with a nation's or even its leaders' personal predilections. The Communazi trade pact and the Rome-Berlin Axis prove that."

The *Vogue* editor said: "Now that I think of it, I don't really know what America's foreign policy is, any more than Mr. Roosevelt's, if it's not just that we don't like the Nazis."

The oil man told her: "You're in the same boat with a hundred and thirty million of your isolated fellow citizens. The rest of them are busy writing books trying to define what it is or what it should be." He grinned at me. "There's another thing, besides what democracy is, that you can find out in Europe: what is Mr. Roosevelt's foreign policy?"

I said: "You know perfectly well I am a very confused woman."

Then we began to talk about Sumner Welles, who had gone to Europe on the boat before us.

The oil man said: "I shouldn't be surprised if he went to Europe to find out what Mr. Roosevelt's foreign policy is, too."

The *Vogue* editor asked: "What do you think of his New Deal?"

"I think the New Deal is a Rube Goldberg machine," the oil engineer replied.

That is the last time for three and a half months that I was to hear anyone talk about Mr. Roosevelt's New Deal, because nobody in Europe thought it had any relation to his foreign policy or the war or our possible entrance into it.

Now we were in the blue Mediterranean, and two days later on a very sunny warm morning we came into the harbour of Naples. Pink and blue and white, and olive green along the hills, with high smoke-plumed Vesuvius over all, Naples looked like all the lovely chromos you have ever seen of it.

TWO

Italy is only a geographical expression.

Prince Metternich,
Memorandum to the Great Powers,
August 2, 1814

◇◇

IN NAPLES we had three or four hours before the electric train left for Rome. So the oil man suggested to the *Vogue* editor and me that we drive out to see Pompeii. We agreed. This is not a travel book—it is a book about the people in the war in the spring in Europe—so I shall not describe the all too familiar sights, sounds, and very strong smells of Naples.

We hired a guide and what he claimed to be "a magnificent motor vehicle" and sped out along the vine-bordered blossoming new motor highway to Pompeii. Of course the first question we asked the guide was whether he thought Italy was going to go in or stay out. His black eyes flamed a little at that, but he replied glibly: "Italy wants peace. Il Duce promised us peace!"

We finally got him to admit what all the American papers

had been saying for months, and all the nice Italians had said on the boat, that Mussolini was a one-man minority for war in his own country. This cheered up the *Vogue* editor and me quite a lot, but the oil man didn't look convinced.

He said: "You girls mustn't draw too much comfort from that. The people never want war. I'm sure the German people didn't want war. At least, when I was in Germany last year they didn't. God knows neither did the French or English. But sometimes in the end they see for themselves they've got to go in, and then they shove their leaders into it. Sometimes their leaders want them to go in and shove the people into it. But a simple desire for peace is no guarantee against war."

"*Si*," the guide said, "and this is very sad. War makes nobody happy. Look what this war has already done to my Pompeii business. Deserted." After that he relapsed into a gloomy silence, and except for his stereotyped patter when we reached Pompeii, he never emerged from it.

Half-way out a tire of the magnificent vehicle *fffted* loudly and burst. The guide and the chauffeur, full of extravagant apologies and excuses, jumped out and began to poke around in the chest under the chauffeur's seat. At long last the guide thrust his head into the car and said: "It is now that we have not the proper tool to push this car up and put a new tire beneath."

The oil man sighed and said: "Two ways of doing things: the right way and the Italian way. This is an axiom," he said, "on which the Allies count heavily."

Perhaps they should not have counted on it quite so heavily, because somehow the chauffeur managed to change the tire without the needed tool, and a half-hour later we were again on our way to Pompeii. But this delay gave us only a very short time to see the lovely ruins of the ancient city, and only fifteen minutes to gobble down a spaghetti luncheon at the little hotel outside the Pompeii gates.

Although this was formerly the height of the tourist season, now there was no one in the little hot dining-room but ourselves and a pathetic moth-eaten group of four old musicians strumming mournful guitars. As we entered, apparently under the impression that we were English, they sang *Doing the Boompsa Daisy* and the *Lambeth Walk* in cracked but true Italian tenor voices. The oil man managed to disabuse them of this notion by giving them each a dollar bill. Then they burst into *Yes, We Have No Bananas*.

I said: "Don't do that. Please sing *Finiculi, Finicula*, or *O Sole Mio*." So they sang those songs, and the *Vogue* editor said:

"I could weep, the whole thing's so damn dismal."

"Totalitarian man is certainly not a tourist," I generalized.

"Oh yes, he is," the oil man said, "but he has a passion for touring in planes and tanks, that's the trouble."

On the way back to the boat the despairful and underworked guide broke his silence only once. It was just before we reached the station. As we whizzed by it, he quickly pointed to a large handsome old building on a little hill and he said, with a happy smile:

"That is the Palazzo Capodimonte of Prince Umberto. He is in it with the Princess. She has just had a *bambina*, called Maria!"

The *Vogue* editor said: "How sweet! War is so depressing: I'm just in the mood for seeing something normal, like a baby."

"That reminds me," I put in. "Just before I got on the boat Elsa Maxwell sent me a telegram telling me to be sure to go and see Prince Umberto; he is one of her most intimate friends."

The *Vogue* editor said: "And what do we do now, just drop the telegram in his mail-box and run?"

I answered, annoyed: "I just mentioned it."

The oil man said: "I can see after we get to Rome I'm never going to set eyes on you two girls again. You know too many important people."

The *Vogue* editor said: "We think you're the most wonderful man we've met in Europe." (She said that to everybody she met in Italy, France, and England. She said if you wanted to find out things, that on-the-face-of-it-absurd remark was an excellent stimulus to conversation. Just because there's a big war going on, it doesn't mean that men have ceased to be human.[1] The contrary was her philosophy. She said the reason professional journalists so seldom found out what important people were really thinking was that they approached their victims as though they were rational instead of emotional beings.)

I said to the oil man: "Oh, I don't know many important people here yet, and I have very few letters of introduction. Mostly I trust to the pot-luck, cross-section Gallup-poll principle, except in a country where I don't know anybody, like Norway or Finland. So there I have letters from Scandinavian friends to Carl Hambro and Halvdan Koth and Sigrid Undset in Norway and to a lot of unpronounceable bigwigs in Finland. . . ."

The oil man gave me a queer sidelong glance. "I wouldn't use those," he said. "If I were you I'd just stay quietly in

[1] In London in June the head of the Military Intelligence told me that most serious information leaks "came from the top." He deplored how often important men "who should know better" spilled into pearly ears secrets that were afterwards innocently blabbed by rosebud mouths all over London.

Rome and Paris and London for a few weeks and then get another nice American boat home from Genoa."

I asked: "You don't think Scandinavia's going to get into this war, do you?"

He replied: "What I think is that anybody who leaves France or London this spring for any neutral country is very likely to find herself going home via the Trans-Siberian Railroad or tracks east out of India."

Now, that's what lots of wise Americans told lots of other Americans in Europe in February. So there really is very little excuse for the numbers of us who got "trapped" in enemy country and had such a terrible time getting home afterwards. The "surprise blows" delivered by the German war machine were not nearly so much responsible for the plight American citizens found themselves in as their own apathy—or curiosity.

When we came to Rome we went to the Hotel Excelsior. Rome, unlike Pompeii and Naples, was crowded. The manager said they were having some sort of Fascist congress. The lobby was jammed with women in almost expensive furs, and handsome dark officers in a wide variety of musical-comedy uniforms, which all looked a little too big for them.

The *Vogue* editor said: "They are just too fr-rrightfully chic, though I'm terrified the poor darlings will trip themselves up with those long swords and assassinate themselves right before our eyes."

After I gave the manager a big tip, he said: "Ah, yes, now I see I have a suite for you. Mr. Sumner Welles has just vacated it." I saw right away I had given him too many lire.

The salon of the suite just vacated by Mr. Welles was

full of large funereal baskets of hydrangeas and azaleas and lilies. The envelopes were still left pinned to the garish ribbons, but the cards had been removed, so I can't tell you who made Mr. Welles these diplomatic votive offerings. It was a big plushy mirrored room, cluttered with marble-topped tables and giant tortured gold chairs upholstered in crimson and bright green satin. Everything in it was outsize. (I noticed later that all the buildings in Rome, the rooms, the furniture looked somehow too big for the Romans. I thought either the Italians had shrunk quite a lot or they intended to grow. Both were true.)

I felt quite happy in Mr. Welles's suite. I felt my having been given it was a good omen. After all, Mr. Welles and I were in Europe for exactly the same reason. (That is, if Mr. Welles and the President were telling the truth when he left.) We were both on a purely fact-finding commission of one for the benefit of the American people. Mr. Welles, of course, was travelling under much more magnificent auspices. He was really going to hear things from the biggest horses' mouths, while I was just going to talk to anybody and everybody I bumped into. But the principle was the same. (As things have turned out, I think my mission was the more successful, because I am telling you everything I found out, whereas Mr. Welles, as a B.B.C. broadcaster said in London in March, returned to the U.S.A., and "maintained his reputation for saying nothing gracefully.")

I had never been to Rome before. The reasons are probably inexcusable for a person who has travelled in Europe as much as I have, but never mind. And although I was very eager and curious to know how people in Rome felt about the war—which meant sitting around for hours at luncheons and cocktail parties and dinners, and calling up newspaper men and nosing around shops and cafés and asking questions of waiters and maids and people on benches in parks, and above all walking through crowded streets until the atmosphere itself soaked into your skin and gave you the true answers—I was terribly tempted to just go sightseeing like any good tourist. Besides, I knew that this first view of the Eternal City was also going to be my last until the war, which of course I knew was going to be very long, was over. So I compromised between the pursuit of permanent culture and ephemeral politics. The result was very unsatisfactory. In the five days I had allowed myself in Rome, I frantically flipped through the city as one flips through a big postcard album, so that my mind's eye became a hodge-podge of stone and brick and marble and bronze images, what the motion-picture companies call a "montage" of old basilicas and great churches and lordly tombs and exquisite temples and majestic colonnades and soaring arches and wide porticoes, of gilded palazzos and broad piazzas and gushing fountains and row on row of flying stone steps, and statues and statues and statues, and through those superimposed images always loomed the great and noble Colosseum and the mammoth and crass marble memorial to King Victor Emmanuel, which on the high hill at the head of the Via delle' Impero banged you in the eye like an enormous white wedding-cake no matter what else you were trying to look at. I raced through Saint Peter's. I tore through the Vatican Museum. I whipped through the Forum and I circled all the wonders of the seven cypress- and pine-crowned hills like a miniature whirlwind. I even followed the Appian Way for fifty rushing miles and took in the exceedingly disappointing Catacombs. And after it was all over, I knew no more of Roman art or history than I had when I landed in Naples. Don't ever do this. It's physically exhausting and mentally unprofitable. Today instead of feeling and knowing Rome in all its separate and yet intimate parts (so different they are and yet so wonderfully blended): the ancient pagan Imperial city, the mediæval papal city, and the modern commercial city, I have only a vague memory of a big town that looked as though it had recently been badly bombed in spots, and its citizens had not been rich enough to quite rebuild it.

Rome is the city above all cities which loses most of its meaning to those who do not bring to it some historical sense, a decent knowledge of art, and a good amount of time. Rome therefore is particularly disturbing to an American. There is something incongruous to an American in walking down a bristling modern thoroughfare, with modern buildings and street cars and shops, and suddenly turning a corner to find himself face to face with a ten-acre lot of crumbling ruins and thrown-down columns and broken arches. You're apt to feel about it the way you would if you paid a visit to an Italian friend in a fine modern villa, only to find all the contents of the attic and his grandmother's bones strewed around the living-room floor. It has been Mussolini's passion these past years to uncover more and more of these archæological bones of a dead world right in the middle of Rome's busiest secular sections. Under the Duce's bold Cæsarean eye the Theatre of Marcellus, the Tomb of the Scipios, the Circus Maximus, the Capitoline Hill, and Augustus' Ara Pacis, the Empire's altar to Peace in 13 B.C., have all been streamlined to their ruined antiquities. And in the suburbs the restoration at Lake Nemi of Caligula's galleys and the whole ancient sea town of Ostia is still proceeding. I said to the oil man: "If this sort of thing goes on much longer, he'll scrap street cars and silk hats and high heels next, and make everybody wear togas and ride on chariot wheels. It's art, but is it progress?" I asked.

The oil man said: "Here is no passion for art or archæology. This is a magnificent expression of the man's Imperator complex. Unable to build an empire, he's had to excavate one."

Then the oil man took me to see the most outspoken advertisement in Rome of Mussolini's Empire psychosis, the maps on the walls of the Basilica of Maxentius on the Via Imperiale near the Colosseum. In 1932 Il Duce had mounted there four great marble plaques which showed how mighty Rome had grown before she dwindled. The first map showed all Europe in black marble, with Rome just a tiny white spot in its midst in the eighth century B.C. The second map showed Rome's greater power in 146 B.C. and what with part of Spain and Greece and a chunk of Africa which the Punic Wars had carved out, there was lots more white marble now. The third map of Rome, A.D. 14, was even whiter; France and all Spain, and Syria and most of North Africa and Morocco now belonged to Il Duce's spiritual forebears. The fourth plaque looked as though a great snowstorm had hit it. Here was Rome's glory at its height. Almost the whole of two continents (except for some unimportant slices of the British Isles) belonged now to the conquering Romans. The oil man said that after enough Romans got the hint Il Duce had intended to give them when he plastered up those plaques, four years later he was able to add a fifth: modern Italy plus Ethiopia. But I thought between plaque four of Rome at its height and number five of modern Italy there was still an awful lot of ground to be covered. I said to the oil man:

"As a matter of fact, I should think that looking at that Rome-in-all-its-glory map would really discourage Mussolini from trying to get anywhere."

The oil man replied: "Not at all. Mussolini is the Killeyoo Bird of Europe."

"What?" I asked.

He explained: "You know—the Killeyoo bird—it flies backwards because it doesn't care where it's going, it just wants to see where it's been."

After that I understood Mussolini better.

Wednesday, March the 6th, was a day that I hope I shall never forget. Because that day at noon I had the great privilege of an audience with the Pope. I am not a Catholic; I am not even very religious; but like all human beings who are not utterly lost to Grace, I am humble and respectful and awed and ashamed, too, before very good men who do God's work greatly.

A Catholic friend in the Vatican had offered to arrange the audience, but partly because I am not a Catholic and partly because, as I say, the look in the face of a man of great good will is so likely to upset one for days and make one think too many painful and searching things about oneself and the whole world (which is, I suppose, why saints in their time were people to be avoided as much as possible), I was timid about going, and at first said I wouldn't.[2] But vanity and curiosity prevailed, so I went.

There was quite a scramble about my clothes. It seems you must wear a long high-necked black dress, and black

[2] The only other "great man" I ever refused to meet was in Germany in 1937—Adolf Hitler. But for quite different reasons. I suppose the simplest way to put it is that I was deathly afraid, being a woman, I might just once smile on him. And all the human curiosity in the world would not, I felt, justify to myself that small but fatal hypocrisy.

stockings, and a black veil over your head. Although I had a long black dress, the neck-line came a little below my collar-bone, and I had no lace veil at all. But the *Vogue* editor had an Italian friend, a lovely dark-haired woman, Donna Cora Caetani, and she fixed me up. She sent her maid with a new paper of white pins and a black chiffon scarf, and the maid tucked it in and pinned it and blocked out the white patch of my throat entirely. Then she draped a mantilla over my head, and I thought I was ready. But the maid said:

"Signorina, where are your jewels?"

"My jewels?" I asked.

And she explained: "Always the ladies wear their great jewels when they go to the Vatican," and I said:

"Well, I have no great jewels." But she looked so sorry for me that I added: "I mean they're all home in cold storage." Really I was shocked at the idea of wearing great jewels to see the Pope, because I am a Protestant of Puritan ancestry. I can't help associating emeralds and diamonds and gold with bare alluring backs in night clubs and flesh-pots like the Metropolitan Opera. That is one reason, I suppose, why Protestants will never quite understand the Catholic Church. We cannot separate, as the Catholics do, the possession of material wealth from the idea of moral and spiritual bankruptcy. Anyway, it's only in Protestant or non-Catholic countries that any substantial headway is ever made in soaking-the-rich for both moral and political reasons.

The *Vogue* editor, who was also going to see the Holy Father, and I went down in the elevator of the Rome Excelsior Hotel at eleven o'clock in the morning, looking like something out of a Goya. In the lobby we met Anabel, the honest and splendid and Junoesque wife of Myron Taylor, the American representative to the Vatican.

She said: "Hello, girls. Bet I can guess where you're going."

The *Vogue* editor answered: "Oh, my dear, dressed like this, at this hour of the morning!"

Mrs. Taylor sighed. She said: "We have a very strange life. My husband gets up at the crack of dawn every morning and puts on his white tie and tails to go to the Vatican. He gets home at night just in time to change into a sack suit for a formal dinner." She waved us gaily to the taxi. "But you'll see—the Pope's a wonderful man—just wonderful."

We drove through a cold drizzling rain past the leafless sycamores by the yellow Tiber, past all the pagan ruins and Christian churches, to the Vatican. In the centre of the piazza formed by the gigantic arms of Bernini's Colonnade, I saw the Obelisk of Pope Sixtus V, and I remembered the inscription on the pedestal that the guide had read to me the day before.

> *Ecce Crux Christi*
> *Fugite Partes Adversæ*
> *Vicit Leo de Triba Juda.*
>
> *Behold the Cross of Christ.*
> *Flee, hostile factions—*
> *The Lion of the Tribe of Judah has conquered.*

And I thought of the other Lion of Judah I had seen also the day before—the great stone Lion of Judah brought by the conquering Italians from the square of Addis Ababa and set in captive splendour on the Highway of Triumph under the Arch of Constantine alongside the Colosseum—which had also known Christians and lions in its day. I said to myself: "Can there really be room in Rome for both these lions: the conquering Lion of the Tribe of Judah who faces all the world from the hill on which Saint Peter died, and that other conquered Lion which is simply a trophy on a pagan highway?" It didn't seem to me that there could be room.

Now we were before the doors of the place where the Vicar of Christ, the guardian of the Lion of Judah, lived. The palms of my hands were wet and I trembled. I asked myself: "What are you trembling for? It would be different if you were a Catholic." But I knew what I was trembling for. I was trembling because I was about to see the one man in all the world who perhaps had the power that perhaps still resided in an organized Church of Christ, the power that comes of God, to stop this war, to give the sad world a little breathing-space of peace. I thought perhaps I was going to see the one man who could perform the miracle, the one miracle for which millions of hearts are truly yearning.

When we came into the Vatican, we went up a long noble flight of steps guarded by soldiers in mediæval orange and black striped costumes, who carried halberds like the Beefeaters in the Tower of London, and then we were met by a little fussy usher in a white tie and tails who whisked us down a long corridor covered with the most incredibly lovely paintings into a hall where the *Vogue* editor left her sables and I left my silver foxes, and then into a small red-velvet-hung anteroom, in the Pope's private apartments. I'm afraid we were a few seconds late, because this room was already full of people standing in a line all around the walls. There were about forty of them, a few men in white ties and tails, three or four women dressed as we were (but with great jewels, so I knew they were Catholics), and about twenty nuns in grey, some of them young, but most of them old, with faint black moustaches, who came from somewhere in South America, as I found out later. The nuns were all talking in hushed whispers, fingering their crucifixes with white and knotted and trembling fingers and cautiously shifting from foot to foot, and looking expectantly with wide, feverishly bright eyes at the little closed door at the end of the room before which the secretaries or ushers were standing. And then the door opened and in came His Holiness, Pope Pius XII, the servant of the servants of Christ. . . .

Everybody knelt. He circled the room, his back to us first. All I could see was that he was very slim, a little bent, and wore a white cap on his head, a red sash around his thin waist, and little red slippers without heels on his narrow feet. Then as he went down the line, leaning over the upturned faces, the faces broke into such good and happy and purified smiles that I could hardly wait to see his face. And then when he came to the nuns kneeling beside me, I saw it. It was so intelligent and so beneficent. He was talking to the nuns in Spanish, and they were hardly breathing. I started to smile too, before he quite reached me. And when he did, he asked me, in very good English, if I were the American lady, and I said: "Yes."

"Ah!" he said, "I loved your country when I was there," and I knew he meant he *loved* it. And then he smiled a thin sweet smile at my smile and made the sign of the cross and said: "God bless America!" Then he went on to the few others, and afterwards he went back through the door. Then everybody got up from his knees and let his breath out in a long gasp, and suddenly we all stopped smiling and began to rearrange our ties and jewels and crucifixes and veils.

So that was the audience with the Pope.

As we went back to the hall to get our wraps, I was still

bemused and didn't want to talk. I felt, for some exceedingly strange reason, so much better in my heart. The *Vogue* editor felt it too, I could see that. Silently we got into a taxi and drove back to the hotel. Now for the first time I noticed how many priests there were in the streets.

I do not know how much part they and the thought of God, and the example of Jesus play in the life of Italians. I hope more than these things do in America. It suddenly occurred to me how for months and months on end I never heard in New York the name Jesus except in church on Sunday, or the other six days of the week as a cuss-word. I tried to think just why we Americans called ourselves a Christian nation, because I suddenly remembered, coming from the Vatican, that Christianity is not just an accepted theory about God, but a whole way of human living. I wondered if the fact that so few important people everywhere in the world were living Christian lives and thinking of everything—politics and business and finance and industry and diplomacy—from a *Christian* point of view could really have something to do with the war in Europe. That, I thought, was the last question you could ask a politician. And you certainly couldn't ask that question of people who think that oil is the answer to everything.... As a matter of fact, I never heard anybody important really talk seriously about God in Europe in the spring—that is, not until the invasion. But the Sunday after the invasion, all the politicians in Paris went with the people to Notre-Dame and prayed on their knees to God to save France for them. They were very shaken. I saw them. . . .

But now, coming from the Vatican, the little black trickle of priests that stole all through the life of the city comforted me. I thought, surely the Pope, who serves these many servants of the Lord, could at least keep Mussolini out. And then I thought, not necessarily, no. The Catholic Church is not so much interested in how or why men die as it is in getting them into a Catholic heaven when they do. The Pope isn't supposed to care what economic systems or even flags men live or fight under so long as Catholics under them everywhere live and die in the faith. Render unto Cæsar Mussolini . . . It was a very depressing idea. Then I thought of the Protestant Church and the Episcopal Church, to which I am supposed to belong. I remembered the Archbishop of Canterbury and how sternly he had refused to compromise with Wally Simpson, and I wondered why he had compromised with the pagan Jew-baiter Hitler so long. Now I thought if the old Archbishop had grabbed a sword or a mitre long before Munich and yelled to the Protestant clergy of all the world: "For *God's* sake, boys, come on!" and they had marched on Munich the way Hitler had marched into the Ruhr or Mussolini on Rome, well, the whole thing might not have happened. But because neither the Pope nor the Archbishop nor any Protestant clergyman got together a gang in the name of God, I could see now there was very little fight left, only talk, in the Christian world. So in the taxicab I had to pray for a Miracle even harder than before.

And then I felt a pin sticking into my neck. I pulled it out of the chiffon scarf at my throat. It was black. I said to the *Vogue* editor:

"Look."

"Oh, a pin," she answered. "Did it hurt?"

"No," I said, "but it's *black*."

"Why not?" she asked.

I said: "When the maid pinned on this scarf I distinctly saw her draw white pins from a new paper of white pins."

She laughed. "What do you think happened, a miracle?"

"Well, I was praying for a big miracle all the time in there. Maybe a little one is all I deserve."

She said: "Oh, don't be silly. We'll look at the paper of pins when we get back." We did. Every second row in the paper was black.

The *Vogue* editor remarked: "I think it's very cute and unexpected of you to hope for a miracle, after a visit to the Pope, but, darling, the age of miracles is over." I know now she was right.

That night, March the 6th, the drizzle of rain which had chilled the warm spring air in the morning turned into snow. And a big wind from the northern mountains whipped the great soft flakes into an enormous blizzard. Frost and sleet and snow blanketed Rome and all its ruins and glories ankle-deep, and withered the palms, and killed all the azaleas and almond blossoms everywhere.

The oil man said: "This is going to play hell with the crops. If Italy gets into the war this year and they don't win it quickly, next winter's famine will starve them to their knees."

Still, a great many people believed in the miracle of peace in Rome in March. For instance, most of the American newspaper men believed it. Naturally they didn't call it a miracle, they rationalized it in political terms. They said: "Nobody in Italy wants war but Mussolini. The Pope certainly not, for obvious reasons. The King and the House of Savoy—which has far more influence on the people than anyone outside of Italy knows—are dead against it. Ciano is definitely pro-Ally, and he doesn't want it. Not even Mussolini's generals themselves want it. That's one reason" (they said) "why Balbo was sent to his Libyan exile, because he thought war would be a gigantic military and economic folly. Naturally, the common people don't want it, because the common people never do—and the rich people because it will dry up dividends and interfere with the season at Venice."

One angle that tickled the American newspaper men in Rome was that practically everybody in Italy thought that if Italy went in, America would instantly fight on the side of the Allies. The Italians had been sold the idea (by their own leaders) that Roosevelt (who they believed was a Jew whose real name was Campo di Rosa [3]) was a plutocratic, decadent Democratic dictator, and that being the case, it seemed very logical to the Italians that he would shove America in the minute things got tough for the Allies. The newspaper men thought that Mr. Welles had probably done nothing to enlighten anyone who suffered from this painful delusion. But the big point the newspaper men made was this: "Italy knows, for economic reasons, she cannot fight a long war on Germany's side. If she was beaten she would be ruined for a century, and that crabapple of Mussolini's eye, Ethiopia, would be lost to him forever. And," they said, "all Italy knows that even if she fought and won, she would be the next victim of Herr Hitler! You can put any bet you want," most of the newspaper men said, "that Italy won't fight with the Germans. She has everything to gain by playing the Stalin game, and just waiting for the proper time to jump in on the side of the Allies, and then make their terms for delivering the *coup de grâce* to Brer

[3] The anti-Semitic policy in Italy never really made much headway among the people. A friend told me a revealing story about a group of players who wanted to produce Edna Ferber's *Stage Door* in Rome. The word got around that Miss Ferber was a Jewess, and the play was officially banned. But not before a government official had called the American producer to say: "Of course if she's only *half* Jewish, we might still be able to get permission for you."

Hitler at the Brenner." They all felt really quite sorry then for Mussolini. They described him as a sick old man [4]—he was variously reputed to be in the tertiary stage of syphilis, to have trachoma of the eye, or a blood clot on the brain—a weary old guy whose fleshy ailments were complicated by the bitterness in his soul as he finally realized that his hand-trained warrior nation wanted to fight nobody nohow. They pictured him as soured to the point of insanity, because he wanted so much to be a real Führer like Hitler, while nobody in his own country wanted to go galloping and goosestepping after him. One newspaper man said to me: "The Italian Fascist legions will march the *paso Romano* with the best of them, but they reserve the right to break ranks whenever they get empty in the pit of the stomach or their dogs get too tired." The newspaper men admitted that because of the Sanctions the Italians hated the English more perhaps than they feared the Germans, but they said that in the end they had more to hope for from the English. They put down a lot of the truculence and bravado of the Fascist party men to sheer exhibitionism.

Now, I don't know what the Romans themselves thought about all this, because the Romans didn't talk in front of foreigners. I tried very hard, over and over again, to make my Roman friends argue and debate with me, the way Americans do incessantly with one another. But whenever I asked a direct question or made a flat statement about Germany or France or England, or even the Balkan situation,

[4] In July, Mussolini got bored with this whispering campaign. He sent for all the foreign correspondents in Rome, and at his Villa Torlonia treated them to the staggering spectacle of himself sailing over nineteen fences on a fire-eating Nazi cavalry horse; then dismounted and played a lousy set of tennis for them just in case they thought all the work had been done by the horse. The press reported that although not a first-class player, he acquitted himself well, but "his *back-hand stroke* was his weakest feature." The Allies would not agree.

which is always so confused that you'd think anybody could risk an opinion on it without being ticked off after, they always changed the subject very quickly, and asked me if I were planning to visit the hill towns, or whether I had been conducted through the beautiful Colonna Palace yet. If I were very persistent they'd say apologetically: "I'm afraid an American wouldn't quite understand the Fascist angle on that." I found out that there was a Fascist angle on everything. I said one day at luncheon to Prince del D–:

"Oh, all right, we won't discuss the war any more. Let's talk about love. There isn't a Fascist angle on that, is there?"

Princess del D– sighed and said: "Ah, *si*, the Fascist angle on love is *make more babies!*"

The *Vogue* editor told me that might be the Fascist party angle on love, but it wasn't the Roman secular angle at all. She told me that the favourite Roman outdoor sport was bottom-pinching, and said that the first day in Rome she had been told the following story (by Italian friends) at least six times: A pretty American brunette, walking down the Via Nazionale, was suddenly nipped from behind. She squeaked, appalled, then whirled around and slapped the very gentlemanly-looking pincher neatly across the jaw. He raised his hat, terribly contrite. "A thousand apologies, signorina," he said, "but I really thought you were a blonde!"

She said that this attitude of gallant but choosy lechery, of romantic lustfulness, seemed typically Italian. She thought that Roman love could best be understood by the people who adored the jokes in *Esquire*, which in spite of its anti-Fascist articles, which nobody bothered to read, was the most popular foreign magazine in élite Rome. She thought that the well-born Italian's gay and lusty approach to sex had a great deal to do with the numbers of rich American women who had married into Roman society. (Although from the Italian side, she thought, money might have something to do with it, of course.) And Italo-American marriages were on the whole pretty successful, she found. Much more successful than Franco-American alliances, because (she thought) in Paris love is a very involved and delicate and intricate science, whereas in Rome it was a very healthy, rowdy, but extremely "chic" *sport*. She thought, on the whole, American women are not either very cerebral or sentimental, so the Roman idea appealed to them more.

(The *Vogue* editor didn't know what "love" was at home.) She explained that the enormous number of Italo-American marriages had had a very salutary and perhaps significant effect on the ruling classes of Rome. They were much more tolerant and infinitely less snotty than they had been before. A sort of gay, good-natured, democratic raffishness pervaded smart Roman society now. And she felt that the very pro-American sentiment of the upper classes and the aristocracy, many of whom were in Fascist government circles, couldn't fail to be reflected in Italian foreign policy. She said the proof was that Count Ciano, who was the pampered darling, the absolutely idolized pet of this Italian-American café society, was the Minister of Foreign Affairs!

Now, I make this digression on love simply to show you that in Rome in February the war seemed so remote and improbable there that some people even talked about "love" as a possible force in human affairs.

The oil man said: "I'm afraid your gentle gal friend rather overrates the cupid motif as a sign that all is quiet on the Tiber now. If any of her Pittsburgh Vere de Veres or noble Roman glamour boys really aired their minds on anything else, they'd probably find themselves dining and wining Addis Ababa fuzzy-wuzzies for the next ten years."

Later I saw that he was right. Except for some desultory abstract conversation about love, punctuated by occasional off-colour stories, highly personal gossip, and exceedingly vague statements of the fact that "peace" was Italy's deepest desire and only goal, I found that in Roman society "conversation" in the sense of the communication of individual ideas on current topics was either a lost or a forbidden art.

But man, in his leisure moments, is a loquacious animal. He must either toil or talk. I suppose that hard blistering toil solved the conversational problem for the vast majority of Italians. The upper-class Italians and the aristocracy solved it in their own way. They danced and drank and rode, and played tennis and bridge and golf,[5] and gambled at poker until they were too exhausted to talk. Rome night life was late and long and terribly noisy in the cafés—young and middle-aged socialites danced a gymnastic version of the cancan on night-club floors that would have left seasoned Lindy-hoppers limp. And in the salons, after dinner

[5] Golf was Ciano's favourite sport. The *Vogue* editor told me that a number of years before, when he had suddenly joined the quiet little golf club outside of Rome, the membership increased from thirty to over a hundred in a few days' time. Then, just as suddenly, at the time of the Sanctions, Ciano resigned. Golf, he said was "a purely British sport" and therefore one which might have a highly pernicious effect on Fascist muscles. . . .

Immediately sixty-eight other Italians resigned. In September 1939 Ciano abruptly joined the club again, and hundreds of rusted golf clubs were wearily dragged out of Fascist closets once more. Definitely, there was a "Fascist angle" on sport. The rising or falling membership of "*le Golf*" tipped off many a journalist as to the diplomatic manœuvres proceeding between 10 Downing Street and the Chigi Palace. One presumes Count Ciano putted his last "purely British pill" on the eighteenth hole sometime in March, and then retired to the nineteenth hole in the Brenner Pass locker room to gloat with Handicapper Hitler, who had all winter given him so many nice strokes a hole.

or luncheon, the bridge tables and poker tables were put up at once, and then until dawn there was a deep smoky silence broken only by the snap of cards, the click of chips, and the little animal grunts and squeals and lunatic laughter and groans that people let out with the fortunes of gambling.

Oddly enough, the only real "conversation" I had with an Italian in my five short days in Rome was on just such an evening. I had been invited to dine in a private suite in the Rome Excelsior Hotel with the lovely half-American Donna Cora Caetani. When I arrived, the small sitting-room was already dense with smoke from twenty or thirty cigarettes, and through this haze came my hostess followed by a dinner coat and a black tie, surmounted by the familiar blond rotogravure features of Count Galeazzo Ciano. Past his shoulder I saw Countess Edda Ciano in a bold print evening gown leaning languorously against the mantelpiece. She was very pale and emaciated, and her red-gold hair and heavy-lidded green eyes slipped by my direct eager glance, like a green wave from the prow of a ship, impersonal, indifferent, curiously cruel and strong. You felt right away that Edda Ciano "met" nobody. In the course of events you came into contact with her, and then moved on, and she was there, sullen and ambiguous as a March sea, and *you* were gone.

The silliest description I ever heard one woman give of another was Donna Cora's description of Edda. She said: "She is a dear sweet little girl."

My feminine instincts told me right away that it would be futile to do anything else but ignore Edda. Count Ciano made that very easy for me. He retrieved me a warm *soi-disant* American cocktail from a slopped-over tray, lighted my cigarette with the other hand, and began to talk in a very pleasant voice, in a quick and flip and pleasant way. He spoke very good English. He asked me a number of questions about my stay in Rome, and whether I had seen the World's Fair Building, the "Olympiad of Civilization," scheduled to open in 1942.[6]

I said yes, it was a swell job daringly and optimistically conceived. I said eagerly that I hoped with all my heart the Fair would open on schedule!

Ciano said there was no doubt of it, no possible shadow of a doubt. (This remark I quoted widely for several months after, to prove that Ciano certainly was not for going into the war; if Italy went to war, how could the Fair open by '42? I see now his statement was not inconsistent with his real policy; Ciano definitely was not for going into a *long* war.) Then he asked me if I'd seen the modern Mussolini Athletic Forum, and I answered yes, and thought it spankingly handsome, but that I felt that the forty or fifty heroic marble statues of nude young men all around it were even for classical art a little outsize. We both agreed that two

[6] I quote here a few sentences from the government's official invitation booklet to the *Olympiad of Civilization* in 1942: ". . . Rome in 1942. An endeavour to assemble all the creative forces in a noble and fruitful competition in the field of human activity. The significance of this appeal is twofold: desire for peace and faith in the future. . . . Italy has confidence in the beneficent and tranquillizing influence of civilization. . . . Of all kinds of collaboration, that which is accomplished under the auspices of the human intellect is undoubtedly the most beneficial to the common weal . . . the peoples of the world [will] take part in this vast and complete synthesis. . . . This Exhibition, created by the will of the Duce, will also show how great has been the contribution of Italy to universal progress. . . . Creations of art which the mind of man has conceived in order to render eternal his visions of beauty and fantasy. . . ." Now, what is so familiar to an American ear about such language? This: It is the super-duper-stupendous, colossal Romanized-double-talk of the Hollywood movie magnates. In Hollywood as in Rome the Imperator-complex boys peddling their escapist dope, their "greatest spectacles of all time," to the brute mass-mind, also try to conceal the cheapness and hollowness of their product and their own lust for wealth and power in astonishingly similar phraseology.

thousand years from now they would give the tourists of that day a very exaggerated notion of the physical charms of Romans *circa* 1940.

Then I said, trying again to be very, very clever and trip him into a politically indiscreet remark: "Oh, wouldn't it be a pity if Italy got into this war, and all the wonderful things Mussolini has built became *prematurely* ruins? It would be so much nicer to have the excavating done by the archæologists of 2042."

He laughed and replied: "The last thing to concern yourself about is the future of modern ruins. They have no future; the kind of ruins you get after a modern war wouldn't be worth excavating." [7]

Then we went in to dinner, which was served at a series of nine or ten little tables, and I sat next to Ciano. But everybody else at the table was Italian, and as I spoke practically no Italian, I understood very little of what they were saying. Ciano did most of the talking, in a jolly, common, confident voice, always half smiling, and everybody at the table said: "*Si, si, si,* Excellency!" to practically everything he said. There was one word they used very often. That was *carbone.* I found out later that it meant "coal," and they were discussing the big news of that week—England's stopping of their coal shipments from Germany.[8]

[7] The truth is, Romans didn't really worry, the way the Parisians and Londoners did, about being bombed. They instinctively knew that no Christian country was going to drop bombs in the purlieus of St. Peter's and the Pope. That was another reason for getting in on Hitler's side: Hitler might not be so squeamish about blasting the Rock that God had founded His Church on.

[8] I said to the oil man afterwards: "If only I had known what Ciano was talking about, I might really have found out something." He answered: "Nothing you would have remembered a week later. This coal business is just one of those incidents that everybody thinks is crucial at the time, and six months later, historians of the period make a note to make a note of it in a footnote somewhere"—which is just where it is now.

So the dinner itself was a great bore, because I couldn't understand or say anything. But I watched Ciano very carefully. I decided he was a nice-looking young fellow, though I didn't like his new crew hair-cut (which he said later he wore because his hair was getting prematurely grey at the temples), but all the time I had a definite feeling he was really quite slick underneath his cocky and casual attitude.

The moment the dinner was over, the waiters whipped the cloths off the tables and brought out cards and chips, and after a little milling around and looking for ash-trays, everybody sat down again and began to gamble. Edda Ciano sat down first alone at a table. She stuck a long slim cigarette-holder into the corner of her great sullen red mouth at a very Rooseveltian angle, and jutted her wide thin jaw at a Mussolini angle, and, narrowing her eyes to two beautiful green tiger-cat slits, reached quickly for the cards and began to shuffle them expertly. You could see that everybody wanted to be at her table, but the guests waited until the hostess, fluttering, told them who could sit where. Edda Ciano paid no attention to the seating arrangements. She just smoked and riffled the cards. . . .

The hostess said to me: "Will you play?"

I replied: "Do they play deuces wild, and spit in the ocean?" and she asked:

"What's that?"

After I told her, she said: "Oh, Countess Ciano has quite a number of original things like that."

So I said: "Thank you, if you don't mind I think I won't play this evening."

Then Count Ciano said: "I don't like gambling either. Come talk to me."

We went into the little sitting-room, where we sat down

alone, and where we were left alone, rather markedly I thought, the rest of the evening.

(The *Vogue* editor said afterwards: "Think nothing of it, darling! Everybody was just observing protocol.")

Ciano said: "Now what shall we talk about?"

I answered: "Oh, anything just so long as we are frank. I'm very, very tired of not being able freely to speak my mind in Rome. It's a democratic vice, of course, but it's the last one I would ever be able to rid myself of."

He said: "Well, now you can shoot the works to me." (Ciano was very proud of the amount of American slang he knew, and I taught him a lot more before the evening was over. I'm afraid he isn't going to find it very useful for a number of years.) "Oh, come," he said, "what do you want to say that you cannot say freely in Rome?"

"I'd like to say," I said, "that the Germans are double-crossing *so-and-sos*, and I think Italy will make the mistake of its history to go in with them."

He said: "All right, say it."

So I made the remark again, and he said smoothly, "Now, you see nothing has happened to you!"

I answered: "Yes, but I've got no reaction out of you."

He said: "Demanding a reaction to what you say is supposed to be rather more Fascist than democratic, don't you think? But even in Italy a man can keep his *thoughts* to himself. . . . Now *I* should like to say something to you. Why should an artist like yourself be so interested in the ugly world of politics?"

"An artist?" I asked.

"Yes," he said, "a successful playwright. I can understand," he said, "why an unsuccessful playwright might get involved in politics—that, for instance, is what happened to me." And then he told me that after he got his law degree at the University of Rome in 1921, his first ambition was to be a writer. He became a theatre and book reviewer on the *Nuovo Paese*, the first Fascist paper in Rome, and then decided to write a play. It was called, I believe, *The Golden Land*. It was, he said, a terrible flop. Reminiscing, he looked a little pale. "You don't know," he said, "what those critics did to me!" He gulped and closed his eyes. "You've never had a failure."

I said: "Oh, yes, I have." Then I told him about my first play, which had been the outstanding flop of its season.[9]

"My God," he said, beaming at me like a long-lost sister, "you *do* know?"

We compared notes on theatrical critics, those snarling if sincere sentinels at the gates of art. After that I understood Count Ciano very well indeed, and why he was at once so indifferent and good-natured in the face of the bitterest personal attacks on him in the foreign press, and so adroit and calm in his most difficult public relations. When your first play (which is as precious and personal and tender and tremulously sacred to a budding author as a boy's first declaration of love) has been greeted with the loud derisive whoops and hollers—the savage, blood-curdling Indian yells of those master scalpers, the critical fraternity—well, no poisoned shaft has ever after any power to penetrate or inflame.

Public life with all its attendant censure has no horrors for a man who—however grievous his theatrical sin—has once been taken naked over the live coals by a group of professional theatre critics. It is the quickest way I know to acquire a spiritual elephant-hide.

Ciano and I decided that all diplomats and politicians should be required by law to have written in their extreme

[9] *Abide with Me*—1935.

youth one unsuccessful play.

It seems that Ciano had also written a second play, *The Luck of Hamlet*—which the title tells you was a failure, too. That was produced in Buenos Aires, where Ciano had been sent as a young Fascist diplomat. With his second theatrical failure the die was irrevocably cast. Politics, which inherits so many inferior talents, claimed Ciano for its own. . . .

And so the evening wore on, and we touched on many kindred topics—Ciano's passion for keeping a diary, his aversion to grand opera (he had refused to attend the fiftieth anniversary of Maestro Mascagni's *Cavalleria Rusticana* at the Opera House earlier in the week), his taste in modern Italian sculptors, his liking for Chinese art, and so on. But if I ever so gently slipped in any question which might have an impersonal or political significance, he slid away from it twice as gently. So at the end of the evening, when Edda appeared in the doorway and flashed her green eyes at him once for a "go" signal, the Count had managed to leave me with the distinct impression that he was a highly peaceful, artistic soul, who had a great love of the theatre (particularly the American theatre), and who adored the American way of life (he had said how very happy he would be if circumstances were only such that he, with his great love for America, could be the Italian ambassador in Washington!). But about Italy and the war I thought I had learned nothing, nothing at all. As he left, I asked a little bitterly: "May I quote you on all these vital matters?" and he answered with his bland, handsome, even-toothed smile: "Oh, by all means, do. . . ."

The next morning everybody in Rome knew that I had sat in that room alone with Ciano for two hours. And although Italians are by nature—quite unlike the French and the English—the kindest and most hospitable people in the world, they were now twice as hospitable as before. A number of people telephoned and said:

"Do stay on in Rome. You'll be able to find out much more about what's going on in Europe right here than in France or England now."

Running over those two hours of conversation in my mind I replied thoughtfully: "Oh, I don't think so." And I felt as if I had let Mr. Welles's suite down badly. . . .

That night at dinner the Marchesa P– said: "Oh when are you going to see him again?" But because the day and its events [10] had passed since the conversation, I naturally asked:

"See whom?"

She said: "Oh, you know."

"Ciano?" I asked.

"Sssh! Please!"

That's when I found out you not only couldn't talk politics in Rome, but you hardly dared call a politician by name when he wasn't around, for fear, I suppose, something you said about him might be overheard and quoted against you. . . .

After that the *Vogue* editor and I always referred to Mussolini as the Big Apple and Ciano as the Little Apple, and all our Italian friends were quite relieved.

The next time I saw the handsome, amiable, and slippery Count was the following night at a movie that Ambassador and Mrs. Phillips showed to a number of guests after dinner at the Embassy. It was *Drums along the Mohawk*. The Phillipses, like the Kennedys in London, circumnavigated diplomatic after-dinner conversational difficulties by showing American films. *Drums along the Mohawk* was enor-

[10] Four hours spent trying to get a Swiss transit visa, three trying to get a French visa.

mously popular with their Italian guests. It was perfectly obvious why: Here were the young pioneers, the nation-builders, carving prosperity out of an untamed land, struggling heroically for their economic and political freedom, and constantly being obliged to slaughter the poor natives who had been sicked on them by the wicked British. The Ethiopian parallel was pleasantly clear.

After the movie Ciano excused himself quickly. As he said good-night to me, he added with a bland smile, "I have to meet His Excellency Herr Ribbentrop at the station tomorrow morning at seven or I would otherwise stay for another of our illuminating talks." Now, the arrival of Ribbentrop, announced the day before by Ciano, had been a diplomatic bombshell that had thrown everybody in all the embassies into a state of panic and fear. And indeed this arrival laid the groundwork for the historic meeting at the Brennero, which in turn sealed the fate of France.

But I think, in the end, I should have remembered how Ciano felt about dramatic critics long after I had forgotten what he might have said about Ribbentrop, because the truth is that in those days I cared almost as much about the theatre and the next play I was going to write as I did about the war. . . . All people, even journalists, have a way of focusing their minds on the things which personally seem most important to them at the time. And if someone inadvertently tells them a larger truth, they often do not recognize it because at the time it doesn't click with a prejudice, coincide with an interest, or square with a preconceived theory. I see now that that night Ciano had told me the truth about himself and Italy and the war. The very fact that he never indicated by word, gesture, innuendo, a flicker of an eyelash, or a half-smile how he as a free individual felt about peace or war—the only topics then worth the attention of an adult mind, which he certainly had–should have proved to me that his mind was hopelessly imprisoned in Fascist ideology, that he and with him all Italy were the creatures of Fascism's master, Mussolini, the one-man minority *who wanted war*. Now I see that the real definition of a dictatorship is: a government in which the Dictator only says what suits him, and nobody else, not even the Crown Prince, dare propound an idea.

Ribbentrop arrived at seven the next morning. At the same hour I left on the Rome Express for Paris. I had talked art and literature and the theatre in Europe in the spring for the very last time. It is, as I say, a significant fact, which I was too dense at the time to see, that this irrelevant talk should have been with one of the few men who really knew what was going to happen.

On Monday, March the 11th, I arrived at the Gare de Lyon in Paris, in France, which was really in the war. Only the painted blue glass in the station, and the paper strips pasted on shop windows, and a few men in uniform in the streets–far fewer than in Italy–suggested the feeling of war. And when I came to the Ritz Hotel on the Place Vendôme, I found that the Ritz was very much the same. There was the same smiling little manager at the reception desk, with his long cutaway coat that almost touched his heels behind, the same smoothly efficient and omniscient red-moustached concierge, and the grey, distinguished Olivier, the great Maître d'hôtel of Europe, bowing as always at the end of the corridor in the dining-room door. I said to the *Vogue* editor:

"But is it my imagination, darling, that makes me think they look a little more solemn and pale than of yore?"

She answered: "Yes, darling, I'm afraid it's just that

imagination of yours." And from the smells of fur and perfume, and the sounds of high bird-babble voices, which when you close your eyes sound like the noises you hear as you're just going under ether, I saw right away that the guests of the Ritz were the same sort of guests that they had always been.

The manager said: "*En effet*, we are rather more crowded than usual, so many people closed their houses during the winter to go to the country, and now they have all come back to Paris. We are surprised—but, be assured, delighted—to see you; we have had very few guests from America since the beginning of the war. Will rooms over the garden do?"

The rooms on the garden with their high French windows and heavy satin curtains and light stiff little oak Louis XVI chairs were full of friendly flowers, arranged as only *la gouvernante* at the Ritz could arrange them in pretty baskets and vases. The *Vogue* editor read the cards.

"My dear, Schiap! Johnny McMullin! Elsie Mendl! Henry Bernstein! Madame Dupuy!" [11] she said; "everybody knows I am here. Where's the telephone book? I can hardly wait to start."

Then we heard the loud shattering, nerve-racking noise of drilling outside. I went to the window. Over the garden wall there were men working in a concrete pit.

I said to the bagagiste who was trundling in my trunk: "What's that?"

He replied: "Ah, madame, they are building an extra bombproof cellar there."

The *Vogue* editor said: "Oh," very thoughtfully. Then she added: "Everything looks so normal, the Van Cleef jewels and tortoise-shell boxes in the show-cases by the

[11] They are all refugees in the Ritzes of America now.

elevator, the awnings down over the terrace there, all these flowers from friends up here—a little too normal. I mean, aren't you, in a way, afraid?"

I answered very honestly: "No." Then I went on: "I've noticed that bombs never make hits—on people who live in the Claridge or Ritz."

She said, laughing: "Why, that's a poem."

I said: "No, it's a political philosophy widely popularized by a man called Karl Marx. I'm putting my entire faith in it now."

And then I opened the cards on my flowers. There was one from the oil man. It said: "Have fun. *These* are the good old days in Paris now."

THREE

It is not by speeches and resolutions that the great questions of the time are decided . . . but by iron and blood.

Bismarck, in the Prussian House of Delegates, September 30, 1862

THE FIRST THING I found out in Paris in early March was that in spite of the savagely bitter and nerve-racking winter of inaction everybody's morale was excellent. Everybody seemed to be full of hope, zeal, spirit, and confidence. There was one phrase on everybody's lips: *Il faut en finir* (This time we must put an end to it).[1] People said it on the streets. Waiters told you so in cafés. The couturières embroidered the motto in red, white, and blue into the corners of gay chiffon handkerchiefs. Jewellers made gold charm bracelets

1 The author of this phrase, which became the war-slogan of the Allies, was the same good, grey gentleman who gave them "Peace in our time"—Mr. Neville Chamberlain.

spelling it. It vibrated the urgent tonsils of every radio commentator. It titled the carefully reasoned editorials in every paper. Every politician rounded his patriotic peroration with it. And in the canteens the soldiers sang it lustily and honestly to music. We must put an end to it! Anyone who didn't believe that they could and that they would was a defeatist or a pro-German. (That omnibus term for all dissenters or critics, "fifth-columnist," did not come into popular usage until after the invasion of Norway.)

Sometimes the French spoke of their morale as though it were something tangible: "The morale of the French poilu," they said, "made him impervious to the longest, coldest winter France has ever had." Or something negotiable like money: "The morale of the home front was such that it supplied our poilus, on short notice, with millions of blankets." Or functional like an anti-tank gun: "The morale of our troops will really begin to operate when faced with the menace of German tanks."

French morale was regarded as different not merely in quality but in kind from German morale. French morale was durable, concrete, natural. German morale was friable, illusory, *ersatz.*

"When they bomb Paris," everybody said, "our morale will be hardened." But: "When we bomb Berlin, you will see how German morale will *break.*" [2]

[2] This often stated view led to a remarkable discovery, however, on my part. I said: "If, when you bomb Berlin, German morale will surely break, why not bomb it *now*?" The answer was: "If we bomb Berlin, they'll bomb Paris, and though it wouldn't break our morale, it would be tragic, first because it is a more beautiful and historic city than Berlin, secondly because the seat of the government is here." Then I asked: "But if it means winning the war? And the government can move." "Yes," they said, "it's already planned to move to Tours. That's what we would hate most of all: to have the government move." I discovered that French people felt Paris was France! In March there was a widespread rumour that Churchill had flown to Paris to demand that Daladier begin bombing-

Indeed, morale was regarded not only as spiritual ammunition but as a decisive instrument of warfare, possessed exclusively by the Allies—entirely lacking in the enemy.

On June 10 Paul Reynaud still believed in the almost physical properties of morale.[3] He said, that in the Battle of Flanders the Germans had embarked on three enterprises: "First, they hoped to crush the morale of our troops, [but] far from collapsing, the morale of our troops and of our country proved worthy of our ancestors. The heroism of the combats in Flanders and of the battles in Dunkirk belongs to history." The second aim, he said, was "to break the morale of Paris [from the air, but] a few minutes after last week's bombing I saw on the spot the proud faces of our men and women workers of Paris, who cannot tremble. We know what the colossal raid means for the people of Paris—nothing." The third enterprise was the Battle of France itself—aimed at the morale of a whole people. But "the dream of German hegemony will clash with French resolution. . . . France, like her ally, is calm and proud."

This palpable if not tangible morale of the French was

---

operations on the Ruhr, but that the Daladier government refused, feeling that this would inevitably result in a loss of civilian life, which in turn would lead to reprisals and to the bombing of Paris. Rumour said this was one of the reasons that Churchill fell out with Daladier and urged belligerent Reynaud, who had small support in a Cabinet dedicated to Gamelin-Daladier defence psychology to take the Prime Ministry if he could get it, promising him Great Britain's energetic support. After the surrender Reynaud was widely criticized by the British for not abandoning Paris for Tours *soon enough*. Churchill understands that London is largely England; he and the British never quite understood to what extent, in the French imagination, Paris was France.

[3] And as late as June 30 England's Harold Nicolson, Parliamentary Secretary to the Ministry of Information, in an impassioned speech at Shrewsbury called upon the English to keep their morale intact, as peoples in other times were told to keep their powder dry. But he envisaged England's morale not as gunpowder but as a super-flame-thrower—"a burst of patriotism, flaming like a furnace, through which no invader, however mechanized, would be able to pass."

not based, as most Americans and many French like to believe, on the noble and spiritual conviction that theirs was a crusade, a crusade for Democracy. Most Frenchmen saw Austria, Czechoslovakia, Republican Spain, Poland, and in early March Finland expire without undue spiritual anguish. Frenchmen were not fighting *for* any of these countries, or *for* Democracy. They were fighting *against* Hitler for France, for France's soil and shops (two thirds of the Frenchmen in France either tilled that soil or owned those shops), for the right to have France run, not by Germans, but by Frenchmen.

In the immediate years before the war, subject to the fierce stresses of Fascist and Communist ideologies, buffeted by the stormy seas of the capitalist depression, France's frail democratic ship of state had been about to split asunder and founder. The declaration of war temporarily caulked the dangerous split and gave all hands on board a common task, a common aim—to avoid capture by the German pirates in order to sink, or mutiny, or sail a little time longer as Frenchmen.

The fact that in their final agonized and not wholly unanimous decision to stem the tide of aggression on Poland's doorstep instead of waiting any longer for it to reach their own, they had also in the eyes of the outside world aligned themselves with the great cause of Democracy, was a pleasant coincidence, but one not without its embarrassments to Frenchmen. To begin with, the crusade for Democracy implied a series of unpalatable and dangerous post-war commitments abroad: namely, the eventual restoration and guarantee of all the "fallen democracies" abroad, and at home the continued observance of a mode of government which many influential Frenchmen now felt was either obsolete or woefully inadequate in a growing world of aggressive totalitarianism.[4] Indeed, the cause of international Democracy had been thrust on France at the very hour when all her instincts pointed to fervent nationalism, and her real self-interests could best be served by both present and post-war totalitarianism.[5]

The dilemma that resulted from France's public and political avowal that she was fighting to make herself and the world safe for Democracy, and the private conviction of both her politicians and her people that France was fighting to make France and France's soil safe for *any* form of French government that seemed expedient to France after the war was over, was responsible for the true accusation that "France had no war aims." She did have one however, on which all Frenchmen were united: France, now and for ever, for Frenchmen.

Somerset Maugham in his book *France at War* glossed this purely nationalistic aim by calling it "security." He wrote: "It is not honour and glory they are fighting for—that will come, but that is by the way—it is *security*."

At long last, after Austria and Czechoslovakia, and Spain and Poland, the French (even then, shoved a bit by the British and egged on by American diplomacy) decided that the only way to have "security" was to fight for it—to win it from the Germans.

So the *morale* of the average Frenchman was the fruit neither of spiritual nor of intellectual convictions concerning "Democracy," but of a natural and physical and purely nationalistic will to territorial integrity.

[4] On June 18, a French broadcaster told the world: "What was our crime? Our loyalty to a way of life that our experience had proved to be unadapted to the times."

[5] On July 13 in Vichy, Vice Premier Laval announced to the world that France was through being "a humanitarian *crusader* for other nations," and henceforth would devote herself to a program of "national reconstruction," the proposed outline of which was definitely totalitarian.

In the final analysis the morale of the French was just a national attitude of confidence based on the reasonable expectation of victory. The morale of a surrounded garrison that dies to the last man, the morale of a Christian on the rack, the morale of missionary bands boiled in foreign oil in foreign lands by barbarian sceptics, *is* something different. One man in a thousand has that. We have words for such men: heroes and saints—and crusaders. A nation is never composed entirely of heroes and saints. And with the exception of the German nation's own perverse crusade for a thousand years of German *Kultur*, and German economy, there is today certainly no nation of crusaders.[6] But the French have never prided themselves on being saints and heroes and crusaders. They are above all, as they will always tell you, *hommes raisonnables*. So when France's reasonable expectation of victory no longer seemed *raisonnable*, their morale vanished—and they laid down their arms and surrendered.

Now, what, in turn, was that "reasonable expectation" based on?

Three things: One, the popular uncritical belief that "History repeats itself," and that therefore the history of the last war would repeat itself. (And the history of the last war was that Time won for the Allies. In 1914 the Allies were disorganized and unprepared. But Time, working exclusively for them, ultimately assured them of victory. Now, better prepared, better organized, had not Time, the

[6] At the beginning of the war, the British proclaimed that all they were fighting for was to destroy the government of Herr Hitler. In April they announced, through Alfred Duff Cooper, that their real enemy "was the whole German people." Now, in July, they have belatedly discovered that theirs is a crusade against "a world revolution of totalitarians." Even in England the crusading idea was very late in getting started. It is, unfortunately, in the nature of true crusaders to be *besiegers* and not the besieged.

beneficent, omnipotent genie of Democracy, already been working for them on twenty-four-hour shifts for the seven months of the Sitzkrieg?)

Two, the less popular, more criticized, but still major faith in the *ultimate* efficiency of the traditional democratic-capitalistic economic process itself, even against that formidable new contender in the economic world—totalitarianism.

And, three, a blind confidence in France's army in being, and France's system of defence. (In England, the counterpart of this was England's faith in the navy, and England's blockade system.)

An acceptance of these three tenets of faith added up to an even more than reasonable expectation of victory.

To be sure, the three tenets which made up the creed of victory were not separate articles of faith—they derived their power to convince, or to convert, syllogistically, one from the other: If you *believe* you have time, your doubts about the slow, bumbling nature of the democratic economic process are comparatively unimportant. If you *believe* in your present system of defence, these same doubts are still a pardonable heresy which time (in which you do believe) will cause you to recant. Believe in any *one* of these three tenets, and you find yourself eventually embracing all of them. The Frenchman who denied all three was either a Hitler agent, a defeatist, or, at best, *pas raisonnable*.

So everywhere in March you heard Frenchmen saying to one another and to Americans: "At the end of the last war we had ten times as many guns and raw materials—and even men—as we began with." But, you slyly asked (being American), where, at the end, did they come from? And they said: "From our own factories, slowly but inexorably mobilized for war industry, from the factories of our Allies —well, from America." And then at this point you were always told (as you pleasantly expected to hear) that the nation or nations which could command America's industrial output ("Never mind its man output, we'll never need it") were unconquerable. There was regrettably one immediate barrier to the Allies' free access to America's industrial output: the Johnson Act. But it was only a question of *time*, every Frenchman argued, before the Johnson Act would be repealed. "Why are you so sure it will be repealed?" you often heard yourself asking. And every Frenchman said: "Because in *time* you will realize this is your war!"

And right there you both stopped talking either current or future Allied war-industry output and began passionately to talk American domestic politics and American foreign policy.

Sometimes Frenchmen, instead of explaining to you why democratic economy must win the war in time, explained why totalitarian economy must lose it in time. Oil, iron, ore, timber, wheat, and butter fats were the theme song of all that. Hitler didn't have much now, couldn't get more, was gradually using up what he had (and if he became desperate enough to attack, would use them all up with fatal rapidity). With a paper and a pencil you could prove that on any French restaurant tablecloth, just the way people were proving it at home.

Look, if Rumania (oil) turned against him, if Stalin (wheat) made trouble in the Balkans, if Norway (timber), if Sweden (ore) or Holland (fat) veered further toward England, if Italy (the big leak in the blockade) could be bullied or bribed or merely awakened to its own "enlightened self-interests," well, the jig was up with Herr Hitler and Company. And as the first neutral went, so would go all the other neutrals. And weren't all these things, in March, well within the realm of possibility?

So many Frenchmen said: "Anyone can see that if Hitler doesn't attack now, at the peak of his strength, he's doomed." And when you asked: "Then why doesn't he attack now?" they replied, with vast logical Gallic shrugs: "Undoubtedly because he knows he's doomed anyway."

So, the stalemate on the western front was widely explained as "Hitler's realization of the economic impasse he's got himself into." His constant threat of an offensive was "just his last war of nerves; he hopes to wear us down nervously, and either force *us* to attack (which we won't do) or wait for French internal dissension (much overrated since the declaration of war) to breed a favourable atmosphere in which he can make peace overtures." In early March a Hitler-inspired peace, a Mussolini appeasement move, was very much the topic of indignant French conversation. The visit of my friend Mr. Sumner Welles, his over-cordial reception by Mussolini, his long hours with Hitler, gave much credence to this supposition. But these expected peace proposals, however violently debated, were questions of only academic interest to most Frenchmen. They were in no mood, in March, to discuss Mr. Hitler's peace proposals.[7] *Il faut en finir* first was their motto. Afterwards "We talk peace—*our* peace," they said to you. Still, thinking on peace, with all its problems (which were, in March, infinitely more perplexing and numerous and even harrowing than the problems of war), you again began to talk Allied foreign policy and domestic politics.

And so while in March everybody posed the urgent ques-

[7] M. Reynaud broadcast to America: "This is no phony war, and we will tolerate no phony peace."

tion: "Will the coming of spring bring a great offensive on the western front?"—or "Hitler's much vaunted hammer blow," as the London *Times* called it—nobody really worried very much about the outcome of that offensive.

It is interesting for the record, however, to note that the author of the theorem that "Defence is the best attack," Captain Basil Liddell Hart, did answer it publicly in early March. In Captain Liddell Hart's book *The Defence of Britain*, published just before the outbreak of war, he had developed the theory that a three-to-one superiority in mechanized weapon power is necessary for victory, and such superiority would be impossible to amass in a war between great powers. In the days that followed September the Allied High Command seemed by every indication to have adopted the Liddell Hart doctrine. Liddell Hart's pronouncement on the coming spring offensive was published in March in all the French, English, and American papers.

"It is obvious that General Gamelin can hardly be expected to achieve now, by an offensive, what he judged that it was unwise to attempt when the Polish Army was in being and the forces defending the Westwall—itself now made deeper—were far smaller. No military information is needed to arrive at such a conclusion, but only a sense of proportion.

"For the Germans, *the prospect for an offensive might seem more promising. But by any known modern process of calculation, their margin of superiority in numbers is not enough to support that promise. So far as can be gauged, only the introduction of some radically new (secret) weapon, or extraordinarily bad generalship on the Allies' side, could give them any chance of real success.*[8] Otherwise they would be inviting a heavy repulse—which might

[8] The italics are mine.

have far-reaching repercussions. . . .

"There remains the question whether the Germans will try a limited coup on the flanks of the main western front for the advancement of their strategic position. Neither Belgium nor Switzerland offers a very tempting target. The water lines in the one case, the mountain ranges in the other, form a formidable obstacle to rapid penetration, while Allied reinforcement to either if attacked would be comparatively easy. An incomplete success might bring more complications than advantages to the invader.

"Holland is a more accessible and more vulnerable target, besides being more difficult of reinforcement by the Allies. And if Germany should be counting on decisive results from an air offensive against England, the establishment of her air bases in Holland would be an important step forward.

"On the other hand, if such an air offensive failed to succeed, and succeed soon, she would have incurred the strategic disadvantage of greatly widening the path and increasing the scope for the Allied air forces which would become an increasing boomerang with every stage of the latter's growth. She would also immediately simplify the British naval blockade."

One French journalist, in the *Paris Soir*, cut this Gordian knot of argument with a remarkably astute and logical observation. He said: "If Hitler attacks this spring, it will be a sign of either great German strength or great weakness."

But wait: I see now that it is going to be almost impossible to give you a clear picture of what Frenchmen and Englishmen were thinking in the spring of the Second World War unless we examine a little more closely the syllogisms which formed their framework of war reference.

French minds were full of these wonderful and happy

syllogisms, some of them with sound military and economic premises and false political conclusions, others with false military and economic premises and sound political conclusions, and each delicately balanced against the others, false against true, like a house of cards (a house of cards, that toppled before the iron reality of the Lowlands invasion). Some of these syllogisms had to do with France, some with England, some with Germany, some with the neutrals, some with America. All together they were the shifting quicksands of false logic on which France's morale and confidence and whole conduct of the war were tragically built. In the light of events, you can say they were wishful and foolish and vain, but at the time they seemed to be highly logical.

The key syllogisms, as I have already suggested, had to do with history repeating itself, and its conclusion concerned "time," which the Allies thought they had, and the Germans didn't have.

> History repeats itself.
> The last war was a long one won by the Allies.
> Therefore this will be a long war and the Allies will win it.

Does that seem now almost simple-minded? Then add to it all the other syllogisms stemming from it, bolstering it up, hemming it around, which made the four-square logical blueprint of Victory.

> A three-to-one superiority in men and material is needed for a successful attack.
> Hitler did not attack in September.
> Therefore Hitler in September had no such superiority.
>
> (And if he didn't have it, then he could not have it now. In fact:)

Germany grows weaker every day that the blockade works.
The blockade has been working for eight months.
Therefore Germany is weaker than when the war started.

(From which it follows that:)

The Germans cannot win a long war.
It must be a long war if the Allies refuse to attack (i.e., stay behind their defences).
Therefore it will be a long war and Germany will lose it.

(Besides:)

Naval supremacy has always decided the outcome of major national conflicts.
The British and the French have naval supremacy.
Therefore the outcome will be victory for the Allies.

(If there is any doubt about this:)

A long war will ultimately threaten American interests.
America will enter the war when her interests are threatened.
Therefore America will enter a long war.

(And suppose she doesn't? Still:)

The productive capacity of the United States is limitless.
The Allies alone have access to that productive capacity.
Therefore the productive capacity of the Allies is limitless.

(What if the Allies' *cash* is exhausted? Then:)

The Johnson Act in America precludes credit to nations defaulting in payments on their last war debts.
A long war will exhaust the Allies' cash.
Therefore America will ultimately repeal the act and extend credit to the Allies (since we have proved a long war will threaten her interests).

All the little neutrals are really pro-Ally, but afraid to act out of fear of Germany.
Germany grows weaker every day.
Therefore as they become less afraid the little neutrals will eventually all become openly pro-Ally, or even Allies.

(This was the syllogism used to rationalize the course that would be inevitably taken by Norway, Sweden, Holland, Belgium, Greece, Bulgaria and Yugoslavia. The open alliances made with Rumania and Turkey seemed to prove this. Still, if you don't like it, try it the other way round:)

With each neutral Germany takes "under her protection" (i.e., conquers), she becomes stronger.
Realizing this, the remaining neutrals must become more pro-Ally (less neutral) as Germany gets stronger (since we have proved they fear a stronger Germany).
Therefore the remaining neutrals in desperation are bound to come into the war as Allies.

(This was the great argument used for eventual Italian and Russian desertion of Germany.)

(There was, of course, a very popular syllogism which contradicted the first premise of the above one flatly:)

With each neutral Germany conquers, she becomes *weaker* (through the "drain" of conquered populations, lengthening of supply lines, internal revolution, etc.)

Belgium, Holland, Norway, etc., are contiguous neutrals which Germany must possess to strike at France and England.

Therefore the Allies are sure to win the war if Germany goes on attacking the neutrals, and getting weaker.

(But the best way to consider the whole problem of neutrals was to bet on human nature:)

Everybody wants to back a winner.
The Allies are sure to be the winner.
Therefore, before the war is over, all the neutrals will be either pro-Ally or Allies.

(This absolutely proved the course Italy would eventually take.)

All Germans are stupid.
It would be stupid to attack the Maginot Line.
Therefore the Germans will attack the Maginot.

(This was the silliest of all. No intelligent, informed person thought it, but it is amazing how many of the people thought it. Remember the Zimmermann note? Remember the "scrap of paper"? Remember how the Schlieffen plan miscarried? Remember the *Lusitania*? If all else failed, from this logical premise of inherent German stupidity you must come to the conclusion that the Germans would somehow blunder fatally and ensure the Allies' victory. Norway was at first widely proclaimed as such a blunder! [9] The best and most comforting syllogism of all was:)

An impregnable defence cannot be taken.
The Albert Canal, the Belgian Maginot, and the French Maginot constitute the "impregnable defences" of France, requiring a far more than three-to-one superiority over a long period of time to take them.
Therefore France cannot be taken; and if France cannot be taken, Germany is beaten.

Now sometimes the French sidewalk-café pessimists and the English week-end spoil-sports said:

"Yes, all that is all true, but suppose Hitler plunks for a Blitzkrieg, because he really has some secret weapon?" Now the scoffing Frenchmen asked: "What secret weapon could he have—besides those dive bombers and tanks he used in Poland,[10] which was a weak, unprepared country, and couldn't take it?"

I remember Colonel (Count) Radziwill, a refugee with the remnant Polish army at Angers, growing very angry one day when this was said in his presence.

He puffed fiercely and said: "You are wrong, it was *not* the tanks and bombers we were unprepared for. It was the

[9] There was in fact a general impression that any attack Germany would make anywhere would be a blunder. The most colossal blunder of all, of course, would be an attempted invasion of Great Britain. Compare the last revealing line of A. P. Herbert's poem preceding the Introduction to this book: "*For it's just the sort of silly thing that silly man would do.*"

[10] Poland, that "weak, unprepared country," which lasted almost as long as the strong, prepared countries of Holland, Belgium, and France put together!

way the Germans used them. They used them in a new way. In a war of movement!"

And a French tablecloth-general said pityingly: "*Ah, mon vieux, comme vous êtes naïf!* A war of movement across the dry Polish plains, *oui*! But through the Ardennes, through the Dutch floods, through the Belgian defences, through the Maginot—through tank-traps and barbed wire and casemates, in the face of our powerful air force—*c'est ridicule!*"

A secret weapon made more sense. So everybody in France freely speculated about gases which might humanely put you to sleep or horribly peel you alive like a banana, and flame-throwers and giant liquid-air bombs, but even while they shuddered as people do always shudder at well-told horror tales, they were quickly consoled, discounting at once such Martian terrors.

There was the asbestos, flame-throwing, bomb-proof shelter of the civilian morale, and there was the French Maginot, and the Belgian Maginot to be got through first, and by that time the British navy's blockade would have starved him . . . and so on and so on around the crazy and happy merry-go-round of false premises.

Now everybody knows what Hitler's secret weapon was: efficiency. The iron efficiency forged in the fires of fanaticism which turned out "those nose-dive bombers and tanks" relentlessly, which coldly co-ordinated military strategy, economics, domestic politics, foreign diplomacy, propaganda, espionage, and the will of the people to his one increasing purpose—to conquer.

Of course, Hitler hasn't won the war yet. (Oh, pray in the vine-clad churches of England, in sombre Westminster Abbey, that God will yet confound this incarnate curse, this shameless renegade, this Hitler! Pray that the navy, or flaming patriotism, or the cliffs of Dover, or America, or something nameless may yet save England! Yes, grant O God Almighty, that this *German* may blunder and miss the last bus yet!) But victory or defeat or the deadlock of a long-dragged-out blood-letting, half of Europe and perhaps all of England will be laid in ruins, and millions of boys—and girls—and old people and babies who might have seen many more lovely, lovely springs will have died very needlessly. And the rest will be in debt, or bondage, or chaos.

All except the lucky or the rich or the powerful (among whom there will be an enormous number of politicians) who will continue to "fight" the war under the bomb-free skies of the United States of America.

But in the spring of the Second World War all this was still "unthinkable." "*Pas raisonable*," the French would have called it. Fortified by many a logical but false deduction of ultimate victory, France, in the spring, marked time, and talked and talked and talked.

FOUR

Never was there a country where the practice of governing too much had taken deeper root and done more mischief.

Thomas Jefferson:
Writings; "Concerning France"

AND HERE was the second thing I now see, but didn't see then: In Paris in March nearly everybody who was talking about the "war" was not really talking about *war* but about *politics.*

Now, in my dictionary "politics" is defined as "the science of civil government." "War" is defined as "armed conflict." They were, I realized belatedly, two quite different things by definition. To be sure, every war, as German General Clausewitz said long ago, has a political objective. But its tactics, its nature, are unpolitical, uncivilian. War is the bloody instrument which a state uses or is forced to use when "politics," when civilian government, fails peacefully to achieve the state's vital political objectives.

To the extent that "the war" was not a state of "armed conflict" from September 3 to the invasion of Norway, it *was* a "phony war." It was in fact politics *in extremis*. That the declaration of war preceded its outbreak by eight months was an unfortunate circumstance which confused too many people's minds about the nature of war. It never confused Hitler's. Hitler used the eight months which followed that declaration to scrap every possible vestige of "politics," of civilian government, and to tighten up the German war machine. To a large extent France used them to safeguard and perpetuate, wherever it possibly could, civilian rights, civilian property, and civilian pursuits. It is a strange, almost insane fact that whereas in the summer of Peace 1939 the people of France were trying valiantly to effect a war economy, in the spring of War 1940 their energies were bent on preserving a peace economy. A disproportionate amount of France's time, thought, and money went into this noble but essentially tragic effort to patch up the framework of "politics," to keep the laws of peace when the spirit of it had fled from all of Europe until the day of victory.

War: armed conflict! That means, of course, guns going off and men being killed and troops being deployed and supplied with food and ammunition while more and more deadly contact is being made with the flesh and blood of the enemy on a chosen field of battle. Guns know no policy except destruction. Plato himself, arguing, would not silence them. Bombs know no ism but barbarism. The laws that successfully govern a peaceful and democratic society do not interfere with the only law bombs know, which is the law of gravity. Neither the Declaration of the Rights of Man nor the theory of free competition nor the sound principles of trade unionism nor an accounting of favourable trade balances, nor gold bars in the vaults of banks can halt tanks in their tracks, and to the statistics concerning America's "productive capacity," nose-dive bombers are remarkably deaf.

The final victor of such a totally unpolitical "armed conflict" may then, and only then, talk politics—his brand of politics, his peace plan, his conception of society. Might does not make right. Right and wrong are spiritual entities that survive alike the bloodiest battle. But only the mighty, *only the strong are free to choose between them.*

When a wise nation is faced with this kind of amoral contact with another nation, it begins feverishly to count not only its own guns but its enemy's guns, and think very hard about its choice, or its enemy's choice, of a field of battle.

Very few people were really counting guns in the spring in Paris—hardly their own, and certainly not Germany's. They were not counting anything except the years of the days of the "Long War" that must pass before they "finished it."

On June 25 Marshal Pétain at last got around to counting. He said: "Today, as yesterday, a war cannot be won with gold only. Men and materials are the answers to victory. . . . On May 1, 1917, after three years of continued fighting, we still had 3,280,000 men under arms. On May 1, 1940, we had 500,000 fewer. In May 1918, we had 85 British divisions. In this May there were only 10. In 1918 we had by our side 58 Italian, 42 American divisions. In 1940, we had no Americans with us, and the Italians against us. . . . This is the *lesson* of our defeat: *Too few guns, too few men, too few Allies*, and their planes were *six to one* against us. We were overwhelmed by crushing *mechanical* and *numerical superiority*."

And then, a logical Frenchman to the end, the poor marshal sought the *reason* why France had allowed herself to be caught in this tragic predicament.

"Since our victory in 1918," he said, "the Spirit of Pleasure prevailed over the Spirit of Sacrifice. We demanded more than we gave. We sought to skimp on effort, and so–we met disaster."

It is of course a little too simple to explain the vast collapse of world capitalistic economy in terms of a perverse love of pleasure, but no matter how true it may have been of France before September 3, it was certainly not true after. Nobody in France was happy. Very few, except a handful of unregenerate fat-cats of the rich families and their congenitally empty-headed plush ladies, were on pleasure bent. Families were split up (one out of two, according to a French poll), business was declining, taxes were crushing. But on the whole few complained; almost everybody made an effort, sacrificed, did his bit as he saw it.

No matter how their leaders may have tried to skimp on money (a practice heretofore conceded to be a virtue in democratic governments), no one, not even the politicians, who talked themselves red, white, and blue in the face, skimped on *effort*. In fact, they seemed to redouble their efforts as they lost sight of their objectives. They, and everybody, honestly thought they were thinking about, doing things about, war. They didn't realize that almost the whole time they were thinking about and practising *politics*.

But everywhere, in every direction, earnest and sincere civilian and political efforts were being made to solve civilian and political problems which were all lumped all together under the general head of "the War Effort." That these problems were essentially civilian problems and not military problems was an error, not of character or heart or honest intention, but of judgment.

Thus: "Our real problem," nearly everybody said, "is how to keep our boys in uniform warm and contented throughout the summer and another hard winter." In a way, you see, they thought even of their troops as accidentally uniformed civilians.[1] So they told you about the "foyers" and "canteens" and "*théatres des Armées*" that the celebrated actresses and elegant duchesses and all the poor but equally patriotic French and English women were organizing and financing 'way behind the Maginot (and right up on the Belgian border) to keep the boys smiling. And they showed you the Red Cross rooms where there were piles upon piles of *colis* or bundles with writing-paper and Chinese chequerboards and sweaters and cigarettes and footballs and belote cards and light reading-matter waiting to go to the soldiers. They were particularly careful to eliminate, from the masses of books and magazines donated, "patriotic harangues." As Maugham put it, "they do not want their patriotism aroused, it is *there*, deep in their bones." [2] They were even more careful to omit all pornographic literature. They said: "The less our boys think about 'pleasure' *in the long months* they are going to spend out there, the more contented they will be." Henry Bernstein, the French playwright, said to me in March: "Ah, the tragedy of this war is that by the time it is over, Frenchmen will have forgotten what Love is!"

[1] At G.H.Q. itself a peculiar battle raged in the spring. Should or should not the soldiers be allowed to do a little spring ploughing in their leisure hours? The farm bloc won. All through the army zones, and right in *front* of the Maginot forts, in the spring, when German soldiers were practising "invasion," many French soldiers ploughed, and planted potatoes.

[2] Meanwhile German troops and German civilians who did not listen to the "political harangues" of their leaders were subject to court martial or arrest.

The French, in their effort to protect their people from the miseries of war thought hard and often, too, of the sufferers on the home front.

In eight months of war they had still managed to do wonders for the 500,000 *évacués* from Alsace and Lorraine. They had found them, through all the countryside of France, schools and food and employment and shelter. They had even got sewing-machines for evacuated prostitutes of Strasbourg, who were, in March, being taught the more useful and social if less popular and historic profession of seamstresses. They pointed with pride to the facts that Daladier had not enforced the totalitarian "decrees" conscripting male and female labour, that everybody was being allowed plenty of gas to motor to the Bois or to the races at Longchamp, that the three-days-without-coal law was being "held over" to the following winter to avoid discontent, that Schiaparelli and Molyneux and Balenciaga and Lelong were showing and exporting collections made of the fine silks still being made in French factories, which were being "gradually" turned into munition plants in order not to bring about too sudden unemployment among the silk weavers, and also because the continued export of silk was one factor in keeping a "favourable trade balance."

After the invasion I saw a French soldier in a base-line hospital. He had a great many pieces of German bomb fragments in his thigh and shoulder. Among his other souvenirs of the war he had in his pyjama pocket a piece of imported French silk from a German parachute. He caressed it with a bitter wonder.

"Look at it," he said. "How fine! You only see silk like that in *this* country on the backs of models in dressmakers'."

And so, in early March in Paris, the Ritz and the Crillon bars were full of ladies in "simple black silk dresses" (but gay flowered Suzy hats) passing tin cans for refugee relief and soldiers' canteens, which were filled to the brim with coins by other ladies in gay Suzy hats who had come there to meet fine-looking French and British officers. Then when everybody was through collecting or giving money, they all drank champagne (that's all the liquor you could get three days a week in France, champagne) and went off, easy in their minds, to have luncheon or dinner.

The Ritz and the Crillon and Café de la Paix and Prunier and Fouquet menus were delicious, if selective. Many of the theatres were open, though after midnight everything was closed unless you knew the addresses of "speakeasies." Yes, everybody ate and drank well while they talked to you about the gigantic War Effort, and explained to you how, because this *was* a democracy, the War Effort was certainly greater than in Germany, because it was voluntary, and how wonderful it was that even in the middle of a "terrible war" a democracy never lost sight of "social objectives." And that would have been all right too, if only it had not lost sight of military objectives.[3]

You see, everybody felt so sure that all a democracy had to do to win a war was to declare it, that if a "free nation" was unified in its desire to win, no "slave-driven force" like Hitler's could defeat it. Everybody felt that: the duchesses and the politicians *and the People.*

Here captious critics are sure to say: "And you, frequenter of the Ritz and crystal-chandeliered salons and embassies of Europe,[4] what do you know of the People and

[3] In late June Stalin himself repealed the five-day work week in still peaceful Russia. One wonders if the party line will dictate a like course to our Communist labour groups here in America. The answer to that is definitely no.

[4] I began by frequenting embassies because embassies are very useful to people who travel, and ended by frequenting them because over a

what they were thinking?"

I have no answer to that except to quote endless anecdotes about *évacués* and maids, and waiters and girls who waited on me in shops, and what the taxi-drivers told me. And everything they said also came to this: "We must put an end to it. It's them or us, this time."

Their occasional doubts concerned, not themselves or the way of life they had had, or had *now*, or wanted to have after the war was over, but their *present* political leaders and the diffusion of France's political leadership.

A taxi-driver said to me, a little sadly: "Russia has a Man, Italy has a Man, Germany has a Man. If *we* only had a Man,[5] we could lick all of them." And then he shrugged his shoulders. "*Mais que voulez-vous?*" he said. "We *like* politics. It is not always *commode*, but we manage . . . ."

Somerset Maugham was not far wrong when he wrote, in March, that the people "have a *sufficient* [6] confidence in their leaders and a *whole-hearted trust* in the *generals* who command their great armies. Everyone who has lived long in France knows how bitter are its political antagonisms, and none can have seen without admiration the way in which, when the country was in peril, these were *composed*; but everyone who knows France must have seen it without surprise, for however bitter the quarrels that agitate the French in times of peace—and really the foreigner gets the impression they are the breath of the nostrils—you can be certain that when the occasion demands it, they will be set aside *to be resumed at a more convenient moment*,

period of three years of European travel I discovered that the embassies of the U.S.A. contain on the whole the most level-headed, best-informed, keenly objective, and efficient men in all Europe.

[5] Draw no hasty conclusions. He may have been a Fascist—or a Communist, or simply, like you, a bewildered democrat.

[6] Again, my italics.

and each man will combine with his neighbour to defend the land which they all so proudly love. What ignorance of the French temper it showed when the Germans thought that in France they were fighting a house divided against itself!"

In the Casino de Paris every night the talented and ardent Maurice Chevalier, idol of the people, came before the footlights and sang a wonderful song which proved that the French people also believed what Maugham believed of them. It was not only the most popular song on the home front, it was also adored "in the Maginot." Its tune was a gay paraphrase of *La Marseillaise*, and the words were the complete portrait of France's democratic army. It is a very long song to reprint here, but then, it was a very big army.

Le Colonel était dans la Finance,	The colonel was in Finance
Le Commandant était dans l'Industrie,	The major was in Industry,
Le Capitaine était dans l'Assurance,	The captain was an insurance man,
Et le Lieut'nant était dans l'Epic'rie,	And the lieutenant had a grocery.
Le Juteux était huissier d' la Banqu' de France,	The adjutant was an usher at the Bank of France,
Le Sergent était boulanger patissier,	The sergeant was a pastry-cook,
Le Caporal était dans l'Ignorance,	The corporal was a dunce,
Et l'deuxième classe était rentier!	And the privates all had private incomes.

Chorus:

Et tout ça, ça fait D'excellents Français, D'excellents soldats,	And all this—makes fine Frenchmen, fine soldiers,

Qui marchent au pas;
Ils n'en avaient plus l'habitude,
Mais, tout comm' la bicyclett', ça n's'oublie pas!
Et tous ces gaillards,
Qui pour la plupart
Ont des goss's qui ont leur certificat d'études,
Oui, tous ces brav's gens
Sont partis chicment
Pour fair' tout comme jadis—
C'que leurs pèr's ont fait pour leurs fils.

Marching in step;
They'd got out of the habit, but
Like bicycle-riding you don't forget.
And all these lads,
Most of whom have kids with high-school diplomas,
Yes, all these good men marched off gallantly
To do for their sons what their fathers had done for them.

Le Colonel avait de l'albumine,
Le Commandant souffrait du gros colon,
Le Capitaine avait bien mauvais' mine,
Et le Lieut'nant avait des ganglions;
Le Juteux souffrait de coliqu's néphrétiques,
Le Sergent avait le pylore atrophié,
Le Caporal, un coryza chronique,
Et l'deuxièm' class' des cors aux pieds.

The colonel had "albumin,"
The major had colitis,
The captain had a bad colour,
And the lieutenant had ganglionitis,
The adjutant had kidney pains,
The sergeant had an atrophied pylorus,
The corporal had a running nose,
And the privates had corns on their feet.

Chorus:

Et tout ça, ça fait
D'excellents Français,
D'excellents soldats,
Qui marchent au pas;
Oubliant dans cette aventure
Qu'ils étaient douillets, fragil's et délicats.
Et tous ces gaillards,

And all this—makes
Fine Frenchmen,
Fine soldiers,
Who march in step,
Forgetting in this adventure
That they were soft, sensitive, and delicate,
And all these nice guys

Qui pour la plupart
Prennaient des cachets, des goutt's et des mixtures,
Les v'là bien portants,
Tout comme a vingt ans,
D'où vient ce miracle là?
Mais du pinard et du tabac!

Who for the most part
Were always taking pills and medicine
Are now in good health,
Like twenty again.
How did this miracle happen?
Wine and tobacco of course.

Le Colonel était d'l'Action Française,
Le Commandant était un modéré,
Le Capitaine était pour la Diocèse,
Et le Lieut'nant boulottait du Curé,
Le Juteux était un fervent extrémiste,
Le Sergent un socialiste convaincu;
Le Caporal inscrit sur tout's les listes,
Et l'deuxième classe—au P.M.U.

The colonel was a royalist,
The major was a pacifist,
The captain was for the high church,
And the lieutenant devoured priests alive,
The adjutant was a violent radical,
The sergeant was a confirmed socialist,
The corporal voted for everybody,
And the privates—bet on the Pari-Mutuel.

Chorus:

Et tout ça, ça fait
D'excellents Français,
D'excellents soldats,
Qui marchent au pas,
En pensant que la République
C'est encor' le meilleur régime ici bas.
Et tout ces gaillards,
Qui pour la plupart
N'étaient pas du même avis en politique,
Les v'là tous d'accord,
Quelque soit leur sort,

And all this—makes
Fine Frenchmen,
Fine soldiers,
Who march in step,
And think that a republic
Still is the best form of government on earth.
And all these nice guys
Who for the most part
Were not really of the same mind in politics,
Now they are united,
Whatever their fate,

Ils désirent désormais	They desire once and for all
Qu'on leurs fiche un' bonn'fois la Paix!	That they be left in peace!

Ah! a democratic army! These were the fine lads with colitis, enlarged colons, corns on their feet, and who knows, finance and pastry shops and stocks still on their minds—who dropped back "weary and exhausted" to a final surrender before the onslaught of the Nazi "fanatics," the long-drilled Strength-through-Joy boys—the soulless slave-driven totalitarian robots. Well, that democratic army of France has won perhaps what in the end it truly desired *most*—not *Liberté*, not *Egalité*, not *Fraternité*, words which had grown too difficult, perhaps, for the little man to interpret—but *peace*. And there was not a big man to say to them, as Patrick Henry said once to us, in the long-ago days when we believed there was something worth dying for: "Is life so dear, or peace so sweet, as to be purchased at the price of chains and slavery? Forbid it, Almighty God! I know not what course others may take, but as for me, give me Liberty or give me Death!" [7]

No, there was only old Marshal Pétain saying with infinite weariness: "I could not agree to the continued shedding of French blood. . . . The fight now has ended. . . . France will be temporarily occupied . . . *but Frenchmen will continue to govern France . . . our honour is safe*. . . . I make to France the gift of my person to ease her sorrow. . . ."

Anyway, after Chevalier sang "All this makes fine Frenchmen" every night in Paris, everybody applauded like mad. I wept myself, my American heart bursting with pride and tenderness at this familiar, voluntary unification

[7] A bitter, disillusioned Frenchman said to me that the motto of the Surrender Cabinet was: "Give us Liberty—or give us Debentures."

of such diverse opinions and interests in time of peril. Then Chevalier bowed, happily, and left the stage, and beautiful half-naked girls sang a *gai numéro* called "We'll Hang Out Our Washing on the Siegfried Line."

(There, as you saw in the syllogisms, was one clue to much of France's "realistic" thinking on the approaching "armed conflict," one of the explanations of France's blind confidence in victory. Nearly everybody in France—the people, the politicians, and the generals were rooted, as immovably as the guns were sunk in the cement of the great fortress of the Hachenburg, in Defence Psychology.)

To the extent that the French admired and believed in the morale and strength of their own democratic army, they despised and disbelieved in the morale and strength of the German army, in March. Nearly everybody said that the Junker military tradition and the Prussian type of soldier it bred had disappeared after the last war. The new army, largely raw recruits, was ill trained, badly manned, improperly staffed. Everybody said the Munich street brawlers had been given high commands. They said the German soldier, today as yesterday, is a dumb totalitarian brute who has no personal initiative, like the brave democratic poilus, and no officers like the French officers, long schooled in strategy, steeped in the traditions of war. All the common German soldier is fit for is to march forward blindly, if he is being enthusiastically machine-gunned by superior officer types from behind. So the French thought, no matter how much the Germans outnumbered them, their own army more than made up for the difference in morale, training, and the superiority of its personnel.

For the rest, as I say, all the "war" talk was politics, and often very speculative politics. Politics that went round and round and came out anywhere, from Petsamo to the Suez.

Frenchmen said: "Since she won't attack, Germany must collapse internally. . . . Civil dissatisfaction . . . the drain of conquered peoples on their resources . . ." (and, parenthetically always: "That's all we really *need* the English for, to blockade them into collapsing"). Ah, but when Germany collapses, will she go Communistic? That's not such a happy thought! Stalin on the Rhine might eventually prove as embarrassing as Hitler. How shall we avoid that? Is it too late to do something or other diplomatic to persuade the Germans to attack the Russians, or vice versa? To finish one another off? Now *that* is the thing to be desired. Then everybody agreed it was too late or too soon or, until the situation clarified itself in Finland more, too dangerous. Italy? Italy would do as she's always done: sit on the fence until she saw the Allies were winning, and then try to make a quick deal and get in on the side of the winners. You know the old gag—Italy is not for sale, only for rent! Ah, poor Mussolini! He had "sat on the fence so long the iron had entered his soul. . . . In the end he would have to sell it for scrap to the Allies. . . ." If anybody said: "But Italy really has a good army, navy, and air force and her immediate self-interests are largely to be achieved by throwing in her hand *now* with Hitler," everybody laughed and said: "Well, let her. You remember the old gag: If Italy's against us, it will take twenty divisions to beat her; if she is with us, twenty divisions to defend her.[8]

[8] The Allied belief that the Italians were cowards never to be taken seriously was one that they cherished almost to the end. Captain Brousse, a French friend, wrote to me on June 5: "Certainly Italy is coming in now at any moment, but the 'aid' she can bring Germany is not of a sort to alarm us. I would even say, quite the contrary, if I did not feel that this

And anyway our poilus are bored to death with this Sitzkrieg. A war with Italy would be a diversion." And then always at this point everybody told the most popular story in Paris: how when General Lord Gort asked General Gamelin what troops he had on the Italian frontier, Gamelin replied: "Ah, mon général, why waste troops there? There we have the *douane*" (custom-house)! [9] The French rather regretted in March that Italy wouldn't declare war on them, because it really was "embarrassing" not to be able to find a convenient front and get on with it.

About this time, Finland surrendered. And while that made everybody in France feel momentarily uneasy in his conscience, because everybody in France had been saying all winter that the Finns were fighting our battle, the battle of Democracy against Dictatorship, and had heartily agreed with Chamberlain that the Russian campaign was "the most brutal and unjust attack ever made on a democracy," they said *now*: "Yes, but all the same we've got to be realistic—what with neutral Norway and Sweden in between, and another long hard winter coming on, it wasn't a very convenient front, really."

A British old school-tie colonel said to me: "Why, it's great luck we didn't get in that war. We'd have sent two

---

is not the moment for too much optimism." And a month later even in the middle of his heart-breaking recital of the most tragic and ironic episode in history, the English "naval engagement" with the anchored French fleet at Oran in July, Churchill paused to take a familiar gibe at Mussolini's wop myrmidons: (they) "kept 'prudently' out of the way . . . we trust their turn will come during the operations we shall pursue to secure effectual command of the Mediterranean. . . ."

[9] After the surrender the fact emerged that the French High Command did not seem to believe the *douane* was really quite enough. They had put 700,000 French troops on the Italian border. The British, who believe in the *douane* defence principle, used this to suggest French treachery—a deliberate diversion by Weygand of troops sorely needed on the Flanders and Somme fronts to a position where 100,000 men would have been quite adequate for defence.

hundred thousand men to Finland and they'd have been captured." (The luck held, until Flanders.) After the surrender of Finland, nearly everybody agreed with Chamberlain's new thesis, that: "the responsibility of this affair rests fairly and squarely on the shoulders of Germany, and not on the Allies. Any suggestion that the Allies in any way failed in their obligations to do their utmost to assist Finland in her need is one that cannot for a moment be maintained. Least of all should the suggestion come from countries far away from the seat of war!" (This meant America.) [10] And everybody said: "Besides why should we go looking for more trouble by actually taking on the Russians? There is more to be gained in waiting for the Russians to take on the Germans," and so on. And then somebody would say: "Is this or is this *not* a crusade of the democracies against the dictatorships, and if it is, what becomes of our crusade if we eventually fight with the Russians?" And that debate often went on for hours. In the end everybody said: "Well, we would have gone to their aid if it weren't for those damn Scandinavian neutrals." Then everybody said: "If it weren't for all the damn neutrals, we could get on with this thing and get it over." And then they talked a lot about how much they'd really like to go into Belgium, or Italy, or through Rumania and Turkey *now* with the Syrian army, but how this would make an "unfavourable political impression on the other neutrals, particularly America," and anyway the neutrals had to "learn their lesson," which

[10] In passing let me note that the three thousand miles of ocean between the U.S.A. and Europe were alternately too *long* a distance from which to judge or advise on Europe's actions, and too *short* a distance for the U.S.A. to avoid the consequences of those actions. The width of the Atlantic Ocean varied considerably in the minds of the English and the French. It was always too wide when we offered advice, too narrow when we said: "All right, work it out your own way." The oil man said to me: "They say: 'Put up or shut up.' They mean: 'Put up *and* shut up.' "

they'd learn as soon as Hitler gobbled them all up, one at a time, like the leaves of an artichoke. And if you suggested then: "But if Hitler gets away with all that, won't he really be winning?" they replied: "Ah, yes, but the moment it looks as though he might be winning, American opinion, outraged by his violation of neutralities which we respected, will surely repeal the Johnson Act and extend credits to the Allies, which in turn will 'ease up' the financial strain on the Allies, and then the material of war, which will eventually tilt the balance of victory, will just pour into France and England."

Of course some people in France in March were not at all concerned with the impression they were making on America. These people were quite sure they'd win the war (either by sitting on the Maginot or by fighting on the Maginot—it didn't matter which) on a strictly cash-and-carry basis. Some of the people in the government even said they'd violently resist any effort to involve them in "political and financial" obligations to America which might thus give her a hand in the peace negotiations or allow her to put pressure on the Allies for a premature armistice short of total victory, as she did in the last war. But credit or cash and carry, nobody really wanted America at the peace table.

I had tea (which was French for champagne) one afternoon with a Madame Pomaret, the wife of Monsieur Charles Pomaret. He was Daladier's Minister of Labour in March.[11]

I began the conversation very nicely. I said: "Madame Pomaret, we Americans who are friends of France feel that American public opinion, which is largely isolationist, is

[11] Made Minister of the Interior in Pétain's Surrender Cabinet and then Minister of Labour, but he has since been retired.

partly so because we don't quite know what France's war aims are."

Suddenly she put down her glass of champagne and got to her feet, and stood over me. "Shall I be frank about America?" she asked.

I said: "Please!"

Then she was very, very frank about America—so frank that I got angry and would have stalked out of their house, only I was sitting there drinking their champagne and couldn't. Madame Pomaret said, with beautiful black eyes flashing: "*Bien, je m'en fous de l' Amérique!*" which can politely be translated into English as "Nuts to America!" She talked very fast and hard and savagely. She hardly let me get a word in edgewise. I thought at the time: "This is the way Hitler harangues unfriendly journalists." In a high, shrill voice she damned old "Uncle Shylock" and cried how after the last war America, clamouring for "war debts," had made poor France "*danser comme une femme entretenue*" (dance like a kept woman).

And when I said, quickly: "You didn't dance long," she replied: "*Écoutez, ma petite*, when your Monsieur Hoovaire relieved Germany of reparations, France was left holding the basket. Why was it wrong for us to collect money from Germany for the rebuilding of our homes and factories, destroyed by German invasion, but right for you to collect from us, who had destroyed nothing of yours, but made you rich as Crœsus? Now, as for our war aims," she went on, "although they are none of America's business, I'll tell you this: We have already achieved one of them. We have destroyed Communism in France for ever!" [12]

[12] Monsieur Charles Bedaux, the Franco-American efficiency expert, told me early in March: "The thing that brought the *appeasers* both in and out of the government into the war at last was the fear that further appeasement meant French Communism."

And for the rest, she said, France was going to win—the Fronts would "present themselves"—without the "unnecessary bother of making America rich," and then split Germany into little pieces, and punish Holland and Belgium for their neutrality by dividing up their colonies with England. And then, she said, the English (who were now rather "*chic*" about admitting their twenty years of hideous diplomatic bungling—which is all that Madame Pomaret could say for them, except that their navy was "useful") were either incurable humanitarians or sly power politicians, but in either case they and their mushy idealism and their balance-of-power politics, were also going to be kept out of the peace conference. France, whose great *army* would win the war (the English, *par example*, with their *ten lousy divisions on the Belgian border!*), would police the Rhine and all of Europe for a century!

At this point Monsieur Pomaret, an energetic, bullet-headed, coarse little Frenchman, came into the room.

Madame Pomaret said: "This is Mademoiselle Boothe. She has been asking me the usual stupid question: What are France's war aims? America wants to know them!" And she told him what she had said, and he agreed: "*Oui, oui, oui,*" in a very pleased voice. Then he said: "I am sorry, Miss Boothe, you must go," and he opened the door.

Madame Pomaret said: "*Oui . . . enchantée. . . .* You will find a taxi on the corner," and closed the door quickly behind me. As I walked down the draughty corridor of the Ministry I heard them laughing crossly. . . .

I repeat all this now in no spirit of bitterness, but only to show you that even in inner Cabinet circles in France they did not talk about War, but about Politics, and they did not really care about Democracy, but about their own nation.

There was, everywhere, a great deal of talk about what

to do with Germany afterwards. One exceedingly popular suggestion was that the Allies should undertake to sterilize all Germans. But nobody really believed the idea was practical. (It wasn't, I'm afraid, sufficiently political to hold their attention. Curiously enough, the Germans are busy sterilizing Poles and Jews in Poland at this very moment.) Everybody agreed that Germany should be disarmed, but nobody agreed on how to keep it from arming again. Some people like Madame Pomaret only wanted to "split it up"; others to leave it intact, but simply to "police it"; others half-suggested an economic union, with Germany against England and/or Russia, in order to remove Germany's economic motives for conquest! In fact people sometimes almost came to blows in bistros and cafés and drawing-rooms about whether or not to be "friends" afterwards with Germany or with Russia and whether or not to put "bastard nations" like Belgium and Rumania and Poland and Czechoslovakia back on their feet or not, whether or not to allow a Danube Federation, whether or not just to declare a Franco-British hegemony on the Continent, whether or not to put things back exactly as they were in 1920, and then rebuild the League of Nations, *providing America agreed to enter it,* whether or not to disarm everybody, or nobody but the Germans, or everybody but the French, or everybody but the French and English, or everybody but the French and somebody else.

This sort of post-war political chatter, posited of course on an Allied victory, led inevitably to speculations about the next war. Here a most extraordinary fact emerged: everybody agreed that, if America didn't get into this war, *all of Europe,* unified economically (and in a suspiciously totalitarian framework) by France and/or England, would probably be "fighting" America for the control of South

American markets! Of course, if America did come in—or rather restore the old 1920 balance of power in Europe, or preserve the present one—then in the *next* war, France would be fighting somebody or other on the Continent—quite likely Germany.

In the drawing-rooms where the high-up politicians were, however, they didn't talk so much about post-war politics as pre-war politics. In any of these drawing-rooms you were perfectly safe in calling any Frenchman you met "*Monsieur le Président.*" Either he had been or he hoped to be the Prime Minister. Anyway, when you called him that, you either restored his confidence or renewed his hopes, a human courtesy you could not refuse him.

I have myself sat in groups which listened enthralled over the coffee-cups to bespectacled, big-nosed Monsieur Blum,[13] to ample, grisled Monsieur Herriot, to hard, dark, white-tied Monsieur Laval, to egg-shaped, near-sighted Sarraut, whose stomach was so high and vast that his belt, like Humpty Dumpty's, seemed also to be his collar; to slick-haired banker Bonnet, to beady-eyed Léger, to smooth, fat-faced Monsieur Mandel, often called France's Disraeli, but who looked more like a male impersonator of Queen Vic-

[13] Half the people at the dinner where M. Blum was present refused to shake hands with him. His *Front Populaire*—the "French New Deal," with its "poisonous gift" of the forty-hour week—was now generally conceded to be the breeding-ground of the Communism and the lack of preparedness and the internal dissension which were the evil stars that lighted Hitler's road to war against Czechoslovakia, and thus ultimately against England and France. The snub that M. Blum received at this dinner did not disturb him visibly. It did disturb the host, Mr. Bullitt, but only momentarily. He asked whether, after all, it wasn't the strength of a democracy that people of such different political opinions, even though they don't speak, can still sit down to dinner with one another. In Germany a clever, fundamentally patriotic man like Blum would have been shot long ago as a traitor. This clever, patriotic man now has a warrant of arrest facing him. He and Mandel, Daladier and others face a term of imprisonment as "traitors."

toria, while these brilliant gentlemen declaimed for hours and hours about each historical political blunder (which individually, of course, each foresaw and struggled against) that was "entirely responsible for the eventual declaration of war in September"! Their favourite phrase was: "The Allies won the war in 1918 and lost the Peace little by little afterwards. . . ." I have followed their tortuous, detailed memoirs, the "inside dope" from Versailles to the evacuation of the Rhineland, from the Rhine to Locarno, from Locarno to Munich, from Munich to the guarantee of Poland. *Ah! quelle folie! La politique de Lloyd George, de Baldwin, de Hoare, de Eden, et de Chamberlain! Quelles bétises incroyables!* French politicians, when they were together, blamed everything on the English. Separately they generously divided the blame between the English and whatever former French Prime Minister was absent from the happy gathering.

Much cynical post-mortem talk, some idealistic prognostications, a little clever opportunism, and the irreducible minimum of performance—hasn't that always been the portrait of a politician?

So the air of the drawing-rooms stank with the fetid odour of political post-mortems. Fascinating detail piled on detail endlessly, the prelude to an unsensed disaster. Precious hours wasted in the spring of the Second World War, regretting, and regurgitating history. The French politicians chewed the past over, as oxen chew their cud, while the slaughterer ("that butcher Hitler"!) sharpened his axe for France—and all Frenchmen of every political persuasion.[14]

I swear to you, in the spring none of these gentlemen talked much about bombs and guns and tanks and aero-

[14] The one to escape lightest was the innkeeper's son of Auvergne, Pierre Laval.

planes and *current* production-capacity. They hardly talked about the cause of these horrors, Hitler. Though I do remember Monsieur Herriot, one night in late April, made a long, impassioned, and really brilliant analysis of the German "metaphysical mind," pointing out how from Hegel to Hitler Germany had by logic (usurping a French monopoly of method) sought to prove that "Might is Right." Nothing about how Germany had always managed to implement this metaphysical monstrosity with shell and strategy.

"*Eh bien, il faut en finir,*" said M. Herriot at long last, brushing the cigar ashes off his billowing waistcoat. And then he folded his square hands stolidly on his big stomach—resting on his greatest and perhaps only conviction. And for the first time that evening all the other politicians in that drawing-room agreed with him enthusiastically, confidentially, almost tearfully. Their morale, you see, was also excellent. They were all very patriotic gentlemen, men of good will really. In fact, the hell that is now France was paved with their good political intentions.

Now I see in the papers, there is a tendency to "smear" France's leaders—to say *they* "betrayed France."[15] I don't really believe it.

[15] The English are accusing Pierre Laval, in cahoots with Marquet, Bonnet, Baudouin, the Comité des Forges, the French Fascist leaders like Doriot, and the bigwigs of the two hundred families, of engineering the coup (using Pétain as front man) that brought about an unnecessary surrender. It is certainly true that Laval, better informed perhaps than Reynaud of the military status of the country and of Italy's intentions, abandoned a reasonable expectation of victory long before Reynaud and began quite early to think what must be done to make defeat less onerous, and to plan how best France after surrender could be kept in the hands of Frenchmen. But this was not "treachery"; it was what he would call "horse sense." It is also true that many of the gentlemen with whom he was supposed to be in collusion were original appeasers, potential Fascists, and that they feared above all else a long war which would either destroy all their properties or result in Communism. But that they had felt this way

The rotating leaders of the Third Republic had been chosen and rechosen times without number by the French voters. It was with the full approval of the people that the French Parliament was largely a great Mad-Hatter's tea-party, at which its premiers moved from soiled portfolio to soiled portfolio, until each in turn sat again a little while at the head of the green baize table. To call all or any of them "traitors" for their presence there at the moment Hitler chose to crash the party is too easy an explanation. And it is not, as the French say, "*raisonnable*." They knew, and the bankers knew, and the financiers, and the tycoons and the élite, and the People, that if France was beaten, Hitler would give them short shrift—little glory, very small "profits," and a subsistence level of existence. They were stupid and blind and egotistic and mean and greedy and opportunistic and human—all too human. But, alas, they were not "traitors." I say "alas" because if "treachery" were the real key to the fall of France, then, to be safe, all England need do now,[16] all America need do tomorrow, to protect themselves is watch for and weed out "traitors." It was not what any one of these gentlemen *did* before or during the war—it was

from the time of Munich was no secret to anyone in France, least of all to the English. (They too have many people at home who feel the same way.) So if this is "treason," we must make the most of it. On the other hand Laval and Company are calling another group of Frenchmen "the traitors": Léon Blum, and Company, for instance; all those elements and figures in the government who, by failing to prepare France for her supreme test, created the dismal domestic situation which made France's surrender inevitable. And Frenchmen abroad are calling the Frenchmen at home who will not "fight for their soil" traitors. Frenchmen at home are calling those "who will not return home and help to rebuild her" traitors. A similar situation prevailed in Germany after the 1918 Armistice. Treachery is the whipping-boy word of defeated nations. The truth is, France collapsed from top to bottom.

[16] The English, who have accepted, if not invented and promulgated, this "treachery theory" of France's fall, are hoping now to avert the disaster of surrender by the expedient of expelling Mr. Chamberlain and all *his* appeasers from the Cabinet.

what all of them didn't do. "The price of Liberty is eternal vigilance." They did not betray France. They betrayed *with* France, over a long period of years, the principles of Liberty and Democracy in all of Europe. That betrayal eventually caught up with them, and with the nation.

FIVE

Furious propaganda, with her brand,
Fires the dry prairies of our wide Waste Land,
Making the Earth, Man's temporal station, be
One stinking altar to Publicity.

Lee Wilson Dodd, in
The Great Enlightenment (1928)

◇◇

THE GREAT CONFIDENCE of their leaders and the confidence of the people, which was based on no inspired effort to find out the facts, explain the third thing one discovered in Paris in March: The French were not at all interested in "making American propaganda."

They had, of course, a *Bureau d'Information* set up in the Hotel Continental, a vast place of labyrinthine confusions, organized, or rather disorganized, under a distinguished French poet-playwright, Jean Giraudoux,[1] who, like

[1] Giraudoux confided to a friend when Mr. Sumner Welles arrived: "Very odd of America to send on a *peace* mission the man who terrified the whole world by broadcasting a Martian invasion. . . ."

an honest artist, loathed the very word "propaganda." This Bureau d'Information was dedicated in effect as well as in intent to the dissemination abroad of France's *a priori* findings that she was invincible. This was neither propaganda nor information. This was tomtom-beating, cheer-leading, community singing. From the Bureau emerged an endless repetitious paper avalanche of "hand-outs" to American and other foreign correspondents, all stories intensely flattering to France, saying over and over that France was democratic and prepared, therefore unified, therefore unconquerable. You could, if you were a foreign journalist in Paris, copy these stories in your own words and either wire or mail them to your own country. But the misty-eyed patriotic military censors saw that your words followed the spirit if not the letter of these flag-waving hand-outs. It now seems no *one* person in France in a position of authority to do something about it really knew all the true facts about the state of French armament. Certainly no one knew what it was compared with Germany's.[2] There seemed to be no process in that democratic form of government for piecing together the mosaic of military facts which might have shown France her own tragic picture of unpreparedness before it was too late. Within France you were perfectly free, in all matters, to question, investigate, make conjectures, criticize, even snoop if you were sly enough. But none of your even faintly pessimistic speculations or facts could be got out of the country.

As an example, here is an omnibus-finding cable I tried

[2] The truth is, the French and British intelligence services almost entirely failed to function in Gestapo-ruled Germany. The Allied governments largely played hunches on estimating German armaments. If their hunches had led them to overestimate instead of underestimate, the story might have been different. Cf., on page 73, Liddell Hart's "By any known modern process of calculation, their margin of superiority in numbers is not enough. . . ."

to send to *Life* magazine. It was censored *in toto*. Much of it has since proved to be nonsense. (You will see how guilty I was at the time of accepting many of the false premises.) But some of it came true days and even weeks later; and all of it was true of the surface situation at the time. The reason that the cable was censored was that from my premises I dared to draw so many unorthodox (although equally false) conclusions. Of course many of the expert journalists managed to inculcate into their dispatches a few carefully veiled hints from time to time that something was rotten in the state of Denmark, but they had to be so carefully veiled that they generally eluded the American public, which is used to having bad tidings conveyed to them in eye-smacking eight-column headlines. Most of the real news about France, which necessarily meant bad news, was either brought back by returning travellers or cabled from neutral sources; and these ill-omen reports were everywhere in America, by the Allies and the Americans, denounced as "vicious German propaganda." Please don't think I object to censorship in time of war. What I objected to in democratic France was that democratic France made it all the easier to go on deceiving herself because she also insisted on deceiving her well-wishers.

March 10, 1940

> Insistent clamour for more vigorous prosecution of war must result in overthrow of Daladier although nobody here knows what anybody means by more vigorous prosecution. Some say diplomatic attack some say military attack some say more speedup in factories and stringent economic totalitarian measures. Likeliest new member of the new super cabinet is smart Laval indeed there is even possibility of his heading it. Another figure to be closely watched is Reynaud. Gi-

raudoux is very unpopular because inefficient [3] and will be eased out at time information minister is appointed over him. Totalitarian requisition of female labour and land laws through enabling legislation decrees may never actually be enforced until military situation becomes acuter. French regard Welles trip with almost unanimous suspicion deeming its outcome at best a fiasco at worst stooging for a future Hitler peace offer based on Allies letting him get away with what he's got already. French willing enough to cede him what he's got if they could believe Hitler would stop there but any peace solution however reasonable is unacceptable to French because they don't believe Hitler and they're unwilling to have to mobilize every six months and want once and for all to settle Europe. Regarding peace aims they are hopelessly divided but there seem to be three main schools of thought in French governing circles; one and smallest can roughly be termed European "union now" school which has plan for federation but would arbitrarily divide Europe into seven carefully equalized economic regions arranged so that each would have suitable population proper economic balance adequate natural wealth etc. Couldn't immediately determine which idealistic bigwigs behind this but think ascertainable with some effort. Second larger school has no real plan at all and conceals fact by clamouring for necessity of warring to death with Germany whether fronts therefor can be found or not. Third and largest school which surprisingly is close to

[3] Perhaps I *was* a little naïve trying to send this when all cables were censored by Giraudoux's own bureau! However, the censorship of this and similar anti-Giraudoux cables did not save his skin. A few weeks later Froissard succeeded him.

Daladier is impatient of America's insistent curiosity about war aims and figures that little neutrals will pay the bill anyway e.g. a nice way to settle this war would be to give Germany some Belgian and Dutch colonies and buy Italy off with Yugoslavia. One fact emerges clearly that whatever happens the little neutrals are going to get theirs from France if they don't get it first from Germany. As anachronisms they've just got to go. As this is also Hitler's theory nobody dares say it openly but most politicians off record believe it. Real and important fact in war is that there's no front. Daladier, Chamberlain, Hitler agree entirely on one thing i.e. casualties of Maginot break through would be impossibly great. New French information indicates fortifications of Belgian and Dutch frontiers make any war there also interminable. There remains eastern front through Turkey and Balkans or Brenner Pass itself but unless Italy joins Allies troop transport to Balkans would be impossible and Brenner obviously so i.e. discovery of any practicable front depends absolutely on Italy which is now focal point. Forget bombing of London, Paris, Berlin, bombing being sensible only as part of real military operations. If military operations are impossible for lack of front bombing is senseless. There being no front discoverable anywhere and counsels on all sides being obviously divided if stalemate continues likeliest outcome might be the gradual search for some workable peace and I expect we'll see definite German peace proposals before summer is much advanced unless Germans risk attack which for above reasons seems unlikely. Some items: German planes production is reliably rumoured among quote defeatists unquote to be still running well ahead of Allies but no way here of checking any sort of military figures.[4]

So you could sit in Maxim's, drinking champagne *rosé*, and tell Frenchmen what every Frenchman told you: that Daladier lacked "all power of decision," that he had to go, but that there was no other "strong man" in France except Laval, who couldn't come back now because he was a Berlin-Rome appeaser; that Gamelin was a politician and not a soldier,[5] that the war of nerves was again growing unendurable, that there were still some Communistic sabotage in the factories and labour unrest, and people who desired peace at any price, and war profiteers; that the peasant poilus wanted to go home—they had never fought except to defend France from invasion since the days of Napoleon—and that unless the war really started, things at home would get tough and there would be serious political trouble—either a Communist revolution or a Fascist coup by next winter—but that when things did get really tough, the slicker politicians would "bring dear ga-ga old Pétain[6]

[4] Well, come to think of it, the whole cable was naïve, considering France was at war—but then, it wasn't a "scoop," it was just what many thoughtful people were saying to one another in the spring *quite openly*.

[5] One French champagne tycoon I dined with thought the opposite. He told a story about how General Gamelin, at a dinner given to the English High Command, at which representatives of both armies and cabinets were present, "put his hand over his champagne glass when the time for the toast came and said: 'I have sworn not to drink *champagne* again until the day of victory." The champagne tycoon was indignant. He said: "Suppose everyone here should follow his example, as Germans certainly would have done if he had been a German general? Why, it would have *ruined* the champagne business in France, on which many provinces still depend for their livelihood." As it is, the tycoon said: "All the vineyard workers are solidly against Gamelin, and I personally tremble for the fate of my country in the hands of a man who can make a remark so flagrantly unpolitic." Subconsciously the average Frenchman *wanted* even his soldiers to be "good politicians." Champagne-salesman Ribbentrop would have been this tycoon's ideal general.

[6] "Maréchal Crétin" to the irreverent ones.

back from Spain and prop him up as an 'out-front man' to give confidence to the people, and to forestall either happening"; that faced with even a few more months of this stalemate war, France, which was the unwilling host of four million political refugees—a tenth of the population—would give vent to its frustration and divert itself at home by increased Communist-baiting and/or Fascist-baiting and rich-Jew-baiting; in fact, that anti-Semitism was on the increase everywhere—as witness the most popular quip in Paris: "The Jews! Invincible in peace, and Invisible in war!" (The trouble with the damn Jews, they said, is that they won't make a stand anywhere.[7]) In short, you could tell anybody you met that France was at the time unified in her desire to win and in her faith in a military victory, but utterly disunified as to where she would win, how she would win, with whom she would win, when she could win, and what she intended to do with that victory! But you could not send

[7] At a New York Zionist rally, in late March, Vladimir Jabotinsky, World President of the New Zionist organization, outlined his plan for a Jewish army of 100,000 men recruited from all over the world, "to assist the Allies in the task of defeating Germany." "This is the time for blunt speaking," Mr. Jabotinsky said. "I challenge the Jews, wherever they are still free to demand the right of fighting the giant rattlesnake, not just under British or French or Polish labels—but as a Jewish Army. Some shout that we only want others to fight, some whisper that a Jew only makes a good soldier when squeezed in between Gentile comrades. I challenge the Jewish youth to give them the lie!" Mr. Jabotinsky received hundreds of telegrams of approval. Meanwhile France surrendered. The army was not raised. But there is no reason to look askance at Jewry for this: early in June, England had just begun to call up her '28s, Canada was only able to pass a conscription law for "Home Defence," 130,000,000 U.S. citizens had not yet provided the recruits for an army of 400,000. On June 30, the Zionist Organization's Honorary Secretary, Ludwig Lewisohn, reported that "100,000 Jewish troops were available to Britain, all to be recruited in Palestine . . . the present Cabinet was giving the offer some thought. . . ." Perhaps the Jews will yet be allowed to make a last stand, and it would be fitting and proper if they made their last stand where they made their first one—in Palestine. But it is more likely, if they do make it, that they will make it in the last-stand place, America.

that news to America. You couldn't even telephone or write it to an Englishman in England, which was France's ally!

When I went to England a few weeks later, I was astounded at the numbers of people, and prominent people, who said: "Tell us what is going on in France. What are the French thinking?" France kept the real news concerning the state of the nation hermetically sealed within its borders. All that Americans needed to know (and even the English) about France was that France was going "to finish it." So America, disposed anyway to be isolationist, was encouraged more and more, as the "phony war" dragged on, to believe that France could settle its own destiny without any outside intervention.

And this is June. And France has surrendered to Germany, and here on my desk lies a book that someone sent me in January just before I went to Europe. Its title leers at me cynically. It's called *From Nazi Sources: Why Hitler Can't Win.* It was written by a Professor Fritz Sternberg, an exiled German, and published by the Alliance Book Corporation in October 1939. Exhaustively documented, with "statistics smuggled out from official Germany," it shows that Germany hasn't got and couldn't get the oil, steel, coal, labour, food, planes, and other essentials to beat a rich, prepared France and England who have "constant access to raw materials. . . ." Now, I do not impugn the professor's motives in writing that book. In fact, I'm sure he got his facts from "authoritative German sources"–German *propaganda* sources. Germany was interested in "foreign propaganda." To many people propaganda, by definition, is putting the best light on a bad case. But sometimes it can be putting the worst light on a good one. Germany's chances of winning were good, but Germany's game was served by having America believe what

France also allowed her to believe: that Germany was weak, that France was strong. People generally believe what they want to believe, and if they don't like you, they are mostly determined to believe what your enemies say about you. Germany generously supplied its many unsuspecting enemies abroad, the refugees and expatriates (like Sternberg and Thyssen) with "smuggled authoritative proof" that she was a weak nation. So Germany by intent, France by wanton stupidity, helped keep France unprepared and America unprepared—and isolationist. I wonder if Professor Sternberg will write another book soon called *Why Germany Cannot Conquer America.* If he does, a great many Americans will buy it, as Frenchmen and Englishmen bought many such books to calm their fears and comfort their egos and save their purses and husband their efforts.

So the French were not interested in cynical or scientific propaganda calculated to induce our help (by arousing our selfish fears for our own ultimate safety) not only because we had expressed as a nation a positive hysteria against Allied propaganda at the beginning of the war, but because they did feel fine and strong, and also because they are a proud, charming, and quite properly conceited people.

I had lunch with Colonel Scheffer, of General Gamelin's staff, one day at the Ritz. I was begging him to uncork the bottleneck of picture-propaganda by persuading the military authorities (who mistrusted the smallest amount of propaganda, as a Dutchman might mistrust the tiniest leak in a dike) to let a *Life* photographer go to the Front.[8] "Ah, America!" he said; "it is in an armed state of photography!"

[8] Five weeks later I consoled this same photographer, who was still waiting: "Don't worry about going to the front any more. The front is coming to *you.*" It did, and *Life's* Mr. Mahomet brought back mountains of pictures of Paris, from Tours, from Bordeaux.

I replied: "Oh, why not make propaganda in America? We are irrevocably pro-Ally. And we couldn't be more isolationist. You have nothing to lose."

"Why should France make propaganda?" he asked with a Frenchman's logic. "Everybody loves France anyway. Besides," he added, although very kindly, "we are not fighting this war for the benefit of American journalists."

I remember I thought a little bitterly at the time: "You are not fighting it at all yet." Of course the truth was (though I didn't see it then; very few people saw it) they were not fighting it, but all the same they were losing it every day, through hours lost in factories, days lost while Allied purchasing committees abroad wrangled with "Uncle Shylock" about prices of airplanes and materials, or turned up their noses at models "not up to Allied standards"—through months lost while they might have been "making propaganda." Instead of saying that, I told the major about how the Germans, who had militarized their photographers and correspondents, kept America wonderfully supplied with interesting stories and pictures.[9]

"*Tiens!*" he said, "if you were *really* pro-Ally you wouldn't publish them."

"Then we should publish nothing," I answered.

[9] A friend makes the point that Germany's propaganda in America to prove that France was strong, and the pictures and stories she disseminated from "official German sources" about her own might, would seem to cancel one another out. To understand this you must understand that Germany's whole propaganda plan in America was—and still is—to keep America isolationist. We reasoned as we were intended to reason: "France is stronger, but, just the same, Germany means business. Therefore let France lick the trouble-makers. But let us keep out of what we gather from Germany is sure to be a bloody business." The same psychology is operating today: Germany has released in America her horrifying film, *The Invasion of the Lowlands*. Our certain reaction will be: "Let's get our own defences ready" (which is bound to conflict with our sending of arms immediately to England) "and stay out of that bloody business over there!"

"*Eh bien*," he said, "why not Europe, since you are isolationist, and just wait and see how it all comes out?"—since, he added with a twinkle, "isolationist America has nothing to lose, whether we lose or win it?"

In England it was the same. The English also were not interested in propaganda. They felt—almost to the end—that any propaganda that was made, America, if she were really interested in the democratic crusade, should make for them, and they honestly believed that the moment America realized that her vital interests were also threatened, she would make all that was necessary.

Here is an editorial published in the London *Times* of Friday, April 19. It was called "No Illusions Left." The "illusions" referred to were not (curiously enough) England's, but America's.

"Germany's brutal swoop upon Norway and Denmark seems to have undone at one blow the effect of months of assiduous Nazi propaganda in the United States. . . . The outrage has exposed the falsity of German propaganda and convinced even the most sceptical that a Nazi victory would be a blow to all the principles in which Americans believe and might well imperil vital American interests."

The editorial then quoted Mr. Roosevelt's speech to the Pan-American Union in which he declared: "Today we can have no illusions. The old dreams of universal empire are again rampant . . ." and went on rather sarcastically to say how fine it was of America to realize what the Allies had realized since September. Still, "the American public had been fed for years [by Germany] with the most one-sided accounts—even the efforts of Mr. Chamberlain and M. Daladier to reach a peaceful settlement with Germany—all these and many more pretexts were found and exploited [by Germany] to balance the universal [American] detestation of the Nazi régime. When the Allies seemed slow at getting off the mark, *preferring to build up their strength instead of providing exciting headlines for the American newspapers,* [*German propaganda*] *whispered to the American public that this was a 'phoney war'*; that the Allied Governments *had no intention* of indulging in any *serious* fighting,[10] but were playing for a patched-up peace; or, worse still, that they were waiting for the Americans to come in and win the war for them.[11]

"This change in the American attitude, as expressed by popular 'columnists' and broadcast commentators, *appeared inexplicable to people on this side of the Atlantic who knew the grim determination of the Allied Governments.* . . . There were many [English] who pointed to the obvious achievements of Nazi propaganda and asked indignantly why we were doing nothing to counteract it. The [British] Government, however, very wisely, not only refrained from indulging in any counter-propaganda but *actively discouraged* any effort of the kind.[12] Nazi propaganda, it was felt, could be trusted [13] to over-reach itself. Something more might have been done to repair the blunder made in the beginning of the war, when the stupidity of the British and French censorships compelled the United States newspapers to get the bulk of their war news and pictures from Berlin, where the authorities took advantage of this Allied short-

10 They certainly didn't, not if they could avoid it. That's what the blockade and the Maginot were for, to avoid it as much as possible. In March, Oliver Stanley, England's War Minister, said: "We intend to fight in our way, not in *their* way. How easy it is [for America] from the ringside, after a comfortable dinner, to urge other people to get out and hit each other. . . ."

11 They were not then perhaps waiting; they are now certainly hoping.

12 The long and bitter memoirs of many a friendly but frustrated American journalist will one day testify to that "active discouragement."

13 In April they were still trusting to this extent anyway in Herr Hitler.

sightedness to give American correspondents every facility to get and transmit the news they wanted. *This mistake apart*, it was a wise policy to refrain from any attempt to influence American opinion and to let *facts* [!] speak for themselves. There are plenty of fair-minded people in the United States to interpret them to their own people. . . . When Hitler gave the word to invade Norway and Denmark, he did more to checkmate Dr. Goebbels than could have been achieved by any counter-propaganda."

There were, of course, some in England and France who were wise, who said: "We must keep America and Americans by our side, inform them, make them realize soon that our war is theirs, even if we have to lie a little by telling them we *might* lose it." Passionate little Paul Reynaud, whose Mexican heritage had imparted to him an odd jumping-bean quality, said that, but he never did anything about it, because it was too dangerous an admission—politically. Raoul Dautry, a sallow-faced, winking-eyed, energetic little Frenchman, who was Daladier's Minister of Armaments, felt the same way.

"We are not in very superb condition," he said to me. "Sometimes I wish that the American people knew that. . . ." And then he complained that military red tape, bureaucratic confusion, the cross-current of political ambitions, and subtle Communist sabotage were interfering with the job he knew he ought to do with guns, planes, tanks. "But for God's sake don't quote me abroad," he sighed wearily. Then he brightened, however. "And besides," he said, "we'll have all we need—in time."

This interview took place late in April. On the 1st of May, worried perhaps lest he had aroused even a small doubt in my mind, he wrote me the following charming letter:

> . . . The magnificent effort of France cannot fail to astonish you. In the trench and in the factory, in the villages and in the fields, men, women, and young people are of one mind and one will. They have only one aim: to escape from servitude and to preserve the liberty of their children. I know that I can count not only on American sympathy but also on American help. How could the sympathy and help of a free people fail to come to the aid of another people, who are defending not only their liberty but the liberty of all! Charged with the task of arming France, I only demand from those who love her that they will facilitate my task and help me to procure the instruments of work which I sorely need. Let each among all the friendly nations do what it can to sell us as many machine tools [etc.] as possible: I must buy *or* produce them by the thousands. They will serve France best who will now save her "work-hours" in her own factories. . . . These can be added to all those which day and night, to the limit of their strength, Frenchmen and Frenchwomen are giving, to assure certain victory. . . .

But even the wiser Frenchmen who felt it might be prudent to keep America informed of the worst as well as the best eventualities, lest one day they might need more than credits or work-hours, comforted themselves mightily with the certain knowledge that really it wasn't necessary to "*do* anything about America"—because French propaganda in America was after all safe in the hands of that master of French propaganda, Mr. Roosevelt.

I complained one day to Monsieur Léger, who was then Permanent Secretary of Foreign Affairs, that I wished that France had a more eloquent, American-wise propagandist as Ambassador in Washington than Count René de Saint-Quentin—somebody like Lord Lothian, for instance.

He was indignant. "Monsieur de Saint-Quentin gets everything for France he asks," he said frigidly.

I replied: "Then your demands must be very much more modest than America feared they might be." [14]

And he said with gentle slyness: "You don't know what Monsieur de Saint-Quentin asks for or gets! He may not be very popular with Americans, but he is a most intimate friend of your President, which is better." [15]

"Calls him by his first name, does he?" I asked.

"Yes, I believe so," said Monsieur Léger proudly. I said nothing.

I think it made many Americans in France angry and unhappy and uneasy to see how everybody trusted Mr. Roosevelt and despised America. Monsieur Léger was no exception.

Nearly everybody in France thought that there was all the rest of America, which was perverse or ignorant or cowardly or grasping (that was your old Uncle Shylock)—and then there was that great statesman Mr. Roosevelt, who always would be President, and who would change all that overnight, if France ever got into a real jam with Germany.

The only slight moment of doubt France had concerning Mr. Roosevelt was when Mr. Welles arrived in a cloud of diplomatic obfuscation. Then France thought, for a split second, that Mr. Roosevelt just might be a politician. A political president just might try to feather his own political

[14] The truth now seems to be that France and England fought "a stingy war." Their demands were modest—criminally modest.

[15] M. Léger is now a refugee in America. The colourless Count de Saint-Quentin has been recalled to France. For Mr. Roosevelt's benefit, the first name of the new Ambassador Henry-Haye is not Henry but Gaston. M. Léger's first name won't interest him.

nest, by announcing "on the basis of the facts that Mr. Welles was able to ascertain, that France and England ought to talk peace with Hitler"—a peace in which Mr. Roosevelt would be the great mediator. (It now seems, on the basis of the facts, that is precisely what a *statesman* might have done. In any case, that is what the French are now saying.) Of course, nobody knows what Mr. Welles really told Mr. Roosevelt.

He told the American people, through the press: "I wish to state categorically that I have not received any peace plan or proposals, that I have not conveyed any such proposals, nor am I bringing back any such proposals." He'd have spared England and France many bad moments if he'd said that before he left instead of after he landed.

Perhaps in Europe Mr. Welles had come to the conclusion that the Germans were going to win, but when he returned and talked it over with the President, perhaps he and Mr. Roosevelt finally decided: (1) that it was not politically expedient to tell the truth to the Allies or to America, or (2) that the course of world evolution would best be served by letting the Allies stew in their own juice. Or perhaps they decided that the Allies would—in time, and with American help—probably beat Hitler. But my guess is that after hearing what Mussolini and Hitler and Daladier and Chamberlain all had to say, Mr. Welles believed what they all had to say, and returned in the same state of confusion he departed in, clarifying Mr. Roosevelt's mind accordingly.

In any case, after Mr. Welles's return Mr. Roosevelt didn't suggest a peace. And he certainly didn't warn France or us about the need for more urgent preparedness.

Well, in March I didn't know, and few if any Frenchmen knew, what Mr. Welles had told Mr. Roosevelt and what

Mr. Roosevelt had told Mr. Bullitt about Mr. Welles's findings on Europe, or about the state of our Union and its productive capacity [16] in a jam. And I certainly don't know what Mr. Bullitt relayed of what he was told to the Premiers of France, who were all his dearest friends and would certainly have believed him.

Mr. Bullitt was terribly, terribly popular with everybody, particularly the French politicians. Without exception, every living ex-Premier of France called him by his first name and gave him his deepest confidence. Not only because Mr. Bullitt was a charming man, an exquisite diplomat, who spoke perfect French and really loved France and its Way of Life, and its streets, and its wines and its literature, but because he was among all the diplomats of Europe the closest to and most loved by Mr. Roosevelt. And because, perhaps, he was known to have said: If it is a long war, in the end we'll be in it. The only case that anyone will ever be able to make against Mr. Bullitt is that he loved France (and still does) too well, but not wisely.

But, as I say, I never met a single man on the streets or a single man in high authority in France who wasn't utterly convinced that if France ever should be on the verge of defeat, Mr. Bullitt would prevail upon Mr. Roosevelt, and then Mr. Roosevelt, their greatest and best American propagandist, would bring a recalcitrant America quickly to heel

[16] Mr. Roosevelt has announced that he is not going to ask any more billions for armaments, because at the moment "industry could not absorb the orders." The ramparts of Industry had in fact crumbled considerably, all unbeknownst to Mr. Roosevelt apparently, while he kept a keen eye on the developments in Europe. The state of "innocuous desuetude" our army had fallen into during seven years of Statesman Roosevelt's administration is something that administration will have to answer to the people for in November. Mr. Roosevelt's best and most logical defence would be an attack on the weakness of democracy itself. I hazard a guess he will prefer to blame it somehow on the Republicans.

and pour all its enormous resources into the breach. I never really found out what Mr. Roosevelt's foreign policy was in France, but I know that this is what most French people believed it to be. I know that in those last awful days of early June it was a bitter, bitter shock to the French people and to tiny, desperate Monsieur Reynaud not only that Mr. Roosevelt couldn't bring America into war, or even repeal the Neutrality Act, but that he could not send what it turned out rather suddenly we didn't have, and which apparently nobody with a big voice had told them (or us) before that we didn't have, "masses of material" and "clouds of aeroplanes."

But the bitterest shock of all to them was that Mr. Roosevelt did not honestly tell the American people what they believed in their hearts *he* believed—that this war was America's war. "What can he lose?" they asked, anguished. Obviously he could lose the third term, but that tragic loss was hard for them to understand when the fate of France hung in the balance. Then in the hideous confusion of retreat and surrender the politicians and the people alike cursed Mr. Roosevelt, cursed America, and might have done worse to poor Mr. Bullitt had he not been in the one safe spot in overrun France—German-occupied Paris.[17]

So France was on the whole trusting itself in the early spring, and entirely trusting Mr. Roosevelt and Mr. Bullitt, and very few people in France or in England or in America sought and published the facts about armaments and told the bitter truths to their people. And if any of the French politicians knew it themselves, they thought of the Maginot, and the English politicians thought of the navy, and I don't

[17] In July Mr. Bullitt rejoined his good old friends Pierre Laval and Marshal Pétain at Vichy. He is currently pleading their cause in Hyde Park, and as Mr. Roosevelt loves Mr. Bullitt, and Mr. Bullitt loves France, so far as America goes, the cause is a safe one.

know what Mr. Roosevelt, who was undoubtedly the best-informed man in the world (after Hitler), thought of, although it was probably a fine Jesuitical argument for believing the Third Term [18] and the New Deal to be the only salvation of a world in which "the old dreams of universal empire are again rampant," and how, therefore, he must assure the certainty of the former and the continuance of the latter before he upset his political apple-cart by telling anybody anything that was too unpleasant.

[18] For those who believe in omens, it is interesting to reflect that President Albert Lebrun was also a breaker of historic democratic tradition. Elected for a seven-year term in May 1932, he ran again in April 1939, and was re-elected, the first French President to violate France's unwritten law of "No second term"–and, incidentally, the last President of French Democracy. It is even more interesting to reflect that he only consented to run because of the "serious crisis that faced France," and as a "personal sacrifice" in the interests of "national defence and unity."

SIX

St. George he was for England;
St. Denis was for France;
Sing, Honi Soit Qui Mal Y Pense!

(Black-Letter Ballad, London, 1512)

AND so you talked Politics and Propaganda and Morale, and meanwhile a mild if fitful March slipped into a delicate golden April. Then began the loveliest crystal-clear spring Europe had had in many years. There was not a little drop of rain, not a faintly mottled sky until mid-June. In Europe that spring, like an ethereal army with blossom-strewn banners, seemed to come on for ever. Before the invasion, the English called it "King's weather." After that the English didn't talk much about the weather because they knew that in Germany everybody was calling it "*Hitlerwetter*," and that in Flanders and Picardy this heavenly boon to mankind, a perfect spring, had become a hideous evil. In such a spring tanks could and did push up faster than flowers.

Now, in April, chestnuts burst into leaf on the lovely avenues of Paris, sunlight danced off the opalescent grey buildings, and the gold and grey sunsets, glimpsed through the soaring Arc de Triomphe at the end of the long splendid vista of the Champs-Élysées, brought a catch of pain and pleasure in your throat. *Paris was Paris in April!* There were not many children in the parks (though more than there had been in winter), but the sidewalk cafés and bistros were thronged with old men and women sipping apéritifs and reading the thin, confident papers, with pretty girls, many of them in Red Cross ambulance-driver uniforms, with little dark-eyed khaki-clad sloppy tough-looking *permissionnaires*. There were American movies and French movies, every few streets, thronged with customers. (Most of them had placards in the lobbies reading: "In the event of an air raid, customers not retaining their seat stubs will not be reseated when it's over.") The shops were open and doing a small stream of steady business, and there was plenty of traffic in all the streets. There were art shows in the Grand Palais, racing at Auteuil, and Soccer games between the tommies and poilus in the suburbs. The fitting-rooms of the couturières and modistes were comfortably filled with foreign buyers.

The show windows of Van Cleef and Arpels and Mauboussin and Cartier sparkled with great jewels in the sunlight. And lots of people, too, bought them. (In fact there was quite a boom in the diamond trade in Europe in the spring. I asked the oil man about that. He said: "War always breeds among the rich what you might call Jewish psychology: Never buy anything you can't hop over the back fence with in an emergency.")

The wide-windowed gilded corridors of the Ritz and its sunny restaurants were fairly well crowded with lovely ladies wearing simple dresses or the smart uniforms of the Union des Femmes de France services. Conspicuous among these was the Duchess of Windsor wearing a dark blue uniform with a little cap cocked over her sleek black hair. She had charge of some sort of foyer or canteen which dispensed quantities of goodies to the soldiers. Also conspicuous was Mrs. Laura Corrigan, enormously wealthy widow of James Corrigan, "the Copper King," and famous for her malapropisms and her erstwhile lavish London hospitality to Britain's ruling classes. She also doled out largesse to the Brave Boys at the canteens and depots. She wore a brown uniform, with a little brown cap embroidered in gold, with the motto: "*Bien Venue*." But Mrs. Corrigan and the Duchess [1] were only two of some twenty or thirty Americans who were doing their bit in the great war effort.

There was lots of jealousy between many of them. I believe each thought the others were striving for a Légion d'Honneur, a decoration much prized by the ladies; at least they often whispered the accusation. Just the same they fought a good war in the Ritz, and many of them fought the real war very well outside of it. You were, on the whole, proud of them.

There were, of course, in the spring, a still large quota of

[1] When the invasion came, and all the soldiers of France and England (except the unfortunate Duke of Windsor) streamed up into Flanders, the Duchess, "on the advice of her physician," departed for Biarritz. Mrs. Corrigan remained in Paris, where she did yeoman's service night and day for the refugees in the stations and casernes. I saw her late one night in June, coming into the black corridors of the Ritz, her hair dishevelled, her little brown cap tilted at a comic angle, her arms hanging limp from having carried baskets and bundles and bandages all day long. I said: "Mrs. Corrigan, you ought to be getting away from Paris." She smiled, and rearranged her cap with its strangely satirical motto: "*Bien Venue*." "Listen," she said, "if the Germans think they can bomb me and my *Been Venoo* out of here, they're crazy! Say, don't I look awful?" It was like that, in Paris in June: Many people you knew saw it through. Many didn't. You had pleasant and unpleasant surprises. . . .

old international bleached-haired bejewelled creatures (some I regret to state American expatriates) dragging chiffon scarves tangled with Pekingese pups down the corridors, who since time out of mind have been known as the Ritz Harpies. In the warm early April sunlight they sat on the flowered terrace under umbrellas, sipping tea or champagne and gossiping about war and its miseries. Bored or wearied with the close war-reasoning of masculine minds, these ladies often took refuge in the vague and happy prognostications of Nostradamus. Nostradamus was the author of a sixteenth-century book of very cryptic rhymed prophecies, among which "everything about the war that was going to happen" was predicted. Happily, the ladies of the Ritz and the salons quoted from it such predictions as these:

"I see the four-power unity of the North menaced by the Orient." (That meant that Italy, Germany, Austria, and probably Poland were going to be attacked by Russia. Anyway, they said so.)

"The betrayed lion will unite itself with the cock, and then the barbarian will be absorbed." (England and France, once Allies, are going to win over Germany, so why worry?)

Their favourite prophecy in Nostradamus was some oblique reference to a personage widely interpreted as being the exiled Comte de Paris, son of the Duc de Guise, current pretender to the French throne, who, according to the prophet, would save France from the barbarians on the fields of Poitiers and reign happy ever after.[2] It was all very comfortable, to ladies who hated Fascism, loathed

[2] After the invasion the Duc de Guise fled from Belgium to Morocco, his son to Brazil. Recently he has returned to France, and the restoration of a Fascist puppet monarchy under the Comte de Paris is being widely rumoured. It may still be that Nostradamus will be vindicated and the Harpies will yet inherit France.

Communism, but felt that democracy, my dear, just *hasn't* worked; now, has it?

A favourite fantasy of mine in the spring was to imagine how it would be if a German parachutist would land ker-plunk among the Graustarkian ladies in the Ritz Garden. I told that to the oil man.

He said: "Oh, they'd all squeal like tail-twisted pigs for a moment. Then one of them would say: 'Aren't you Baron von Bozzle's oldest son? *Oh, grandson?* You know, your father was very fond of me when I was a girl in Monte Carlo. You've come such a long way down. . . . Do have a cup of tea before you mount again."

I asked: "But what if the Germans came to that revolving door *en masse*?"

The oil man answered: "The waiters would bow, the manager would bow, Olivier would bow, all very coldly but correctly, and Olivier would say, in excellent German: '*Guten Tag*, General Brauchitsch, we have not seen you in some years.' "

(That is, I suppose, the way it happened, because the Ritz never closed its doors.) The oil man felt this was no reflection on the Ritz or its personnel. "The Ritz," he said, "like the Vatican, is a kingdom apart—international temples of Mammon and God."

So in early April it was a ghost war, in the skeleton of peace, but it wasn't as unpleasant-looking as that metaphor suggests. The worst that it was for people with a little money was boring.

British war-correspondents, week-ending in Paris, groused about the "phony war" and the dearth of readable dispatches, and told how they had written letters to their editors asking to be sent to the "trouble spot of the Balkans," to Turkey or to the United States to report the political situation in America. . . . "It is, of course, of vital importance that Roosevelt be re-elected. . . ." [3]

Sometimes, just to break the monotony of "war stories," these correspondents collared visiting Americans for interviews. The questions that were troubling the British public in early spring are somewhat reflected in the questions they asked visiting firemen. Here is a list of such questions which one London newspaper man submitted to me in writing when I refused "offhand" to be interviewed:

Are the Allies being too patient?
Should we bomb Germany?
Why do you think we should bomb Germany?
What would be the effect of bombing Germany?
What do you think of British women in uniforms?

(This was answered for all time, and for everyone, by an irate Scotsman in kilts, pictured in a comic magazine glowering at a trousered lady in khaki. "Wuman, ye look *tarrible!*")

What do you think of the British versus the French black-out?
What do you think of Britain's leaders—of Chamberlain, Churchill, etc.?
Which British leader is the most popular in America?
What is your view about the British policy of allowing 65,000 aliens to move about freely in Britain?
When do you think the war will end?
Will the United States come into the war this time?
Will Roosevelt be re-elected?

[3] A cable I received from London yesterday says: It is now of vital importance that it be Wendell Willkie. It is a great relief to realize that no matter how our presidential election turns out, England will be pleased with it—if there's still England.

What do you think about the Nazis?
If Hitler goes, whom should we deal with afterwards?
Will Britain be stronger or weaker after the war?
Should Britain try to negotiate peace now, and, if so, what should we demand that Germany give up?

Needless to say, I answered none of these questions. I had a decent respect for the sensibilities of my French and English hosts, and I didn't want to be accused of being a war-monger.

Real war-weary A.P. and U.P. men were drifting back from Finland via Sweden, via Amsterdam, skipping "dull Brussels" to go to Turkey and Syria. "There's a hell of a good soldier out there called Weygand—you remember—saved France with Foch in '16, saved Poland in '18, saved Russia in '20. Best of the fighters. Exiled now, they say, because he doesn't get along very well with this crowd of bumbling, inefficient politicians." [4] By the troop movements of the press you began to see that everybody was now sure Hitler was going to sit the war out until the following spring or, at worst, move into Rumania or Hungary.

This later supposition, which definitely.portended a long French Sitzkrieg, started endless uneasy and heated debates as to whether or not the British blockade was really effective: "Italy is 'the big leak.'" A lot of people said: "We ought to declare war on Italy at once—to plug it." Everybody began to grumble quite violently that Daladier and Chamberlain (not, significantly enough, Gort or Gamelin) ought "to take the military initiative somewhere."

"The trouble is," an English colonel said to me at wise Sir Charles Mendl's [5] luncheon at Versailles, "we are

[4] The English are now saying he was exiled because of his well-known Fascist leanings: the Treachery motif again.

[5] Formerly Press Attaché to the British Embassy in Paris, now a refugee in America.

gentlemen. There are so many nasty things they can do, and we simply can't and won't be nasty."[6]

Sir Charles Mendl himself was much tougher: "We've *got* to be nasty—take off the kid gloves—get at them!" His charming white moustache bristled fiercely. We've got to—bomb Baku—bomb Batum! Extreme, of course, but it will end the war quickly!"[7]

But precisely why Sir Charles thought bombing Baku would end the war quickly, I never found out, because Sir Charles was interrupted by a pretty little Frenchwoman

[6] In Berlin on June 30 Alfred Rosenberg, chief Nazi Party ideologist, generously offered to eliminate this trouble for ever. He said the war will "put an end to British gentlemen . . . the British prototype of the capitalistic age . . . living on the work of others . . . will be replaced by the German worker-type. . . ."

[7] This theory may sound absurd to you now. But it was so widespread in April that A. P. Herbert, sensitive always to the follies and daydreams of his nation, wrote a poem about it in *Punch*:

BAKU; OR, THE MAP GAME

It's jolly to look at the map
  And finish the foe in a day.
It's not easy to get at the chap;
  These neutrals are so in the way.
But if you say "What would *you* do
  To fill the aggressor with gloom?"
Well, we might drop a bomb on Baku,
  Or what about bombs on Batum?

The scale of the map should be small
  If you're winning the war in a day.
It mustn't show mountains at all,
  For mountains may be in the way.
But, taking a statesmanlike view,
  And sitting at home in a room,
I'm all for some bombs on Baku
  And, of course, a few bombs on Batum.

Sometimes I invade the dear Dutch,
  Sometimes I descend on the Danes;
They oughtn't to mind very much,

who didn't know where Baku or Batum was, and, after being told, wondered if they were by any chance anywhere near Batik, where the shawls come from.

A Rumanian diplomat, anxious to remove the seat of war a little farther from his own back door, suggested that the English might instead take Narvik to cut off Hitler's iron-ore supply—but nobody else except Sir Charles, who preferred Batum as a jumping-off place for an invigorated policy of British nastiness, seemed to know just where Narvik was, so we all dropped that subject.

I remember at another such luncheon I suddenly felt as though every country in Europe had been exhausted as a possible battlefront—every country but Spain. I had a letter in my pocket from an American friend who had just returned from Spain. I thought: "I'll read it to them just so

---

And they don't seem to have any planes;
I slip through the Swiss and say "Boo!"
I pop over the Alps and say "Boom!"
But I still drop a bomb on Baku,
And I always drop bombs on Batum.

Vladivostok is not very far;
Sometimes I attack him from there.
With the troops in a rather fast car
I am on him before he's aware.
And then, it's so hard to say who
Is fighting, precisely, with whom,
That I'm keen about bombing Baku,
I insist upon bombing Batum.

The next person seriously to consider the question was Paper-hanger Hitler, who, in hanging White Paper No. 7 on the British, tried to prove that they had a full-fledged plan to bomb Baku from Turkish air bases, a plan nipped in the bud by the invasion. Add, in all fairness to Sir Charles Mendl, that experts have since testified that whereas bombing Baku might not have put Hitler out of business, it could have slowed up Stalin and his mechanized agricultural production considerably. The reason that the Allies didn't bomb away was probably that the governments couldn't decide whether or not they really wanted to slow up Stalin.

we won't have to go all over the same old ground from Sweden to Turkey until coffee." I read it:

April 4, 1940
Basses-Pyrénées

I was so glad to get your letter. . . . Address me here, I will get your letter whether I have left or not. It may be that I shall have to return to the land of bull-fights, grandees, castanets and mules. Madrid I found much restored since my visit there last summer. Shell holes have been filled in, windows replaced and many buildings rebuilt. In spite of these outward changes, however, it is a sad and disturbing town to visit—to begin with there is great poverty—in the poor quarters the people look more like phantoms than human beings —and even great dissatisfaction. Only the Falangists go stamping about with proud military smiles on their faces, saluting each other, building roads, when houses are needed, and concocting God knows what dark schemes. Everywhere one sees Germans, fat middle-aged men wearing swastika buttons in their lapels and smiling with that self-conscious fatuity of the most unpopular boy in school who at last finds a friend who appreciates him. And they are right. There is no doubt that the present government is completely in sympathy with the totalitarian ideals and as much opposed to the democracies as either Hitler or Mussolini. Whether they would actually march against France and England I doubt, owing to the great unrest at home. . . .

Then there is another reason why I feel Spain will not take active military action—a large part of the present army, which looks well-fed and quite well turned out, fought against Franco until the very last weeks of the revolution. One officer told me that 90 per cent of the men serving under him now had formerly served in the Republican Army. I asked him if after facing death for three years for one ideal he thought so many men could change their beliefs overnight. He said, "Oh, yes, because they know *we mean to make a great Spain*—and *Spain* is *their* country." He then began the usual Nazi-Fascist lecture about "*espacio vital*" and I could not help replying that a country that had been open to colonization less than fifty years ago surely had enough room for its population today, that it seemed to me that he was mistaking "*espacio vital*" for irrigation. A remark that did not go any too well and one that I should not have made as no one is allowed to talk freely. All telephone calls are apt to be "listened in" on and all publications, letters and telegrams strictly censored. But to go back to Spain and the war. Neither Hitler nor Mussolini conducted what they now openly call their "Spanish Campaign" for love. Nobody can be fool enough to believe that. Therefore what Spain does to help them depends largely, in my opinion, on what Mussolini does and whether France and England oppose him. If they do, then quite aside from man-power Spain can provide naval bases, flying bases and certainly the most vulnerable point from which to attack Gibraltar—the only point from which it could be attacked by infantry troops. To have Bordeaux, Toulouse, Marseilles and Toulon within easy flying distance of the Spanish frontier would also be a most serious menace—not to mention the route between North Africa and France open to attack from both east and west. God knows whether all this may happen, but there is the possibility and one must remember that even those parties opposed to Franco are antagonistic to the Allies, the Republicans because the Allies did not help them, and curiously enough, the Monarchists and Carlists because the Allies did not help Franco—though these last are much less bitter than formerly. Of course, as awful as it would be, a new revolution in Spain might prove of enormous assistance to the Allies—at least I cannot help thinking that. In any event, I am convinced something is going to happen in that poor half-starved and throttled country before the present European show is over.

Jamie

There was a pause after I read the letter. Nobody had thought much about Spain. There were no political clichés for dealing with her.

The British colonel laughed. "They'll be in a bloody mess if they try to take Gibraltar," he said. "Quite a rock! Quite a rock!"

I said: "But it's one of the nasty things they could do, isn't it?"

And he replied, vaguely: "Oh, rather!"

"Speaking of bull-fights," an English major at the other end of the table said, "any of you ever see pig-sticking?"

We talked about India.

There were, of course, many English people in France in the spring—staff officers, diplomats, business men, even wives of B.E.F. officers. There had been a great debate in Commons in March on leave for B.E.F. wives. Was it "demoralizing"—or vice versa? The effects of war were so far-reaching that the English even pondered *publicly* in the spring: Do men need women? The consensus of English *public* opinion seemed to be No. Privately Englishmen said: "Well, occasionally—anyway, at not too long intervals." The French, of course, thought otherwise. And the French military, according to their immemorial habits, had arranged things at the front accordingly. So in England, in April, Lady Astor threatened in the House of Commons to strain Anglo-French amity for the first time since the war began by stirring up trouble about the licensed French brothels at the front.

Of course the English were not "gay" about the war. But they never were ones to grouse as much as the French, what-what? The English in April couldn't help being amused by many things; for instance, America's absurd preoccupation with war-and-peace aims!

The major said: "I say, I wish you Americans would forget all that tripe like 'Federal Unction,' [8] and 'A New World Program, Inc.,' and 'Out of chaos with a little Effort.' All *we* want to do is pry loose this bloody rat Hitler. That'*s all*," said the major.

"Is that really all?" I asked.

He said: "Oh—er—we might pop him off to some filthy hole like St. Helena, and shave off half his moustache as a punishment. But *he's* the real bird we're after!"

I insisted: "But then what will you do with the German people?"

The major looked baffled. "I haven't the foggiest idea," he said. "But, I say, if they surrender *now*, we might be sporting about it. If this war goes on for a decade or two, we're sure to get the wind up and think of something fruity!"

They were also amused by the extraordinary severity of

[8] The Federal Union idea was one of the favourite jokes of the English. But when, in June, Winston Churchill, with a magnanimity and vision born of desperation, offered just such a union with Great Britain to the French, they were very unhappy indeed when the French laughed.

the French rationing system [9]—"You get Baba on Tuesday, rhum on Wednesday, Baba-au-rhum only on Saturday—even in the Ritz," said the major. "Why, you can get all the sweets and liquors you want every day at Claridge's!" [10]

The notion that England might be invaded or that there might be Englishmen—speaking English—who were traitors, potential or actual, in England was really hilarious in April. As a British wit put it: "The German army is now entirely mechanized. The only cavalry unit left is the Trojan horse. But how to land it?"

Above all, the English were amused by Lord Haw-Haw, who every night broadcast to them of Germany's might and told them all of their own weaknesses.

I said to the major: "But he is a very persuasive propagandist. Some of it *must* stick."

And the major answered: "Not really. We all laugh too hard to really hear what he's saying." Besides, they pointed out, it's a jolly feeling to know that when you listen to him, you are doing something people are shot for doing in Germany.[11]

English luncheon and dinner guests in Paris also talked English politics. On the whole they didn't really like Chamberlain. But who else was there?

The colonel said: "A lot of the more intelligent people in your country don't like Roosevelt. But who else is there

[9] Three meatless days, three sugarless days, three days without liquor. My April birthday fell on a sugarless day. Good friends found it impossible by bribery or cajolery to wheedle a birthday cake out of Olivier, at the Ritz.

[10] English rationing of meat, butter, sugar, and gas bore down largely on the middle and lower classes, but even they, as an M.P. pointed out in the House of Commons, could eat all the snails, frogs, liver, kidney, tongue, oxtail, sausages, meat pies, and tripe (no reference to the Speaker's) they cared to.

[11] By early June there was a newspaper campaign in London, urging the government to make it a public offence to listen to Lord Haw-Haw.

in America?—if you follow me."

"I don't," I said. "I refuse to believe two nations of hundreds of millions of people like ours have only one man apiece fit to lead them. Besides," I said, "you have Churchill."

The colonel shook his head dubiously. "England," he said, "mistrusts Churchill. He's the dictator type, and he has an ancestor complex. He'd like to be the Duke of Marlborough, if you follow me. . . . He's a brilliant hothead of course—eighteen ideas to the minute in Cabinet meeting, one of them corking, but the other seventeen bloody awful."

"The virtue of Chamberlain," the major said, "is that he can always be trusted to pick the very best of the bloody awful ones!" Everybody laughed—they thought that was funny. I thought it was very disquieting.

"No," the colonel said, "Halifax would be the man if Chamberlain is ever got rid of." This didn't seem likely to the colonel, "since," he said, "one doesn't swap horses. Also, like your Mr. Roosevelt, he still glows a bit in the sunset of his 'promises.' Chamberlain promised us peace in our time," he went on; "Roosevelt promised you prosperity in yours. Well, neither of them could deliver. Sooner or later all politicians die of swallowing their own lies, but meanwhile there isn't anybody around now who can tell us better ones, who can, you know, promise us anything but war and misery; [12] and who's going to elect a man who can't promise you *something* pleasant?" What-what?

The major felt that Chamberlain was, on the whole, a drip, but that it didn't really matter, because the English had plenty of time. Look at the last war: three years get-

[12] In May, Churchill said to Britons: "I have nothing to offer but blood, toil, tears and sweat," but even that was not an original offer. It was made first on September 3, 1939, to Britain by Adolf Hitler.

ting rid of Asquith. On the whole both the colonel and the major felt the English were functioning *politically* as might be expected. They explained that a long war needs money. The Conservatives had (a ten-year inheritance) the confidence of the propertied classes. There was really no man better fit than Chamberlain to conserve "the wealth of the Empire." He was securing, on matters of government loans, for instance, the *voluntary* co-operation of the people.[13] It was muddling through perhaps, the colonel thought, but it would do for another twelve months.

The American oil man, at my end of the table, whispered to me: "After that, they'll either extract it by involuntary methods, or we'll have to carry them on the cuff for the duration."

The colonel went on: Chamberlain's government was building up England's export trade to keep favourable trade balances. A careful adjustment was in progress between the needs of export industries and the urgencies of armament production. The government was bringing about "political" adjustments between the labour groups and the Conservatives gradually. It was spending its money in America judiciously, getting every ha'pennyworth out of airplane purchases, giving English and colonial factories their chance first to expand and then to supply and sell to the warring Empire. A political necessity.

In a budget speech in April Sir John Simon said: "Why should we suppose that the willing exertions of our people, if properly aroused and directed, will produce less [revenue]

[13] Of this voluntary economic and financial method, Professor John Maynard Keynes had already warned in February: "To depend on voluntary methods when the treasury has to take one half the national income to run a successful war is comparable to relying on these methods to raise an army of 5,000,000 men." Of the new budget which Sir John Simon presented in early spring, and which met the approval of the whole nation, he said: "It's a cowardly budget. Of course it's popular."

than if we attempted to apply a cast-iron formula to compel our people to lend. . . . Nobody has better reason than we who enjoy freedom to be willing to pay the full price necessary to preserve it!"

But on the whole, the colonel felt the picture was a bright one. Ingenious economic dodges of the treasury plus judicious purchases under enemy noses in neutral markets, and the daily tightening of the stranglehold blockade, were rapidly putting Germany in the same spot in which she found herself in 1916—after only seven months of war *this* time! Indeed, it was all wise, cagy, methodical. Not really, when you came to think of it, "muddling through," this, at all! *Or was it?*

(The only minority report I ever heard on the British vice of muddling through was from the American oil man. He said: "If the English don't start muddling through quick, they're going to lose this war." I asked: "What do you mean?" He said: "Now, take oil, my business. The first week of the war they formed the United Kingdom Oil Pool —assembling all British oil companies under one government department. Good idea, so far. But then they began to *organize* the department. The English have no gift for organization. Committees were named to organize the committee that ran the Pool. Subcommittees were appointed to organize the organizing committees, and steering committees were appointed over them. . . . Result: in March, in the Mediterranean, one oil tanker often received from London three sets of orders to report to three different ports for three different types of cargo. Now," the oil man said, "it was *impossible* to accomplish that, in a week's time!" This sort of thing, he said, was prevalent in all branches of "war effort"; for example, the A.R.P. had organized its spending so well that it was now buying cosmetics and sanitary necessities for female air wardens, the Food Administration had organized food so well that masses of butter were spoiling in warehouses, and so on. Said he: "The British genius is for muddling through *at once*. This sort of thing is neither British muddling through nor German organization.")

Sometimes, because I was an American, the English in Paris asked me in serious, uneasy whispers: "Do you think the French will stick another year or two of this kind of war?"

And I would always say, because it was so obvious: "No *democratic* nation can exist as an armed camp for years and still stay democratic." "*We* can," the English always said, and I would retort: "You're not really an armed camp, the way France is. Your navy, 'mobilized' for hundreds of years, has long been integrated with your peace economy; in fact, it assures the continuance of that economy. But five million men have been yanked from the shops and fields and factories of France, which cannot produce and function for very long without their consumer-producer power. This Sitzkrieg makes that daily more apparent to them. That's why everybody in France now has begun to clamour so loudly for action. It's action or else—or else some sort of revolution, ending in Communist or Fascist dictatorship. Though on the whole," I always said, mischievously, "since you've asked me, a separate peace with Hitler might still be a preferable solution, if France really wants to stay a democracy. . . ."

This always made the English you saw in Paris very mad and truculent. And this is the fourth thing I found out in Paris in the spring. The English didn't really like or trust the French any more than the French liked or trusted the

English. They agreed with Shakespeare, who said three hundred years ago: " 'Tis better using France than trusting France." Between perfidious Albion and fickle Marianne there had in the past been too much treachery, too much Continental jobbery and Punic faith; too many "heads I win, tails you lose" diplomatic gambles, and irrevocably too much blood spilt to make the alliance a thing that was cherished by the friendly heart, or ratified by a brotherly instinct. Not even the rivers of blood they had spilt together in the last war, and the trickles in this one, were thick enough to wipe out this historical enmity. The current French joke that "every Englishman is willing to fight to the last drop of French blood" was certainly not justified in March. England had since the war's beginning lost some 4,000 sailors at sea, against 1,500 French on the Maginot. The losses in pilots were predominantly R.A.F. men. And in the last war one million of the Empire's dead ought to have given the lie to that mean-spirited remark. But the French went right on making it. That's because the French hated the English for their twenty years of blundering diplomacy, which had left France's manhood holding the bag in the fabulously expensive Maginot, and France's taxpayers, who had to build the Maginot because of those blunders, holding it at home. The French felt it was a grim irony to have as your ally the fellow who'd got you into this mess. "Hitler is England's Frankenstein," they said to you. "Our blood will be spilled, thanks to the stupidity of Englishmen!"

Some of this I indicated to the major. He exploded. "Can't trust these damn Frenchmen, can you? I knew it. Their wine, their women and their filthy money! Put 'em in any order you want. But that's all Frenchmen care about!" He glowered at me. "Well, *we'll* stick it, and stay

English, have no fear of that."

I had none then. I have none now. England may have a head of clay, but her feet are firm and unfaltering.

But in France in April, the kettle called the pot black, only in the presence of an American scuttle.

SEVEN

We are so well equipped that if the war were to last ten years, we should not have to buy the button of a soldier's gaiter.

Marshal Le Bœuf, on the eve of the Franco-Prussian War, 1870, speaking of the preparedness of the French army

◇◇

NOW LET ME be honest. In early April I had also believed with all of the English and most of the French that the requisite for victory was largely "sticking it," wearing down Germany. All the follies and fancies of the Allies I have told you so far, I didn't really believe were follies then. I was impatient of the few I did perceive, but I never doubted the Allies would survive them. So like most of the French I also might have cherished the reasonable expectation of victory until the very day of the invasion if I had never gone up to the Maginot.

Like every American in France, I wanted very much to

see this famous defence system. In the middle of March I directly requested permission of the Bureau d'Information to do so. Many journalists and "distinguished visitors" had gone, of course, but the difficulty lay in the fact that I was an American woman,[1] and the Maginot was "firing." I won't tell you here the hours, no, *days* spent thereafter in trying to arrange it. From the first moment when I realized how unorthodox the request was, I said to the Information people: "Well, never mind; if I can't go, it doesn't really matter." But without my volition—indeed, in spite of my own genuine efforts to drop the whole thing—I was caught up in a series of telephone conversations and rendezvous with Bureau d'Information officials, with their wives and girl friends, with Cabinet Ministers and *their* wives and girl friends, with staff officers and their wives and girl friends, until at last it seemed to me *tout Paris* was divided into two warring camps: those who thought "an American woman should be allowed to see the Maginot," and those who thought it "might establish a dangerous precedent."

There were days when my telephone rang steadily. Some quite strange voice would say: "Madame, I am Colonel X. You will see, tomorrow you will receive the permission. I have heard of your case, I have used my influence. It is arranged for you. . . ." And other days when my phone rang, another strange voice would say: "Madame, I am the Duchesse de Z. I met you with Captain Y at luncheon. . . . I hear that Colonel X has botched your affair. . . . But my cousin is a friend of Paul Reynaud.[2] Tonight she will use

[1] As it turned out, I was the first American woman, Dorothy Thompson the second and last, to go officially to the Maginot Line.

[2] This was the ill-starred Countess Hélène de Portes. She also took a hand in my affair. I now read in the papers that she is being called the evil star of France. She was a dark, homely, talkative little woman, in her late forties. She looked as much like a *Hausfrau* as a French *maîtresse* can. She was patriotic, energetic; she had many friends and

her influence. . . ." Still other days someone from G.H.Q. telephoned to say: "Madame, we regret to tell you again, your request is *impossible* . . . but be assured, we shall all continue to use our influence." It was all very confusing and mysterious—and disquieting. I thought: "Is there no one whose yea means yea, whose no means no, in this country?"

At length Colonel Scheffer telephoned from General Gamelin's office to say that Gamelin himself had received the request and had refused it categorically. "There, now," I said, "that settles the matter." I reported to all my Maginot workers (some thirty or forty by this time) the generalissimo's irrevocable decision. The news spread like wildfire through *tout Paris*. Everyone seemed highly indignant. "*Ah, que c'est stupide*," everybody said. "France doesn't know how to make propaganda!" (I may add in passing that at those moments when it looked as though I might be allowed to go, the Bureau d'Information had made one condition of the trip that I should never write anything about it until the war was over!)

And my telephone rang even more incessantly. Madame A would smuggle me out to the front in a Red Cross ambulance, disguised as a volunteer driver. . . . Madame B had an aged uncle who lived in Reims; his nephew was a colonel in a Maginot regiment. We would lunch with the uncle and just pay a call on the colonel. . . . Madame C was going to a *foyer* near Metz with a group of artistes. I would pretend to be a *chanteuse*. . . . The plots were many, allur-

---

a lot of notions about everything. But to call this plain little woman who bustled and fiddled about the important man she loved, and who interceded for friends and causes rather indiscriminately, the *Du Barry of France* gives the same cockeyed impression of her role as would a French newspaper man were he to call Mrs. Eleanor Roosevelt the Cleopatra of the New Deal.

ing, and ingenious. I no sooner said no to one than it became an integral part of another fresh plot offered to me.

On April 4 I went to see Monsieur André de Laboulaye, head of the North American division of the Ministry of Information, and France's Ambassador in Washington from 1933 to 1937.

I said: "Please, monsieur, tell anyone, tell everyone who has become embroiled with this *cause célèbre* to lay off'n me! Please tell all the strange and charming and gallant men and women who apparently all over France are working on my behalf that I don't really want to do anything incompatible with the military policies of a great country in the throes of the greatest war in history. The 'No' of a generalissimo of France is 'No' to me anyway. Please, I don't want to go to the Maginot any longer. It was just a feminine whim. I am the *marraine* (godmother) of a fort in the Maginot, and I just thought it would be cute to see it. Now I realize the request was presumptuous, the idea fantastic." (And, I thought, my nerves and health wouldn't stand very much more of the cabalistic goings-on of which I was rapidly becoming the victim.) "In fact, monsieur," I said quite truthfully, "I am going to Norway and Sweden next week."

And he, with great relief in his voice, replied: "That, madame, is an excellent solution. And it is very generous and charming of you to offer it."

I said: "Then may we consider the matter settled?"

And he, very, very relieved: "*Absolument!*"

"It will not be necessary," I asked, "to broadcast my decision on Paris Mondial?" and he smiled and said: "Ah, no; that might just reopen the question, which is settled."

So (this being France) on April 5 I received the following note from an army liaison officer with the Bureau d'Information:

Dear Miss Boothe:

Be ready please for morning. You are going. You will visit your Maginot Fort that you are the Marraine of. But I have spend the whole day to raise the mountains for it. In France the things get done if you are patient with enormous efforts. All the safe conducts are signed.

Very respectfully,

(Captain) Charles Emmanuel Brousse

And the next morning Captain Charles Emmanuel Brousse, a handsome, forty-year-old Frenchman, with snapping brown eyes and a soft thick Perpignan accent, called for me at dawn, and in a shiny new little G.H.Q. staff car we set off for *la zone des armées*. . . .

Captain Brousse said: "You see, General Gamelin was so full of admiration for the firm stand you took against all *les intriguantes* of the Paris salons, which Monsieur de la Boulaye told him about, that he relented, and said: 'Perhaps this is the sort of person who *should* see the Maginot. Perhaps she will understand it.' " It was, as I say, all very confusing.

I answered: "I don't understand anything, but I am happy to be going."

He said earnestly: "I wish so much you should go, because sometimes I feel Americans get the wrong impression of France's war effort, never leaving Paris. You will now see—the war in the Ritz is one thing; the war out there is quite another!"

We stopped at Châlons-sur-Marne for luncheon. Now, Châlons was well in the army zone, and just in case you feel that the Ritz was no standard to measure France's war-effort by, here is the menu served to officers and non-commissioned officers, in Châlons's one hotel, La Haute Mère de Dieu:

Les Hors d'œuvres
Le Saumon maître d'Hôtel
Le poulet de Bresse au champagne garni de fonds d'artichauts au beurre
Les fromages
Les fruits
Les vins—specialité: Champagne rosé

Captain Brousse said: "Keep the menu for a souvenir. No matter what happens to France, it will prove to your friends that her officers will always dine like kings."

(And Somerset Maugham, who feared that there might be some discrimination in the matter of food, in favour of the officers against the soldiers, "made it my business to ask a number of men how they ate [in the lines], and I found none who had a complaint to make . . . the morning, a cup of black coffee and a hunk of bread; at ten . . . sardines or sausages, with another cup of coffee . . . the midday meal . . . hors d'œuvres, meat with rice, potatoes, or lentils, cheese or stewed fruit, a quarter of a litre of wine. . . . The evening meal . . . the same . . . the ration of wine has now been increased to a litre. . . .")

Alsace and Lorraine in April. . . . How beautiful they looked, how rich, how fair the fresh-ploughed fields were in the pale shimmer of spring sunshine! And then, speeding through miles and miles of this sweet countryside, when I looked closer, I saw that innocent haystack after golden haystack was punctured by the ugly protruding snouts of field guns. Half-built cottages everywhere housed machine-gun nests. And on the little green brows of hundreds of tender hills nestled a vast nasty brood of camouflaged cement pill-boxes. Plains bristled like porcupines with thick-growing, short, vicious iron quills to repel tanks. Wide, deep-dug holes pocking the valleys yawned for them. And far-flung across the uplands lay wide, unbroken lines of barbed wire, like vast rows of fakirs' beds of shining nails, defying Nazi mystics to immolate themselves upon them painlessly.

And Captain Brousse told me proudly that in every green wood, in every copse and thicket, in every wide shadow-drenched forest, thousands of guns were concealed, and hundreds of thousands of men were camping.

"It looks peaceful," he said, "but let one German division move over the Siegfried, and it will all—all turn into the inferno!"

Then I saw that all this lovely, lovely part of budding France bristled with hidden death, like a beautiful woman with a dread disease. Woe, I thought, to the men who sought to embrace her! I had an uneasy, fleeting thought: "The Germans are really smart—why should they try it? The Germans are really smart—they must be thinking up some way to avoid all this massed murder. . . ."

It had taken the better part of the day to motor from Paris to Metz, the largest town in Lorraine, behind the north end of the Maginot.

There in the small, dark, cold little Hôtel Royal, which like all the little hotels in the evacuated army zones was largely patronized by officers, I was delighted to find in the dining-room an old friend. It was young Lieutenant (Count) René de Chambrun, a very able peace-time lawyer, famous on this side of the Atlantic for being the son of a Longworth, a great-great-grandson of Lafayette, and therefore a hereditary American citizen. In France he was better known as a Frenchman who was the son of General (Count) Aldebert de Chambrun, nephew of Senator (Marquis)

Pierre de Chambrun, nephew of Charles (Count) de Chambrun, former French Ambassador to Rome. But most especially René was known as the husband of José Laval, pretty daughter of shrewd Pierre Laval, an ex-Premier, but still one of France's most powerful politicians. Currently, of course, Laval was a man more feared than followed. He was no friend of colourless Gamelin, of vacillating Daladier, of cocky, dynamic Reynaud. But he was a great friend of war-glamorous Marshal Pétain and General Weygand. A turn of the tirelessly revolving wheel of French politics might always bring him, or them, back. The house of Laval was not one to be ignored or trifled with. Here was a man to be listened to and from time to time propitiated.

Son-in-law René had spent eight months of "phony war" now in one sector of the Maginot, doing liaison work between the French and the English, occasionally showing "the might of the Maginot, and the force of France" to really distinguished visitors.[3] Lord Gort and the King of England were perhaps his two most famous Maginot customers.

That night, in the dining-room of the cold little hotel in Metz, René was enthusiastic, in fact impassioned, in his faith in France and all she was fighting for. The Maginot, he felt, was the supreme expression of France's determination to preserve her own nationhood. "And if anyone in America doubts for a moment," he said, "that *peace* is our only war aim, and *defence* our only strategy, tell them this: that we have anchored all our millions of dollars' worth of great guns in five hundred million dollars' worth of concrete." That is when I had my second uneasy thought. I remem-

[3] A few days after I saw him, I heard that his liaison work had been so well done that France had made him a captain, the youngest in the French army.

bered what Count Radziwill had said: "Their new weapon in Poland was the War of Movement . . ." and concrete, I thought, heavens, that's *very* immobile.

Because René was in love with the Maginot, he was also in love at that time with the province that had inspired it.

"You must do an article," he said, "about Lorraine [4] for the American papers. Lorraine is the immemorial gateway used by the barbarians for the invasion of France since the time of Attila the Hun. Here in Metz is a very ancient stone ruin of a gate, called La Porte des Allemands, to prove it. This city," he said, "is the very rampart of the province which is the rampart of the nation! Monsieur Maginot, who conceived La Ligne Maginot himself was a Lorrainer."

Now, I had the greatest respect for René de Chambrun's intellect, his powers of analysis and deduction. I said eagerly: "But, René, are they *sure* to try to come through this way again?"

He paused a moment. "They always have," he answered, "though of course the last time they did come through Belgium. But we have urged the Belgians to see to their own defences. And anyway," he said, "we are now rapidly extending our fortifications along the Belgian border." I thought: "Is that true? Then why haven't we heard of, why haven't we read about, why haven't we all seen more pictures of these new fortifications? We have seen so many, so very many, of the Maginot. . . ."

I said: "Oh, René, why didn't you build them *before?*"

And he replied: "Well, partly because they cost so much,

[4] A few days after this, in Paris, I read a strange story in the French papers, its authenticity vouched for by a dozen Maginot soldiers. It said that "in Lorraine there is a miraculous spring which started flowing exactly three months before the end of the Franco-Prussian War of 1870. It flowed again in August 1918. On February 19, 1940, the miraculous spring began to flow once more. Will Germany collapse by the end of May?" asked the papers.

partly because we haven't had time, but mostly because the Belgians, seeing our guns and forts facing them, might have thought *we* were growing too aggressive."

"Even," I asked, "if all the guns were anchored in concrete?"

He said: "Very well, it's a mistake not to have had them there before, but it's one which in time will be remedied." (Now came another uneasy thought: "Why does everybody always go on saying 'in time' everything will be all right? How many things are wrong here and in England which only time will cure? Are they sure to have time? Has Hitler promised it to them?")

And then, because René had been cooped up in the Maginot for months and had had little news of the outside world he said: "Don't let's talk about the war. I long to hear everything about America! Tell me quickly: will Roosevelt get a third term?"

I answered: "Well, you see—"

He interrupted: "Of course he will!" And then he asked: "But can he get America in before November?"

I said, apologetically: "Not unless he or France can paint a much blacker picture of France's chances than the situation seems to warrant."

He laughed half-heartedly. "No chance of that," he said.

You see, everyone was very proud in France, so nobody really wanted us to be in a position again to say: "All right, now we'll win the war for you." So René said: "The picture is grey and murky, but it certainly isn't black. The real reason why the Allies would like America to come in now is for the moral effect on the other neutrals."

It was a funny thing in Europe that although both the Allies said very pointedly to Americans: "*All* of us democracies are really in this thing; we all sink or swim together," each Ally wanted most of the credit for winning, and no matter what America did they were both agreed that America should never get what was left over. As the oil man said once, they felt quite able to manipulate the pool, and sell out at the top. All they expect of us is to underwrite the original issue.

The next morning we left Metz early, and an hour later we came to "my fort," Le Mont des Welsches, a typical fort of the Maginot Line—that vast row on row of cement catacombs, of sunken earth-bound battleships along the whole length of the German border. Outside the Mont des Welsches was a great mound of insulating wooded earth whose bald head was studded with bomb-proof turtle-neck gun turrets. The small camouflaged entrance in the side of the hill was guarded by barbed wire and tank-traps, and bristled with machine-guns.

The inside of a Maginot fort is too familiar to need much description . . . the great air-conditioned galleries threaded with rail-tracks, cut off at strategic intervals by fireproof sliding iron doors, guarded by spaced machine-guns . . . the floors that could drop in, hurtling the besieger who penetrated so far (a desperate supposition) into fifty-foot pits . . . the great guns on the "first floor," the control and chart rooms below them . . . the prodigious supply rooms, glutted with food, medicine, and honeycomb racks of shells . . . the bewildering mazes of machinery, of oil tanks, of electrical gadgets, thrice duplicated in every detail lest any part should be put out of order. . . . A Maginot fort was (and is) an impregnable Trojan city of sinister Martian ingenuity.

The simile was provocative: After I had seen all these deadly mirabilia and asked all the questions I could think of about them, I said timidly to the dapper dark little Commandant of the fort: "It is impregnable, of course, unless—"

"Unless what?" the Commandant asked happily. He knew all the answers. He had given them to experts. "*En effet*," he said, with Gallic gallantry, "so far Madame has asked me all the same questions the King and Lord Gort asked when they came here."

I smiled a sweet acknowledgment of the obvious compliment, but I went right on: "Unless," I said, "you import a Trojan horse."

"Ah, sabotage?" he said.

"Yes," I said, apologetically.

He looked stern. "Lord Gort," he said, "didn't ask me that, madame. He knew the answer."

"But *I* don't," I said sweetly.

Then, very patiently, he told me that the men of the Maginot were the most carefully picked, carefully watched, best pedigreed soldiers in all France. "Besides," he went on, "our system of exact triplication of every mechanism would make effective sabotage impossible."

I said, even more apologetically: "In that case, the Achilles heel of the Maginot must be the morale of the soldiers within it? A long siege, perhaps—a *very* long war—?"

He looked rather hurt. "Come here," he said to a big cross-eyed soldier standing at the door of the gallery.

"*Oui, mon Commandant.*"

"How long have you been here?"

"Six years," said the cross-eyed one very cheerfully.

"And are you still very happy?"

The cross-eyed giant looked embarrassed. "*Eh bien, mon Commandant*," he said, "*je fais mon métier* (I'm doing my job)."

Now the Commandant fixed him with a fierce direct black

little Mediterranean eye and shouted: "Now tell Madame—would you or would you not die for France?"

The soldier gulped unhappily, looked at me with one eye, with the other at the Commandant. "*Ah oui, madame,*" he said with shy but deep sincerity.

The Commandant dismissed him with an indulgent and paternal gesture that Napoleon might have used to a soldier he had just told was carrying a marshal's baton in his knapsack.

"*Voilà, madame!*" he cried triumphantly.

I laughed. "Now suppose that poor man had said no!" I said mischievously.

"No?" the Commandant asked, incredulously. Then he pushed his Maginot beret slyly over one eye, and said with some Gallic wit: "In that case this poor man would *also* have died for France—but a little prematurely."

"Then, look, *mon Commandant,*" I said earnestly. "There is no way from within or without that the Maginot can be taken?"

He nodded energetically. "That is the inescapable conclusion, madame."

(Again the uneasy thought: "The Germans are smart, they know everything: Either they have got some secret weapon or they are going some other way." I—even I—had now quite definitely figured out that one.)

"Then why should the Germans try to come this way, *mon Commandant?*" I was nothing, in the Maginot, if not tenacious.

"Ah, madame," he said with melancholy enthusiasm, "what have we got our two great armies for, except sooner or later to hurl them at one another? And you don't understand the Germans? *Ils sont bêtes*—they *will* try to come this way. Imagine if they didn't! How foolish they would look—

France would look! . . . *Non, madame, ce n'est pas raisonnable!*" said the little Commandant.

I persisted: "But can't they get into France some other way?"

"What other way?" The Commandant laughed, and all the junior officers standing by laughed quickly after him.

"Holland? Belgium?" I asked earnestly.

They laughed even louder, and then they all began to explain at once why this was also impossible. They said: "First, the Germans will get their noses very wet in the floods in Holland; second, we are reliably informed that the Belgians have a very good small Ligne Maginot, and, thirdly, they don't want to take on three million more Dutch and Belgian soldiers." "The Germans," the Commandant said, "are stupid—but not *that* stupid."

At last my tour of the Mont des Welsches was over. The Commandant and all the junior officers escorted me up the long subterranean ramps to the entrance. I blinked for a moment in the sudden sunlight of the April heaven.

"Au revoir," I said, "and thank you. You were kind to let me come. I think your fort is the most wonderful fort in the whole Maginot. And I hope to see you all again in happier circumstances."

"You will, madame. . . . *Mais il faut en finir,*" said the Commandant happily.

Now there was a disturbance at the black mouth of the fort's entrance. A little white-faced poilu, holding both arms behind his back, was suddenly catapulted by other friendly arms in my general direction. His white face went red as he skidded to a halt, breathless, before me. "*Madame,*" he stammered, "*Madame . . . est . . . est très brave. . . .* We could not let you go without . . . *eh bien, c'est la guerre, n'est-ce pas?*" And from behind his back he whipped out a small bouquet of little slightly wilted store carnations and red roses. And he stumbled away, as the other soldiers at the entrance applauded the motive, the deed, and his personal bravery.

I wanted to cry. I said to the Commandant, who was smiling with enormous pride: "Out of those great dark steel and stone caverns—red roses! Where did he get them?"

The Commandant replied: "*Bien*, when they heard you were coming, he walked to Metz at dawn this morning. He's just got back—just made it!"

Then I thanked them all again, as you would, very tearfully. And while I was saying au revoir all over, I wondered if a lady visited the Siegfried Line (if they allowed such a thing!), would a German soldier walk twenty miles to bring her a little bunch of red roses?

I asked Captain Brousse. "No, madame," he said, "and that is only one of the differences between the French and the Germans. Even in war Frenchmen do not forget that the pretty ladies deserve red roses."

And still I was very sad, that morning, I knew all of a sudden (though I forgot it, after, as you will see) that the Maginot would one day break their hearts, as it had almost bankrupted their exchequer.

All the way back from the fort to Metz I worried about the Maginot—how the French would feel about it if the Germans never attacked there.

"Captain Brousse," I asked, "won't you all be—well—terribly disillusioned if after the war is over the Maginot has never been used?"

He said, cheerfully: "You mean if the Germans collapse before they attack it? *Pas du tout*. They will see that five hundred million dollars was a small price to pay for all the French lives it will have saved." And then he laughed. "But we'll get that back too," he said. "After the war it will be the greatest tourist attraction in Europe!"

Now the war in France is over, and the first official tourist to the unused Maginot was a German in a grey ulster called Adolf Hitler.

But the Maginot will always lie heavy on my heart. Le Mont des Welsches was my fort. They had made me its *marraine.* I had sent them their cigarettes, their champagne, their brave flag embroidered in gold with the Maginot motto: *Ils ne passeront pas.* What comfort is it now to that gay little Commandant, to the cross-eyed one, to all the men of my fort who asked nothing better than to die for France, that the Germans didn't pass—*that way*? [5]

On April 8 we again set out from Metz to visit the 11th Regiment of the Foreign Legion, billeted in a Lorraine sector. We drove first to the regiment's staff headquarters. They were in the little *Mairie* of a "village somewhere in France." On the old stone steps of the *Mairie* the colonel of the regiment, a red-headed, vaguely unshaven man with a fierce scar running from one ear across his chin down under his collar, flanked by five or six smart-looking junior officers and several sloppy, much decorated, and (traditionally) bearded legionnaires, saluted and greeted us. They took us at once into the little stone building.

There, in the dining-room, on a long wooden trestle table they had laid out a little buffet of champagne and wafers.

[5] I have been reading stories, date-lined July, from Vichy and Berlin in which the Germans claim that the Maginot fortresses were made of very inferior material and cement that could not stand up against the German guns. I am absolutely certain that this is false. It is probably propaganda calculated to soften the bitterness and disillusionment of the people because "the Maginot was never used," and to make the "crooked politicians and contractors" who built it so flimsily the whipping-boys for unhappy France. Having destroyed French morale, the Germans must now build it up along Fascist lines.

The stems of the glasses were twisted with ivy from the village church wall.

"Look," said Captain Brousse, pointing to the low casement windows.

I went to the window, and there outside, seated between the neat rows of a vegetable garden, was the band of the Legion, some twenty men with drums, fifes, and battered brass trumpets. My appearance at the window was the signal for the band leader. He lifted his baton and then, there in the heart of war-time France, I heard the loud though unsure strains of *The Star-Spangled Banner.* It was as noisily and as badly played as I have ever heard it, and yet, I strangely felt, with better will, and more courteous intention. And it evoked in my mind the broad image of my dear country, so strong, so safe, so far away, and so wilfully isolated from Europe's imminent disaster. I thought: "God bless America! I hope with all my heart she will be spared this war, as she wishes. . . . I hope with all my heart America is right, and this war is not really about Liberty, and Justice for *all*. . . . Because if America has any meaning, that is its meaning. And if this war should really turn out to be about that after all," I thought, standing at attention among those foreign legionnaires, "how shall America answer one day to history, that she was not here to fight for Liberty and Justice?" I cried a little then, because, you see, I am really a very average American, which is to say I am at heart idealistic, evangelical, and easily stirred by crusader emotions.

The band then played—very much better—the March of the Legionnaires. And after I had clapped and waved to them out of the window, and they had half grinned and half glowered back an acknowledgment, the colonel, with a barely perceptible nod over my shoulder, dismissed them. (It came to me a long time afterwards that what they played as they filed out of the garden was *The Blue Danube*. I asked Captain Brousse about that. "What is strange about it?" he asked. "Since when is Strauss a *German*?"

Then we all drank toasts to France, to Victory, to America. The colonel, whose chest was absolutely jammed with medals, said: "Madame, I have only one complaint against America—the false impression she has given the world in her motion pictures of the Legion."

I replied: "I don't understand—my impression gathered from those movies is that you are all incredibly reckless and romantic and idealistic."

He said stiffly: "*Précisément*, madame. We are neither reckless nor romantic nor idealistic. We are the world's most sensible and cautious men—professional soldiers. Our ranks are not, as your cinemas suggest, made up of men who either despair of life or fear the law. They are made up of men who love life so much they have nothing but contempt for death, her enemy. We enjoy life, so we enjoy fighting. We are not like the average poilu. He really hates fighting. He only fights because he must. He dreams of nothing but the day when he will return to his wife and children. A legionnaire thinks of his wife and family—if he has a family—only once a month. *Voilà*!" He drank to it.

I asked: "Why only once a month?"

He answered: "That, madame, is when he sends them his pay cheque. This is an unfortunate rule in the army."

The rest of what the colonel said to me or showed me is of no importance. The thing that I remember now, and thought of all the way back to Metz that day, was that he had said the French poilu doesn't like fighting. And that, too, made me uneasy. Why should he? I argued with myself; neither does the tommy or the Ger— But the Germans do, I thought. If we know anything about the Germans we know that they have always liked fighting. And then I thought of France and its rapidly declining birth-rate, and how the blood bath from 1914 to 1918 had so terribly weakened the nation. "They are hating and fearing, with all their collective social and national instinct for self-preservation, a repetition of *that*," I said to myself. In 1918 there were fifty million. Today they are forty. What will they be if this war goes on as long and is as bloody as the last one? "The average poilu hates fighting. . . . The average poilu wants to get back quickly to his family." So a long active war, or a long stalemate war, the average poilu doesn't really like it.

I confided these fears to Captain Brousse. He confirmed them; "but you forget one thing," he said. "The average poilu *loves* the soil of France more than he *hates* anything. And the only alternative to fighting it out or sitting it out is to let this Hitler take it from him."

I was comforted. But now, in the end, I see the French poilu loved his soil so much that he preferred to turn it over to this Hitler rather than see it destroyed utterly.

As for the Foreign Legion, the last I heard of them, two days after the surrender they were still holding a French fort near the Swiss border. And when the Armistice came, they announced that their intention still was to fight their way back to Africa, from whose shores their further intention was to go on fighting.

On April 9 I was the guest of honour at an officers' mess in the headquarters of the 7th Division of the 3rd Army, stationed behind the Maginot. The headquarters were in a small *presbytère* of a little French village called Kemplich. The small, clean, family-smelling dining-room, hung with cheap chromos of Madonnas with bleeding hearts and Jesuses with lambs, was a strange background for the gold-braided general and his ten level-eyed, stern-looking officers.

For me, an American woman, and for them, French soldiers, this meal was a strained and awkward occasion. Small talk, the gossip of Paris, was remote from their daily doings. Big talk, the gossip of politics, was not their métier. Soldier talk, military shop-talk, was a terrain on which I knew—and they knew—I could only make a fool of myself. After the first expressions of greeting, welcome, and admiration for my country (to which none of them had ever been), and my expressions of admiration for their country (in which I was, and that seemed to be that), the conversation degenerated into amiable mutters about the weather, and a pleasant exchange of smiles. But then I realized, suddenly comforted, that conversation wasn't really necessary. All the officers were quite pleased just to sit and look at me, just because I was a woman, and most of them hadn't seen a woman (of their own class) in months. An occasional feminine chortle or gurgle from me was quite enough to evoke a whole train of nostalgic memories of other chortles and gurgles and the high thin voices of the absent women who were dear to them, and to keep their minds and hearts busied for an hour. In this pleasant atmosphere of understanding non-communication, the officers of the regiment and I settled ourselves at luncheon.

It was an excellent-looking luncheon with mounds of crusty bread, tinned sardines, and olives and tomatoes and carafes of red and white wine, spread on a great red and white checked tablecloth. The first course was, mysteriously enough, oysters. I was just about to ask the general how, in the heart of war-time France, he had been able to come upon such alien fruit, when a pale-faced radio operator burst into the room, saluted in a frightened way, and handed the general a small piece of square lined paper covered with delicate pencilled French handwriting. The general looked at it gravely and then, after digesting its contents with a barely perceptible spasm of his facial muscles, read it with a blank face aloud to the table:

Bulletin

NEW YORK: Communications being cut off between the Scandinavian nations and the other countries, we cannot get confirmation of the news from New York according to which the Norwegian Minister declares that his country is in a state of war with Germany.

The news of the occupation of Denmark at 4 o'clock this morning was cabled to the *New York Times* by its correspondent from Copenhagen, who added that he had succeeded in transmitting the message before the intervention of the censor.

PARIS: According to the news from Norway, the German troops have occupied Bergen. The Norwegian government has left Oslo.

AMSTERDAM: About fifty German warships left German ports yesterday going north. At 11 o'clock the German forces were in the Kattegat toward the northwest.

The radio operator shifted from foot to foot. The general said, crossly: "*Eh, bien!* No orders," and the radio man departed. There was silence.

We all looked solemn and utterly bewildered. The general said, after a long, thoughtful pause: "*Donc!* This is the affair of England. They have the navy."

There was another silence.

And because, as it turned out, very few of the French officers at the mess knew, except in a general way, where Oslo was and certainly not where or even what the Kattegat was, they found they couldn't ask the general any bright questions about the German invasion of Norway.

Captain Brousse whispered in my ear apologetically: "You've heard—a Frenchman is a fellow with a beard, who eats lots of bread, and has no knowledge of geography."

Then the general handed me the paper with a pleasant smile. "This interests you as a souvenir, perhaps?" he asked, and I replied: "Oh, yes." "*Alors voici*," he said, and reached for another handful of oysters.

So the general and all the officers dropped the Norwegian matter (which was England's affair) with relief and alacrity. But you felt they were happier after the news. No matter what it signified, it meant Allied action, and Allied action was the prayer in every good French soldier's heart in April. So the general smiled silently and cheerfully all through the chicken and cheese.

With the coffee he began to explain to me the duties and excitements and dangers of the "*corps francs*"—the volunteer patrols which went out to reconnoitre and get prisoners in the outposts of the Siegfried Line. I was very much interested and I, too, forgot about Norway. (It was, after all, such distant thunder.) Then the general sent for a lieutenant of a "*corps franc*"—a second-lieutenant—for me to talk to.

He was a thin, tall, pale young Frenchman who had enlisted in the army in spite of the fact that the doctor and his mother warned him that he had chronic appendicitis, and that his appendix might burst at any moment. He told me this only because I said: "You look very ill; are you?"

"But I feel better now than I've felt in years," he said. "There is no cure for imaginary fears like real danger." He had been in real danger. In the black night before, armed with sawed-off machine-guns—"like those American gangsters use," he said—he and his patrol had prowled around a

German patrol that was prowling around his patrol. Both sides had fired some shots, but nobody was hurt, and he had brought back some highly useful information to the general. I expressed great admiration for his cunning and bravery.

He blushed and refused to admit he had done anything very gallant. "Somebody has to do things like that," he said simply.

Captain Brousse whispered to me: "He is being given the Croix de Guerre tomorrow." In those days of the "phony war" nearly every French officer who came within gunshot of the German lines received a decoration. But there weren't too many passed out, because on the entire front from September 3 to April 10 there were only fifteen hundred casualties.

(God knows how many thousands of acts of glorious, unquestioning sacrifice, how many deeds of eternal fame, were unrewarded, will never be rewarded by any government, in the horrible mêlée, the hellish confusion, that was "the front" during the thirty-nine terrible days of the invasion!)

Then the young volunteer, blushing again, gave me another souvenir, a small fragment of a German shell which had burst behind his patrol lines one night. The shell had a date on it—1936.

"You see, the Germans began to get ready a long time ago," the general said indignantly. "But they'll be using shells marked 1946 before they can even make a dent on the Maginot."

The young lieutenant said timidly: "It's quite heavy, madame; you can use it for a paper-weight."

(I am using it now to hold down the bitter pages of this manuscript, and when I look at it, I am not really worried about the fate of that nice French volunteer. If he died, he died peacefully and bravely. If he still lives, I know his appendix will mercifully burst before the Germans conscript him to build flat-bottomed boats for the invasion of England. What worries me when I look at the date on that shell is this: Will the 1946 series of German shells be dropping behind our Maginot, which is to say: the Atlantic Ocean?)

So then, having seen Lorraine and Metz and the Foreign Legion, and my fort in the Maginot, and a regiment's mess, and guns on roads and in ditches and in woods and up trees, and the ample promise of imminent death everywhere, I went back to Paris.

There I wrote General Gamelin a letter, thanking him for letting me see "the power and magnificence of the French war machine." But I did not tell him that I had had a very uneasy feeling that this machine was somehow wrong, because it wasn't on wheels—because it was strangely immobile, and because the poilus who were running it really hated running it and wanted so much to get back to their wives and children.

But now, back in Paris, everyone was very excited and happy about the Norwegian campaign. Everybody but the politicians—that small band of former Prime Ministers of France who were always waiting for a crisis that would allow them to crawl into office by their own connivings, or be catapulted back by public opinion. In early April such a crisis had been nicely brewing. The French people were a little jealous when on April 3 Churchill was named British Defence Co-ordinator. They said: "There is more action in England than there is here—we must also do something." This created a public mood favourable to a political putsch for a Cabinet crisis which was slated to reach maturity about April 9. Four days before in the Baltic, unknown to the French and the English—this now seems a certainty—Hitler had started a putsch of his own which wound up being called the Invasion of Norway. On April 8 everybody was saying that Reynaud, who had come into power with a majority of one in late March, had simply revamped and added to Daladier's old Cabinet. The only difference that either the politicians or the people could see in the conduct of the war was that Reynaud was *in*, and Daladier was *out*, but with one flat foot and both rounded shoulders pressed against the door of Reynaud's office. This was not *la guerre à outrance*. It was in fact the same disgusting Sitzkrieg. And since, as *Time* put it once, the French public has no qualms about "yanking the pitcher out of the box in the middle of the ninth inning," Reynaud was about to be yanked, on the very eve of the Norwegian invasion. Flandin, Herriot, Chautemps, Daladier, Bonnet, Laval—each had that glassy-eyed mesmeric stare which came into the French politician's eye when he saw the brass ring coming up again as he rode on the merry-go-round of the Third Republic government.

But the invasion snatched the coveted bauble away from them. Reynaud, echoing Churchill and Chamberlain, proclaimed the invasion as an Allied master-stroke. He said: "Once Germany has devoured its ephemeral booty she can no longer be replenished by way of Denmark and Norway. We have closed henceforth those two windows looking on the North Sea." And everybody else said: "Yes, and the Germans' nerves are cracking, they are growing reckless—they have reversed their policy of not extending the conflict and are extending it into the sea where the Allies are superior. They know we have them cornered!" So Reynaud's government stood popularly acclaimed by the people as the first to begin a "more vigorous prosecution of the war." As I say, everybody except the former Prime Ministers was happy!

But by the middle of April, in France, recriminations had begun to grow, although mostly they were directed against the English. Where had the British Intelligence been while the Germans were planning this? Where was the navy? Where was that British Expeditionary Corps which was supposed to have been assembled for Finland? Why didn't the campaign get under way? Several tense days passed, and then as the good British news from Norway of the successful landings at Andalsnes and Namsos came to Paris, a strange thing happened: in the streets, for the first time, sloppy, indolent French poilus saluted British officers smartly.

The British colonel said to me: "I've always thought they didn't salute before because they didn't know any better. Now I know it's because, even though we are their Allies, they had no respect for us even as soldiers until this moment!" He was much pleased that at last they were really respected.

Captain Brousse said, when I asked him if that were true: "*Oui*, but now at last we are *really* Allies. Not since the affair of Jeanne d'Arc," he said, "have the English and the French so well understood each other."

By the middle of April everybody thought this was the beginning of the end for Hitler, that at last a front had been found, and that, as Chamberlain said in Commons the first day, Hitler had missed the bus and, as Churchill said, made the worst military blunder since Napoleon's Spanish peninsular campaign.

I was jubilant. I forgot all about my doubts in the Maginot. Everybody was right. Why worry about the war since the Germans were sure to win it for you? Oh, the Germans *were* stupid. Stupider even than the Commandant of La Mont des Welsches thought they were! I decided now to go to England, which was going to be closer to the war and to victory. I went to the American Embassy to arrange my exit permit to England.

That's when I met our military attaché, Colonel Horace Fuller. He is a lean, weather-beaten, drawling former artillery officer from the West somewhere. His natural amiability is obscured somewhat by the fact that he does not suffer fools gladly. That day I was one of them.

"Oh, isn't it wonderful?" I said.

"What? What's wonderful?" he asked suspiciously.

"Norway!" I said beaming as an Englishwoman would beam if Englishwomen beamed as easily as I do.

He looked very sour. "Oh, sure," he said. "Hitler's missed the bus all right, but he's caught a transport plane instead."

I looked bewildered, so he said: "Innocent, come with me."

In his office he showed me maps of Norway and explained what it meant to force enemy-held fiords in ships, how much tonnage and what kind and how many men it would take, and how many guns; and he explained, very patiently, how Norway of all countries was the kind of country which, if you "got there fust with mostest men," [6] you couldn't be got out of in a day or a year, perhaps ever. And Hitler had got there fustest. And then he told me how many miles it was from Stavanger to Scapa Flow as a bomber flies, and what it meant to Germany having many more submarine bases so close to Scotland and the Channel. Then he called in a bright, hard, scar-faced little bulldog of a man with clear, keen, blue American eyes. This was Lieutenant Colonel George Kenny, the air attaché.

"Ask him," he said cheerfully.

[6] "Gittin' thar fust with the mostest men" was the recipe for victory offered by Civil War General Nathan Bedford Forrest, the only officer in the Confederate Army who was not, according to Southerners, "a gentleman." They were quite pleased with his soldiering, though.

Rapidly Kenny told me how many airplanes he thought the Germans might have, and the cold-blooded, ruthless, effective way they were using them in Norway and had used them in Poland. "Like forward artillery," I remember his saying. "They won't use gas," he said. "High explosives weigh about the same, and do ten times as much damage. In fact, gas won't *destroy* the Channel ports, the industrial centres, the air bases, the railway system of France—that's what the boys are after.[7] Maybe they will use gas one day, but that will just be the cherry on the charlotte russe," he said—"just a topper. It makes me sore when I see all the money the French and English have spent on gas-masks, most of which are full of leaks by now, when they ought to know—what everybody who's been in Germany since the war began knows—the German people have no gas-masks."

Both colonels were terribly, terribly gloomy about the Norwegian campaign. But they were even gloomier, Stygian in fact, about the "real offensive" they said was coming "sure as death" through the Low Countries in May or June. And then they showed me other maps, of the Belgian and Dutch frontiers, and told me how many *panzer* divisions they guessed the Germans had there and near Luxemburg.

I was uneasy in the Maginot, but now for the first time I was frightened. I said: "But the Germans haven't enough raw materials to—"

They said: "Stop talking economics."

I retorted: "But if the Belgians and Dutch decide to make a military alli—"

[7] This is the real reason, probably, why the Germans didn't waste bombs on Paris, and won't on London either, except in the dock areas, or to strafe Mr. Churchill, who has announced that he is hell-bent on defending it. If they can get in England what they got in France, first, Claridge's is still the safest place in Britain.

Colonel Fuller said: "For God's sake, stop talking *politics*. This is *war*, and if you don't know the difference between politics and war, look up the definitions in the dictionary."

"Gee," Colonel Kenny said, "I'd like to see the show, but I must get going." The colonel was in a great hurry that day, because he was going back to the U.S.A. with an urgent report based on a study he had just made (in the face of violent political and military and diplomatic obstruction and red tape) of French planes and aviation production and of German sample planes brought down behind the French lines. He continued: "I've got to get home and help undo a hell of a lot of mistakes we've been making in our plane construction. If we don't pull ourselves together and undo them fast, we might as well throw half our air force into the ash-can, it'll be so out of date for the kind of war the Germans are going to unload on their next victim."

"Next victim?" I asked unhappily.

"Yop," he said; "all off at Paris and London—next stop Washington."

"You're joking," I suggested.

"I'm a funny little guy," said Colonel Kenny, grinning.

"We won't let them get away with that," I asserted.

Little Colonel Kenny said: "I knew a little guy once who used to say: 'I learned very young in life never to call a big guy a sonuvabitch without a brick in my hands.' We haven't enough bricks to call names at the moment."

"Oh, we'll get them in plenty of time," I said.

Colonel Kenny nodded reassuringly. "But on the other hand, Confucius say: 'He who follows is always *behind!*' . . . Well, don't you stay too long. A bomb might put that good clear mind of yours permanently out of working order. So long," he said, and he left us.

I said: "Oh, Colonel Fuller, *you* don't really believe the Germans are going to win, do you?"

Colonel Fuller replied: "Don't you understand English? Yes, if some miracle doesn't happen. They've got the guns and the tanks and the planes and the men, and a plan, and the initiative."

I asked: "Is there really no hope—"

He answered: "You want me to say something vague and comforting that has nothing to do with war—or with politics? Literary, that's your style. O.K.: The British never know they're licked. On, on, into the jaws of death, no matter if it is a lousy piece of strategy. Yes, the British will always keep on fighting. That's the best hope."

I wanted to cry. I did.

He said, kindly: "You think too much about the war. Come have a drink."

Now I see that both the colonels were terribly, terribly right. They were two objective cold-minded army men, not talking politics or patriotism or morale or economics; talking *war*, which was their profession. And that's the first time in all that spring in France I heard anyone talk war exclusively. I've often wondered since what became of the reports Lieutenant Colonel Kenny and Colonel Fuller wrote for their Embassy and for the War Department in Washington. Were they hidden away in some dusty military file? Were they thrown in some politician's bulging wastepaper basket, after Mr. Bullitt and Mr. Roosevelt finished with them?

Colonel Kenny did miss the show—he went back to America. But I saw Colonel Fuller after I had got back from Belgium, in June. It was a few days before Paris was really bombed.

I said: "Tell me, please, please tell me, what's going to happen?"

His hands trembled. His eyes were quite bloodshot from loss of sleep. He tried to smile, but he couldn't. He said: "Oh, there's hope of course—the morale of the French—maybe the newspapers are right and we *can* deliver a thousand planes a month soon. Maybe this has opened America's eyes —and if we come in—"

"Oh," I interrupted, "don't talk morale and economics and politics, talk *war*. What do you really think?"

He answered wearily: "I don't want to use my bean any more; I want to use my heart. You see, I want them to win so much, so *very* much. I fought with these babies at Château-Thierry in the last war . . . and, oh, they've been so God-damn dumb; but, dear Christ, I love them. . . ."

On June 14 I read in the paper that Ambassador Bullitt with Colonel Fuller, military attaché of the American Embassy in Paris, and all the members of the Embassy staff remained indoors behind closed curtains while the German troops paraded past the Arc de Triomphe.

Now it would be very untrue to say that nobody in France was thinking in *war* terms, even after Norway. I'm sure there were many wise English and French men in the army and out of it who were thinking—even trying to make themselves heard, which was of course impossible over the frightened or excited or contented gabble of the mob, and the cross cackling of the politicians.

(I remember someone once told me a parable about a Chinese sage who said to a flock of geese: "If you will *all* be quiet, I'll tell you something that will turn you into human beings," and then one was quiet, and another was quiet. But they were never *all* quiet at once, and the sage silently waited and waited, and grew grey and old as the days and years went by, and in the end, one by one, the geese were all caught by the farmer boys and eaten for dinner.)

For instance, René de Chambrun was thinking. The little captain I had left, so concerned with the heroic destiny of Lorraine, the "Rampart of France," had begun suddenly and furiously to think out there in the quiet Maginot. By the end of April he had marshalled all his thoughts on paper. He sent them to his wife, requesting her to forward me a copy of the letter. I had gone to England and so I never received it in Paris, until the week after the invasion of the Low Countries.

But here is the letter:

> . . . The colonel of the corps [8] gave me some very precise information on the Norwegian campaign. It can be summed up in this sentence: On sea and on land the Allied navy and the expeditionary force have been bludgeoned by the German aviation.
>
> For the first time since the origin of the world war a fleet has met bombing squadrons. On the first day the *Rodney* (England's largest battle cruiser) was severely hit on the bow so that it had to turn back. Churchill had counted on leaving the large units permanently in the narrows as the navy used to do to blockade a port. He changed his mind rather quickly. On land it was total disaster . . . bombing of air bases, crossroads, the troops on the march, mercilessly and very effectively.
>
> In announcing several weeks ago "the Norwegian victory," the first "mistake of Hitler," Paul Reynaud declared:

[8] An English corps which was, one presumes, in Norway.

1. The Narvik-Lulea railway is definitely cut.
2. Not a ton of Scandinavian iron can ever be transported into Germany.
3. Allied divisions are on the way to Norway. [The French ones at that time were between Bouzonville and Metz.[9]] Only a brigade of Chasseurs Alpins have debarked at Narvik.

But let us examine the first two points:

Germany imported before the war six tenths of the Swedish ore. She has just, as I will prove, assured herself of the *whole output*.

In fact, by a military occupation of Norway she places Sweden in a vise between herself and Russia. Thanks to the occupation of Denmark, and to her aviation, she shuts off both sides of the Baltic-Atlantic passage. Sweden then can only export to Germany, or to Russia—with Germany's permission. Even if we succeed, which is *improbable*, in holding Narvik for a long time, we cannot prohibit Sweden, a neutral country, from working her own mines. During the six summer months the ore from the north, the production of which can be intensified at this period, will use the route Lulea-Stettin—during the winter, that of the south-bound railroad. Thus, by the occupation of Norway and Denmark, Germany has just obtained absolute control of Sweden. What this all represents to Germany is *iron, chromium, nickel, cobalt*.

But here is what is also very serious: England and France used to control the Norwegian cellulose business (which is used in the manufacture of gunpowder

[9] It now seems that the regiments of Savoyard mountaineers threatened mutiny rather than embark for Norway. The defence of their own soil was the only ideology understood by many of the unquestionably "patriotic" French peasants.

and of which Norway is one of the principal producers) and of nitrogen and timber. These businesses now pass into the hands of Germany. Denmark exported to England forty per cent of the English imports of butter, milk, and cheese. All these immense supplies of foodstuffs are now Germany's.

After having taken account of the fact that Sweden (and all her produce) falls directly under German domination owing to the occupation of Norway (because of the failure of the Allies, the Swedish press has already become very pro-German), you mustn't forget to add that Hitler has further procured as a result of the war against France and England:

The armament industries of Austria and Czechoslovakia (Vienna and Skoda);

The Czechoslovakian mines;

The coal and other material of Poland. (And anything else in all or any of these countries of which she chooses to avail herself.)

But ore, cellulose, nitrogen, timber—*that* is what three or four of Churchill's cruisers and destroyers would have been worth to the Allies!

Let us go back: As soon as Hitler attacked Poland, French propaganda cried out: "Hitler makes the mistake of Wilhelm." I answer no, no, and no! While he was constructing the Siegfried Line, and while making the Russian-Polish operation, Hitler proved to his own satisfaction that we were mobilizing merely a *defensive* army on his west. Meanwhile Hitler had got rid of his enemy on the east for all time. *Wilhelm never did that.* And now, having hardly fought, Hitler has obtained almost everything which was necessary for him to wage war against us. Wilhelm never did that. While attacking us Wilhelm had to scatter his forces—and fight Russia, Serbia, etc.

As Hitler, I now believe, intends to attack us this summer on all fronts from Belgium to Tunisia, focused on the Maginot Line,[10] he rectified before starting all the faults that Wilhelm made.

In short, from 1914 to 1918 Germany had to combat fifty powers on five fronts: Russian, French, Italian, Greek, Yugoslavian.

In the summer of 1940 Hitler will be able to fight the great armies of France and the absurd British army on one front two thousand kilometres long—from the Belgian to the French Colonial front, with the acquiescence of Stalin and Mussolini—and perhaps the help of the latter! Worst of all, it will be a long time before we have attained air parity (March 1941 according to an article I read in an informed American magazine).

So, compared to the obvious weakness of Wilhelm's position in 1914, Hitler will have these advantages before beginning:

1. All the mineral production of Scandinavia at his disposition;
2. Norwegian submarine and air bases on the Atlantic facing England;
3. The ability to close the Baltic;
4. Control of Polish ore and coal;
5. No enemies on the east or south, but, on the contrary, providers of wheat, oil, and—maybe allies;

[10] This wishful thought died hard, even in as clear a mind as de Chambrun's.

6. Fifty-five per cent of Rumanian oil exports without bothering to occupy the country;
7. The power of Italy, to whom he can always offer the inducement of Yugoslavia—or if that fails, several angry German divisions, at their own Brenner—a pretty powerful "inducement."

And militarily *we* have no plan of attack, because since the war we have entrenched ourselves softly and complacently behind our Maginot Line and our small *inadequate* casements on the north.

The announcer said this morning on the radio: "*The Allies are 'ready to face' all eventualities.*" Here is our own extraordinary denial that in tactical matters we are not willing at any point to take the military initiative. (Shades of Frederick, Napoleon, and Joffre!—what can you be thinking?)

Further, by being diplomatically all over the lot aiding Red Spain a little, Poland a little, Finland and Norway a little, we have played the game of our adversary, who attacks with considerable force at *one* point at a time (Austria, Czechoslovakia, Poland, Denmark . . . and tomorrow in the Balkans?). In his effort to forestall German aggression your father[11] was *right* when *he* tried in 1935 to attack diplomatically at one point —Rome—and that with all means. It was not his fault that he failed to do so.

Before I left the front the other day, two German officers were caught, by chance. For two weeks they had been spying behind our lines, trying to steal the plans for major works of defence which we may have finished since September. None, alas, have ever been finished!—because our High Command doesn't know

[11] Pierre Laval.

here, as they do in Germany, how to create the "mysticism of work" and above all to make plans for *such* "eventualities.". . . The fellows were volunteer spies. I for one see, in the fact that the Germans seek volunteers for carrying out this sort of mission, a sure indication of an attack this summer. There are many other indications. (For instance, the growing espionage in Belgium and Holland.)

I am one of the few who stayed for eight months in one sector of the front. Since the beginning we have always captured from the German patrols Austrian and Czechoslovakian material. This proves (to me anyway) that the German High Command is keeping back *elsewhere*, for the real attack, its formidable reserves of *German* material. Further, the repeated German strategy on all points of the front since the beginning of the war has had but *one* aim—to take prisoners from us. Now at the end of seven months they know, thanks to our relief-corps system, the *whole* number of *our* army divisions.

Again, judging by the prisoners we have taken, the spirit of the German army is magnificent. It possesses above all things *Faith*. The corps commander told me of the incredible boldness of the German bombers who in wave after wave dove on the ships in Norway.

Now the Führer of these fanatical people will be able to present himself one year to the day after the last meeting of the Reichstag (September 1, 1939) and announce if it has not begun by that time—the *final offensive*. And he can expose a table of victories uninterrupted; above all, those since the beginning of the war—Poland, Denmark, Sweden, Norway (and the Balkans??). The position of Germany, he will say, has nothing in common with 1914. Now we have come (he can say) to the last phase of the struggle, to avenge for all time the shame of 1918 and wipe out for once and always the imperial capitalism of the plutocratic democracies.[12] And to do *that* Hitler will have the disposal of *170* divisions, and a vastly superior air force to which the Polish and Norwegian campaigns will have given confidence and vastly useful technical information. Hitler will even be able to offer himself the luxury of sending 20 divisions to the Polish front, to keep Stalin quiet, in case all this should annoy Stalin —and still have 50 divisions more than we to fight us with! Moreover he will be able on north, east, and south to strike his blows where *he* chooses, on a line going from the sea on the north to Tunisia—while trying to break through at some soft point with a massive tank attack on flat ground, with aviation and motorized divisions.

This can be very hard for France!

Clare Boothe told me the other day that the only chance of drawing America into the war was to paint a very dark picture—

Is this one? I made it for her, but above all for you and your father. And I add that it isn't the good little Mexican [13] with his thirty-five ministers who can prepare our country in time for tomorrow's Gargantuan struggle. It isn't *he* who can create *before* the summer the war power we shall need, a power beside which the force that shakes the earth under nine million Turks annually would seem nothing. . . .

Late, too late, the smart young soldiers of France had begun to count divisions and guns and measure fronts and

[12] Which is precisely what Hitler did say, ten days later, when he launched the final offensive.

[13] Paul Reynaud, whose grandparents lived in Mexico for a time and made a fortune there.

question merits of *defence*, for the benefit of their napping political elders.

Late in May young Captain de Chambrun, after three dangerous and adventurous weeks of liaison work in Flanders, escaped from Dunkirk to England, and at once returned to Paris. The night of his return he saw his good friend Ambassador Bullitt. Now his brilliant analysis of the situation brought about by the Norwegian expedition could not have failed to be followed by an equally brilliant one of the situation brought about by the evacuation proceeding at Dunkirk. Perhaps for the first time ardent Francophile Bullitt was desperately alarmed. He paid a call on Weygand the next morning, and at his request the generalissimo ordered de Chambrun to proceed at once to Washington with a "message to Garcia" for the long-promised Roosevelt aid. (For those who are astonished that Ambassador Bullitt had such instant access and influence with the military as well as government high command, it must be stated now that it was often said, and not jokingly, in the spring in France, that Bullitt was His Grey Eminence, the most powerful man in France. What tacit commitments he had made, or the French government may have erroneously believed he had made, for America, or rather for Roosevelt, that the French government so gladly let him play this role, is a riddle only historians will resolve.)

De Chambrun saw Reynaud, saw Dautry (France's Knudsen), who said only "a blood transfusion will now save France." No longer did Dautry plead for *machine tools* to construct French plants, as he had a few weeks before, when France was fighting the war on a three-year plan. But guns, planes, the perfected products of instant death-dealing, and—battleships, was his, Reynaud's, and Weygand's anguished plea. . . .

On the 20th of April 1777 Lafayette set sail from Pasajes

on the Iberian Peninsula, for the American colonies. He wrote to his mother: "I'm enlisting my heart in the cause of American independence. . . ." On May 11, one hundred and sixty-three years later, his great-great-grandson sailed in the Yankee Clipper from Lisbon, on the Iberian Peninsula, to try to enlist the heart of America (as represented in the person of Franklin Delano Roosevelt) in the now desperate cause of French independence.

It was already too late. Roosevelt's promissory notes to France, which shrewdly bore no date, went by default. A personal predilection for France was not a policy (as the President no doubt pointed out with heartfelt regret to de Chambrun) which could save her now. On June 15 Reynaud made his last hysterical tragic plea to Roosevelt on the radio of the world. Roosevelt deeply sympathized . . . but America, he sadly explained, really did not have the things that France needed. Nor, indeed, did it have the will to war. Sorry, Lafayette's descendants, can't come this time. And France surrendered.

The day after the Armistice, de Chambrun's father-in-law became Vice Premier of France, under eighty-three-year-old "front man" Marshal Pétain. And still the spirit of Lafayette, who fought on the flimsy barricades of Paris streets, was not dead in France: I heard on the radio this morning (July 8) that seventy-year old Senator Pierre de Chambrun, René's uncle and therefore the great-grandson of Lafayette, and also an honorary American citizen, cast his vote, one against six hundred, against Laval's suspiciously totalitarian government and in favour of the old democratic form.

One in six hundred. That was about the ratio in France of men who were willing to die on the last barricades of the last province of France for the ideals that Lafayette stood for.

May their sons be many!

EIGHT

Of all the sarse that I can call to mind,
England doos make the most unpleasant kind,
It's you're the sinner ollers, she's the saint,
Wut's good's all English, all that isn't ain't;
Wut profits her is ollers right an' just,
An' ef you don't read Scriptur so, you must;
She's praised herself ontil she fairly thinks
There ain't no light in Nature when she winks;
She's all thet's honest, honnable and fair,
And when the vartoos died they made her heir.

James Russell Lowell, in *The Biglow Papers*

In these troublous days, when the great Mother Empire stands splendidly isolated in Europe . . .

The Honorable George Foster, in the House of Commons, 189

Whether splendidly isolated or dangerously isolated, I will not now debate . . . I think splendidly isolated, because this isolation of England comes from her superiority.

Sir Wilfred Laurier, in the House of Commons, 189

◇◇

ON April 25, burdened with the sore knowledge abou Norway provided by the only two men in France who ha talked war straight to me, I went to London. In that late April, London was lovely beyond even an Englishman's belief. There were bright azaleas in the window-boxes of hotel and home windows, and tulips in the court of Buckingham Palace. Sheep browsed in park enclosures, ducks splashed joyously in park pools, and hordes of pink-faced people lounged happily in tuppenny "deck chairs" on the Hyde Park greens, feeding the pigeons. The cuckoo and the nightingale and the swallow had returned to all the parks of London—or so said *The Times*, occupied now as always with the multifarious and mellifluous bird life of England. For the cuckoo and the nightingale and the swallow the public air-raid trenches in the park and the barrage balloons over them had no meaning. And looking at this happy breed of men, these sunning English, you felt they had little meaning for them, either. The little barrage balloons seemed no more than silver toys, disporting themselves innocently high up against the blue sky, twinkling in the warm sunlight. Traffic tooted and jostled in the crowded thoroughfares, smart-looking officers (both male and female) and smart-looking men in mufti with smartly furled umbrellas clipped along the streets, avoiding at corners and building entrances the high-piled sandbags. The sandbags you saw had long since lost their pristine plumpness. Most of them sagged limply, many had begun to split their seams and trickle their anæmic contents into the streets. Some of these bags were even pleasantly sprouting green things. (In March this was a minor scandal—who had profiteered, filling these white bags with cheap black earth instead of insulating sand? someone had asked in the House of Commons. Nobody cared much. The question seemed to have only a political significance.) No one except officers and government people carried gas-masks. As the lady in *Punch* put it, "Frankly we've never had any occasion to use them."

Now even the pitch-black-out, the most horrid and real manifestation of the war during the winter, which, when you emerged from the warmth of a bright interior, fell over your head like the sack of a kidnapper, had lost its terror. On a clear starry night, on a bright moonlit April night, it was wonderful to walk in the streets, seeing the myriad black chimneypots of London, and its dear familiar monuments, Trafalgar Square, the Houses of Parliament, the beautiful bridges, silhouetted against the midnight blue, looking at once safer and more solid, and picturesque and romantic. And permanent, as only British tradition can be permanent.

London at night was altogether gayer than Paris. There was good Hungarian music in Claridge's, played for women in low dresses and men in dinner coats; fine Italian food at Quaglino's, where young frilly girls danced with young sleek officers. There were cocktail bars and night clubs everywhere, and dozens of theatres were open. ("You must see John Gielgud in *King Lear*, and Emlyn Williams's *Light of Heart*—no, it's *not* a war play.") There were a half-dozen musical comedies, and a scandalous rash of strip-tease burlesque shows. When Mr. Pethick-Lawrence testily suggested in the House of Commons that so much frivolity, so much "splurge of wealth," might in war-time convey the impression to less fortunate Britons that the rich were getting off too lightly, Sir John Simon ticked him off neatly. He said that if every income in the land above two thousand pounds was totally confiscated, the Treasury would be only sixty million pounds the richer—a drop in the bucket, said Sir John, when it came to war financing. This answer didn't cast much light on the problem of who would finance the war and how, but it quite silenced Mr. Pethick-(soak-the-rich)-Lawrence. And so London night life was only momentarily threatened.

The English are a race with a highly individual but none the less strong sense of humour. They made many jokes in April. The winter's black-out jokes, sandbag, gas-mask, evacuated-children, women-in-uniform jokes, the jokes about rationing and barrage balloons and Hitler's secret weapon and "scuttling" and stupid censorship and the trials of not being able to talk about the weather had given way to a newer and timelier crop: about Lloyd George's ill-fated domestic agricultural program, "digging for victory" ("The Second Battle of Waterloo will be won on the turnip fields of Little Muggleton"), parachutist and Quisling and fifth-columnist jokes, and war-time cricket and racing jokes. Jokes about Hitler, Göring, and Goebbels, the neutrals, and the invasion of Britain were old stand-bys, hearty-laughing perennials.

The Paris papers had long since been reduced to one sheet. Now, "foreseeing a possible paper shortage owing to the situation in Norway," the periodicals and press of England were cutting down again on newsprint. (The English, never a talkative race, have always more than made up for that in their passion for printed wordage.) But the once ponderous *Times* could still not be called puny. In England there was still plenty to read, to eat, to wear, places to go, and all together a working pattern for pleasure. There was, in short, little gloom certainly few outward signs of what the *Times* had called Britain's "grim determination." I do not for a moment mean that England was radiant. The immediate future was too uncertain. Taxes were high, families were split up (but only one out of six, according to a Gallup poll in March), and no matter how you looked at it, war was a rum business which interfered everywhere little or much with the normal business of Englishmen. Paris was Paris in April, but, looking back on it now, I saw that everybody had been really rather openly gloomy, because, after all, a "long war," with an enormous army kept mobilized, was bound to be harder on France than on England.

Add that in April the triumphant progress (in the newspapers) of the Norwegian campaign was lifting every Englishman's spirits. There were not even any published casualty lists to depress them. To be sure, the war communiqués were dull, or, to be more exact, cryptic. But in this official black-out of news, the newspapers relied on "reliable neutral sources" in Holland and Sweden and Geneva. These proclaimed gigantic German losses, few Allied ones, and Allied progress everywhere in Norway daily.

I wonder now whether this also was "Hitler-controlled" propaganda to encourage the English people to believe they were in sight of a great victory, only in the end to learn the bitter truth from their leaders, so that to defeat would be added the demoralizing shock of disillusionment and the poison of resentment.

Something had happened to me when I first began to suspect in the Maginot (you understand I am no seasoned journalist; I was just beginning to suspect, whereas every wise American newspaper man in Europe probably knew for a certainty what I now merely suspected) that France and England had been dangerously lulled to sleep by the self-induced illusion that they had both time and impregnable defences. I believed the American colonels completely about Norway, and although, in a few short hours of wishful thinking after I left their dour presences, I had avoided a full acceptance of their tragic conclusions about the "inevitable outcome of an inevitable invasion of the Low Countries," still, in the back of my mind their prophecies and my own uneasiness about France remained dark and brooding. Even though I was unable to understand and evaluate Hitler's might and horrible force (as they did), I could still sense its imminence, as one senses a thunderstorm, even before a cloud appears in the sky. I felt afraid, as you do when you enter a familiar but black room, and the squeak of a chair or a moving drapery reminds you that you read in the papers this morning that there were burglars in the neighbourhood. I was afraid for England, for France, afraid of that nameless, faceless, inhuman, unseen thing, *the enemy*.

It is curious to note that at no time during all these months I spent in Europe did I really give any serious thought to the horrid fact, which only emerged early in June, that my country was also the victim of all of England's and France's illusions; we also were unprepared to meet a terrible enemy.

The next ten days were difficult days for me in London. I both trembled for and resented bitterly the smugness and complacency of the British, their almost criminal tolerance of the ineptitudes and inadequacies of their government, which they all had now begun to admit, rather grudgingly, but said they didn't know what to do about. I read with a sinking heart (and also, paradoxically, with a sort of furious *American* smugness and complacency) signs like this in a late April copy of *Picture Post* that *some* Englishmen felt as I did, baffled and frightened:

"At home, in 1915, seven months after the war began, we were talking freely about the war. We were free to criticize the conduct of the war, and it was criticized beneficially. We could throw out a government that had lost our confidence. Now already, after seven months of renewed war, there is much more suppression both of opinion and news. Everyone knows our Government is grossly incompetent, so incompetent that it may even fail to win the fighting, and yet few people dare demand its replacement."[1] It was a shocking thing to me that long after Mr. Hitler had blown Mr. Chamberlain's *Pax Umbrellica* inside out, they still let him hold the twisted framework over their heads for protection. And their intolerable self-confidence, based on the paradoxical notion that no matter how entangled they might be in a European war they were eternally isolated from the bloody brunt of it, made me even more than normally sensitive to their constant open, smoothly stated criticisms of American isolationism, or what the *London Economist* called "America's deliberate myopia."

Although the French probably resented American Isolationism as much as the English, they were never quite so outspoken about it to the average American. Madame Pomaret was a notably disagreeable exception. Possibly this was so for two reasons: The French instinctively knew France was a dangerous place for an American to visit, and your courageous courtesy in doing so they complimented to some extent by refraining from openly insulting your country. England, on the other hand, was presumptively as safe as New York. You did not in any sense flatter their cause by being among them in their "hour of danger." It was, they felt, an "hour of trial," which is something different. Second, the French had no feeling of "blood kinship" with us. We were to them completely foreigners, who could only be counted on when friendship coincided with self-interests. But the

[1] The author of this was that perennial prophet without honour in his own country, H. G. Wells. Another British author struck the note prevalent among his contemporaries when he said to me of Mr. Wells: "Don't take him so seriously. He's just a crusty old gentleman whose liver wants turning."

English felt we had a family relation to them. A favourite phrase they used in arguments against isolationism was: "We are, after all, your older brothers." In fact, many of their arguments were *ad captandum*, a rank appeal to our traditions and sentiments. They invoked "family loyalty" quite as often as they argued wherein lay the manifest self-interests of their younger brother. Anyway, the English felt they could be a little rude to Americans in London, since it was, after all, a matter of consanguinity. Personally, I, too, believe it is partly a family matter. But before the war I had more envied than resented the certainty (and it was a certainty) of our English cousins [2] that they had more brains, more beauty, more wealth, more history, fine poetry, noble literature, charming architecture, more breeding and manners, and elegance and glamour and gallantry and loyalty and *noblesse oblige*, and even more lovely gardens, and more exquisitely manicured scenery per square inch in the British Isles than was to be found to the hundred square miles in all the rest of Europe, not to mention the three million square miles of the United States of America. Their pre-war pride was sometimes galling, but it did seem justified. Even the uncomplaining servile acquiescence of the sometimes starving, always abused lower classes in the British way of life then somehow seemed picturesque if not admirable. You were almost willing in those days to define this unquestioning self-abasement and bootlicking humility as the upper classes did, as "the dauntless decency of the British people." But when you perceived that this very pride of the rich and humbleness of the poor were paving the way for a tragic collapse, when you began to feel that from *laissez-faire* to *laissez-tomber* was a very short distance, when you saw that

[2] After September, it seems, they began to look on us "more as brothers."

they were giving all the history of a glorious past as indisputable evidence that an equally glorious future was assured to them, when you realized that nearly everybody in England was sleeping on his ancestors' laurels, you suddenly found yourself feeling either pity or contempt for their wilful blindness, and a vast rage at their "altruistic" efforts to pluck the mote from the eyes of their American brothers.

So when, as an American, you heard them remark: "If this war spreads, the two yellow races, Japan and America, will be fighting each other," your blood boiled, and you found yourself defending the weak cause of isolationism simply because you resented the premise of the attacker, which was that he *alone* was the alert and awake and ready Defender of Democracy.

In April in England I became argumentative to the point of stupidity. I said appalling, mean-spirited "deliberately myopic" things like: "Why should you expect a conglomerate race of people, with the blood of every European country in their veins, three thousand miles away, to see the economic and spiritual importance of the British Empire if you can't even convince the Irish in Eire of it, who are only a stone's throw from here?" [3] The English replied wearily: "Oh, the Irish! They were the first extreme case

[3] In the spring I.R.A. terrorists were planting bombs in London railway stations and threatening the lives of important personages like Anthony Eden. Eire was violently isolationist at best, pro-German at worst. Inadequately defended, in fact almost defenceless from sea or air, Eire strongly suggested itself to any objective mind as a possible point of German attack. But most of the English, even after the Norwegian campaign seemed doomed, shrugged off the Irish as historical potato heads, and refused loftily to think about the invasion of Eire. As Sydney Smith once said, "The moment the very name of Ireland is mentioned, the English seem to bid adieu to common feeling, common prudence and common sense." Now, in July, Northern Ireland is jammed with British troops, waiting for the uncivil kerns and the wild Gaels to erupt, waiting for the Germans to "protect" the groves of belligerent Blarney.

in this modern world of the mental disease called 'Nationalism.' They are madmen, like the Germans. They make no pretence of caring about democracy the way you Americans do." Then I said, nastily: "We tried to help you make the world safe for democracy last time. We got nothing but debts and insults out of winning *and* footing the bill for it. And look what you've done for democracy—put it into a worse jam than ever. Oh, we know Europe's motto: When bigger and better bags are made, America will hold them!" The answer to this was naturally seldom more polite than the statement.

In their long post-mortem political evenings, while the English admitted their Continental diplomatic blunders from '20 to '39, they inevitably traced the current disaster right back to Woodrow Wilson,[4] to his quixotic ethnological solution of economic European problems, which had arbitrarily divided Europe up into a series of unsound sovereign states, to his League of Nations, "which the rest of America ratted on." "What fools we were," they said, "to rely on *one* man to deliver the American nation!" Whereupon, thinking on American presidents, they promptly drifted into eulogies of Mr. Roosevelt, telling me how important it was for England

[4] One of the few dissenting voices I heard in England from the accusation that the fruit of this war was of Woodrow Wilson's planting was that of the American oil man. (He was there in April to help the English. How, exactly, I don't know. There was some legal hocus-pocus about putting Norwegian oil tankers in foreign ports under American [oil company] flags. I remember he said: "In our small way we oil guys are fighting for England at every oil outpost of the British Empire.") He said: "Odd, nobody anywhere ever traces this mess back to F. D. Roosevelt. When, bitten with New Deal economy, and the managed-currency ideas of the Brain Trust, he scuttled the World Economic Conference in London in '33, he gave the death blow to the gold-standard age, to the age of investments. The World Economic Conference was the last hope for a peaceful solution of Europe's problems, which were, and are, economic. Guess you could say F. D.'s scuttling of that conference paved an easy road for the German revolution of Mr. Hitler."

that he should be re-elected. When I said: "Oh, it doesn't matter at all; if our vital interests are clearly threatened, we'll go into the war if we're led by a Hottentot" (the English felt anyone but Roosevelt would fully answer to this description), all the old school-tie politicians, and the lords and ladies who were their cousins, would answer: "Mr. Roosevelt wants to get in, and that's half the battle for us." If I said: "I thought you were going to win this war without us, anyway, so what do you care who's president?" they would reply: "Now, let's be coldly analytical. You're sure to drift in toward the end. A Roosevelt shove might help. Though we all hope he doesn't shove *too* soon—we want it to be quite clear by the time you do come in who really won the war!" I'd say cagily: "How do you know Roosevelt wants to get in? Has he ever said so, definitely?" "No," they'd answer, "not exactly." I'd get madder and say: "I can't see why you think he is so wonderful. He has done very little to clarify American public opinion about the real issues involved. He has in fact influenced it far less than events themselves. Why, he's just bobbing about now like a beautiful gilded cork on the topmost crest of the wave of indignation about Norway. What we ought to do about Germany, the steps we must take to assure ourselves of either peace or defence or an effective entrance into Europe's war he never speaks about forthrightly. He just bellows eloquent denunciations of "Nazi aggressions" and murmurs melodiously in his fireside talks about the sanctities and beauties of liberty. If he really believes that we may also perish if the European democracies do, why doesn't he say so in stentorian tones without waiting for a mandate from the people?" [5]

[5] In late July, even after President Roosevelt had denied to the American people any desire to go into the war on Great Britain's side, the *London Economist* in an editorial rooting for his re-election said: "Mr. Roosevelt wants to act. He is merely awaiting a clear mandate from

To that they'd say stubbornly: "Well, we know he wants to get in. We don't know exactly what he's told the Prime Minister, but the P.M. told my cousin's brother-in-law how important for us it was," etc., etc.

Again in the matter of Italy, which had now begun to bother the English a little, "Roosevelt," they said, "is putting pressure on Mussolini to keep him out."

"What sort of pressure can he put?" I asked.

"Well, if Italy goes to war, he'll stop all shipping."

"That's a foregone conclusion, implicit in the Neutrality Act," I answered, "and that's no news to Mussolini!"

"Well, he's offering to give Mussolini a seat at the peace table on the same terms as the Allies, when the war is over."

"Oh," I said, "when is the war going to be over? Are you sure to win it? Will Roosevelt still be President if it's a very long war?" (They thought so, and so does Mr. Roosevelt.) "Will you agree if you do win it to allow neutral America and Italy to sit at the peace table on equal terms with the Allies? And how can Roosevelt promise that?"

"Well," the reply was, "maybe he's promising Mussolini a big loan."

"Without the consent of Congress?" I asked.

The American oil man said: "You're all talking nonsense. Mr. Roosevelt knows exactly what he's doing. He's appealing to Mussolini's sense of sportsmanship!" That shut up everybody.

The end of all this sort of exasperated and admittedly badly informed chatter (in which the English and I both behaved, as I have said, very rudely) was that I began to see

the people." One of two things must be true: either Great Britain misunderstands the President, or America does. As this book went to press, the only person who can clear up that misunderstanding has failed to do so.

clearly that although they were sure they could win the war without us, they really resented winning it without us, because it seemed damned unfair to them that we should be the beneficiaries of a victory for which we made absolutely no sacrifices.

I said to our Ambassador, Mr. Joseph P. Kennedy: "You know, sometimes they are so insolent, so sure of themselves, so smug, I feel as though it would do them good for once to be beaten." He said, "Please remember, miss, we Americans can live quite comfortably in a world of English snobbery and British complacency, but we can't live–I should hate to live–in a world of Nazis and German brutality. Though they snub us or sneer at us, yet must we love them and aid them, because their heads may be a little thick, but they've got the right end of the stick. In the end they stand for all the things we stand for, and if they go, we shall be the losers. Above all," he said. "they're the only crowd honest men can do business with."

And because I knew that Mr. Kennedy wanted the English to win, more than he wanted anything except to serve America as she thought he ought to serve her, I hated the way many of the English politicians talked about our Ambassador. They said it was due to a remark he had made in a speech in Massachusetts on his vacation: "All *hell* is going to break loose over there," and to his saying on his return to London in February: "America still doesn't know what this war is all about." He said to me on May 9, when I reminded him of that undiplomatic remark: "No apologies. The English can't know what this war is about either–or they'd get ready fast to win it." And when I said to him: "But the English ask why you don't explain to America what it is all about," he replied: "My job is to explain America to the

English, and I've told them over and over the American people don't want to go in, and the chances are they won't. Naturally, that makes me about as popular as a poison-ivy pedlar at a Sunday-school picnic."

On April 25, in spite of our indignation over Norway, we still didn't know what the war was all about, and we never shall, I suppose, unless the English navy is sunk, surrendered, or scuttled. Everybody said Kennedy was a "defeatist" who went around saying the most terrible untrue things: that America wasn't going to have time to get into the war—that America couldn't help much even if it wanted to help, it was even more unprepared than the British—and that it would probably "all be over by Christmas." As every Englishman knew it would be a *long* war ("fought in our own way"), that could only mean one thing: Mr. Kennedy thought it was going to be a short war won by the Germans!

In short, Mr. Kennedy (if he was pestered enough) said all sorts of things that were undiplomatic, and true as only bitter truth can be. Quite naturally the English didn't like Mr. Kennedy. They felt it was a peculiar misfortune that Poland had got a Biddle, who liked Poland, and France a Bullitt, who adored France and said publicly that everything the current French government did was perfect, and that England had got an Irish-American isolationist like Mr. Kennedy. Whatever Mr. Kennedy goes down in history as, it will not be a second Walter Hines Page, of that you can be certain.

In the drawing-rooms where they knew little of his efforts to aid the Empire in matters of trade and shipping and armament, their political aversion to him (as a "typical isolationist") was couched in very personal terms. They accused him at once of being a publicity hound and a recluse. They pointed out his shocking lack of "protocol," his gaucherie and American bad manners. One of many instances they quoted was his asking the Queen to dance before she had sent her equerry to ask him to ask her. Indeed, Halifax was rumored to have privately reprimanded him for his brash diplomatic red-tape cutting, and it was said that the entire diplomatic corps had decided that for the winter he was to be disciplined by being invited nowhere. It was a further cause for complaint that Mr. Kennedy didn't seem to mind that. He was nothing if not unsociable. Every day after he left his London office he retired quite happily to his country home in Windsor. Even this philosophical resignation was viewed with a dark suspicion. The English implied that he wasn't a sportsman. In fact, "Run, rabbit, run" they nicknamed him, because he not only went to the country to be safe himself every night,[6] but he had sent his wife and nine children to America. Why, they said, he was absolutely *terrified* of bombing, or (ha-ha) an English invasion. On the day of the Lowlands invasion Mr. Kennedy closed his place at Windsor and moved into his London residence, which has no bomb cellar, for the duration of the hostilities.[7] And today England is trying desperately to send thousands of its own children and mothers to America, and Mr. Kennedy and all the members of his staff work day and night with very eager hearts to help them.

Mr. Kennedy was a poor "diplomat" because he touched

[6] When the bombing of the English countryside began at last in July, Windsor took its share.

[7] This started a rumour that Mr. Kennedy was "closing up to beat it to America." When Ambassador Bullitt left France in the winter for his vacation, the French were delighted. Everybody said: "He is going to work some more on the President." I asked Mr. Kennedy after the invasion if he were, as the English euphemistically called it, "retiring." He said, grinning: "Oh, I may be going back for good any day now. Tell me, how do you think I'll look best when I land? In pine, mahogany, or copper?"

on their sore spots roughly, but he was an honest Ambassador and a very good prophet. His war case-history, however, has very little to do with Mr. Kennedy as a person. Before the war he was personally quite popular. Afterwards he just became a symbol—a symbol of "intolerable American isolationism," of "the other yellow race," of our "deliberate myopia." I mention all this now in no mischievous spirit, but merely to show you that even in late April in London our English brothers badly misunderstood themselves and us.

There were here (as there had been in France) men who felt that this antagonism based on gross misunderstandings between England and America, whether overtly expressed in drawing-rooms or covertly in political cloak-rooms, or subtly implied in the press, was a bad thing, which should not be permitted to grow. Lord Lloyd, Sir Walter Monckton, Sir John Reith, Anthony Eden, Sir Stuart Campbell, Duff Cooper, were only a few of at least twenty men I talked to in the government who yearned for a better understanding between our peoples. This naturally brought up interminable arguments on propaganda. The English had also laid down a policy early in the war of "no propaganda" and because anything an Englishman lays down is apt to be laid down for posterity, it was hard now to pry up that policy. Add that the English (like the French) had no feeling for or mastery of—hardly a conception of—the new science of propaganda as wielded by the Germans, and you can guess that these arguments were fruitless.

A. P. Herbert envisaged proper propaganda as frankly "telling Americans the Truth." This was not an alternative to telling them lies, but simply to telling them *nothing*. In a London magazine in late April he wrote:

"Why 'propaganda'?

"The word, I see, has at last become as unpopular as it deserves to be. In the United States, I believe, you cannot say 'Hitler invaded Poland' without being accused of doing 'British propaganda.' . . .

"The British Government with wise and even miraculous foresight . . . provided for this from the very beginning. They said 'We will do no "propaganda" in the U.S.A. Hitler himself will do our work for us: and truth will prevail.' At the beginning this looked good enough. . . . But the Germans cheated, as usual. They did a lot of clever 'propaganda' which was not labelled 'propaganda' and was not suspected; and nobody in America believed for a moment that we were *not* doing propaganda. We were being, not too clever, but too virtuous by half—and not for the first time. The result appears to be that our poor old Truth is always labouring along in the wake of Hitler's nonsense. She will of course prevail in the end; and it seems to be true that whenever Hitler's propaganda gets him a few holes up, Hitler himself does a master-stroke of strategy, piracy, bestiality or what-not, and the match is squared. But meanwhile much time, trouble and money (not to mention life) is flowing to waste. . . . Should we not now confess that we were wrong, though virtuous, and start telling the United States the Truth, loudly and openly? Open 'propaganda' would be bad of course; and veiled 'propaganda' would be bad, likewise. *Any* 'propaganda' would be 'bad,' because it is a bad word, and the people have rightly come to regard it as the name of a bad thing. (Even 'Information' is a suspect word.) But there is nothing bad about the Truth. Or is there? Why don't we say to the United States: 'We are sorry. We thought you would get the Truth without having it served up on a plate. Some of you have: but not enough of you. Henceforth we are going to serve it up on as many plates as we can find—openly, and without shame (for why should anyone be ashamed of telling the Truth?)."

Then Mr. Herbert said the Truth was an explanation of "the real meaning of 'British Imperialism.'" Of course the only Truth they really wanted to tell us was that this was our war and we'd better get in it, if not with men, with everything short of men. But that was precisely the sort of thing Americans in April would have called rank British propaganda. Someone told me that Mr. Churchill had said at a dinner where he had been urged to "make propaganda" in America: "Impossible! If we said: 'God is just,' that would be called British propaganda." (The oil man said: "Judging by the shape the Allies are in, that statement is rank British propaganda.") In April the Truth about Propaganda still completely eluded most of the English.

An Austrian refugee novelist in London told me sadly: "They cannot understand it, really. It is an instrument wielded deviously or openly, by word of mouth, by argument or auto-suggestion, by whispers, by editorials, by microphones, radio or any other known means of communication, illicit, illegal, unfair, or the contrary. Its sole purpose is to make your nation, or the other fellow's nation, believe whatever truth or whatever lie suits your immediate purpose. Sometimes it wears the fierce face of terror, sometimes the face of peace. It spreads panic and confidence with fiendish discrimination. Above all, it is not an instrument for the dissemination of truth or information. If it ever serves either, that is merely a coincidence. That the end justifies the means is its only motto. Unfortunately the democracies, based on the theory that public opinion forms policy, can very seldom wield propaganda effectively.[8] A nation whose policy-makers have a free hand in the forming of public opinion can wield it very effectively. It has to be highly organized, subsidized, and integrated with long-term and therefore generally undemocratic objectives. Perhaps propaganda is a lost cause for the Allies—and for America." After that I didn't say anything more about propaganda, because I believed the Austrian.

By May 2, although there was still no shadow of doubt about the eventual outcome of the war in the minds of the English, there had begun to be a little doubt about their own "grim determination" to win it. The sore spot, the ungrim point of disaffection in all this determination, was easily identified as Mr. Chamberlain. And although Mr. Chamberlain said bravely in the House of Commons: "We have no intention of allowing Norway to become merely a side show,"[9] there was a general uneasy feeling that the Chamberlain government was running it a bit too much like a peep-show.

The *Evening News* published an editorial called "Rose-Tinted Spectacles"—and this time (*mirabile dictu*) they were not American, but English spectacles that were referred to. Said the editorial:

"The battle in Norway is rushing to a climax. Within the next few days—perhaps within the next few hours—we shall know what the future holds for the Allies in the moun-

[8] The Gallup and *Fortune* polls, with their clear mandates for isolation, have made any intelligent foreign policy almost impossible. Politicians are faced with a clear choice: to reform American public opinion by telling the American people the truth, or to wait (when it may be too late) for events to reform public opinion. Being job-holders, not statesmen, the vast majority of them will wait.

[9] When the Allies finally abandoned Narvik on June 10, the news rated little more than a line in French and English papers. The Norwegian campaign sputtered out like a little wet snow-soaked firecracker among the great guns that were booming all over burning Flanders.

tainous north of Europe. . . .

"It is idle to pretend that the war *as a whole* is being waged by the Government with success, or with the incessant energy and tireless determination which alone can enable us to win it.

"Complacency is still the most powerful captain in the State. Until that most dangerous of all the Quislings is expelled from his high place in the Cabinet and in the Government Departments he will continue to lead us through a fool's paradise towards disaster."

The editorial then quoted a speech of Mr. Ernest Bevin's: "It is no use disguising the fact that ever since the war broke out those who, like myself, have been constantly in touch with Government departments are intensely dissatisfied with the kind of obstruction, lack of drive, absence of imagination, and complacency which exists. Then there is a complete refusal to take into consideration the kind of foe we are meeting."

The climax came. It was most humiliating. And although Mr. Churchill made a very fine speech about what a "splendid evacuation" it was, so splendid in fact that many of the papers were encouraged to call it a victory, everyone knew in his heart it was a defeat. That knowledge broke the first faint fissure in the wall of British conceit and complacency —a fissure through which, in the drawing-rooms of Mayfair and the big week-end houses, leaked a tiny trickle of disturbing rumour: "Things are worse even than Churchill said. He didn't tell all the truth: he was, as he was accused in Parliament of doing, 'using his popular person as a bomb-shelter for the Prime Minister.'" This sporting gesture of Mr. Churchill's vis-à-vis his superior was denied by other rumours: He was saving his own skin. It was Churchill himself who ordered, unknown to the War Ministry, that the fleet turn back from Trondheim, when he might have forced it and held it before the Germans had got their Big Guns set up there. "Hotheaded Churchill has cold feet for the first time in his (and the British navy's) history." "The Expeditionary Force was not ready to go to Norway because the Finnish Expeditionary Force, of which it had been composed, had never really been assembled." "Our Intelligence didn't know about the invasion." "The government never asked Norway and Sweden for permission to pass through with their armies." "Mannerheim had appealed months ago for aid. He was asked not to make the appeal public for fear it would 'encourage' Hitler to invade Norway and Scandinavia." "One still can't quite figure how the Germans took Norway with fifteen hundred men and three brass bands unless the brass hats slipped up at home very badly." And over and over again: "We haven't really enough airplanes. Why haven't we? A Minister told me that if the truth were known about our airplane contracts and the way they were given out, and the way they've been filled, the scandal would topple the government." And so forth and so on.

But while this crack of doubt, and the ooze of rumour that came through it, marred the smooth glossy face of British conceit momentarily, it was everywhere instantly plastered over with the cement of faith and tradition.

For instance, I asked my chambermaid what she thought of the end of the campaign in Norway. " 'Orrible," she said cheerfully, " 'orrible. But I 'ear we gave 'em what for: killed millions more of them than they did of ours and that's certain." [10]

[10] All through the hostilities the peoples of Great Britain and France derived enormous and violent comfort from the greatly disproportionate losses the Germans were reported to be sustaining. Three to one in tanks, six to one in planes, ten to one in men, were given out time and time again as the official figures of losses. A French officer

I said: "But doesn't it worry you that England lost the campaign?" "Aooh," she said, "I dunno. Maybe we wanted to. Hi expect the government knows what hit's doing."

And in the drawing-rooms in early May the upper-class English said: "England always loses every battle but the last one." Perhaps they were so proud of that tradition that they had subconsciously allowed it to become their only blueprint of military strategy. They were also, as I have said, proud of "muddling through." So they made that their political policy. I remember an Italian Fascist in Rome saying to me in February about the English: "A nation which is overripe with tradition is overripe for ruin." I pray that this is not true, that they will still muddle through, still win the last battle. And now that it's come to what it has come to, they know better even than we do the agonies they might have been spared if they had broken with tradition and planned to crash through, and to win the first battle.

Still, by the first week-end in May the English were willing to bury the blame for the Norwegian affair quietly. They had even an overt desire to bury Chamberlain with it. "'E's dead, but 'e won't lie down," somebody quoted a Gracie Fields' music-hall song.

"And we certainly will get rid of him when we have a real crisis," an under-secretary said to me at tea on the terrace of a big ancestral home. It was a place of wide lawns flowing down to the "liquid history of the Thames," and gardens which cuckoos and nightingales frequented, and immemorial grey walls, and great oak-panelled rooms hung with old

said to me in June: "When this battle is over, you will see how small our losses have been. The day in, day out toll taken by massed infantry attacks in the old trench warfare is a thing of the past." In July French newspapers published a government memorandum claiming that 1,500,000 Frenchmen had been killed or wounded during the war, and that this justified the armistice. France, in surrender, took great comfort from its own losses then.

English masters, and hunting portraits of the lordly owners by new ones.

"A real crisis," I repeated, feeling uneasy again as I had in the Maginot. "What do you call a *real* crisis? By that time it may be too late!"

A plane droned overhead. Nobody looked up, as everybody looked up with white faces and suddenly parted lips at planes that flew over Paris.

At this tea there was an old, untidy, very distinguished Gladstonian-looking gentleman named J. L. Garvin, editor of the London *Observer*. To the astonishment of all the conservative lords and ladies and brass hats and politicians there assembled, he set down his teacup with a clatter, rose from his chair, and raised his voice in trembling anger. He said: "I have heard those words before, in March in the House of Commons. Lloyd George said them: 'It is the same trouble . . . too late with Austria, too late with Czechoslovakia, too late with Poland—certainly too late for Finland. *It is always too late or too little or both. That is the road to disaster!*'"

Everybody looked pained and surprised. This was a conservative household. The name of Lloyd George still evoked a certain melancholic displeasure. But Mr. Garvin went on. His yellow old eyes filled with angry tears that blurred the white light of prophecy in them, so that he looked, alas, not so much like the Daniel come to judgment he really was as a weary old gentleman with a grievance. He said he now saw clearly (and, God willing, not too late) all that was wrong with England—its inertia, its smugness, its fatal unpreparedness, bred of too many years of easy victories and physical immunity. Eloquently, with many a quotation from the classics and from the *obiter dicta* of contemporary politicians, he held the mirror up to his country. He said that

England must wake up to the "iron veracities" of the war and then face them with "comprehensive British energy." So far the British *people* had done all that had been asked of them, were willing to do more, but that for the one Chamberlain in office there were hundreds, no, thousands sitting around today in the drawing-rooms of England's ancestral homes and the groaning boards of Mayfair. He said that *their* government, supplied with great wealth and power, had staked too much on the theory that "long purses make strong swords"; that Hitler's very presence in Norway belied it; that the pressing need was for two things: immediate mastery of the air and, second, a smaller, strongly led War Cabinet—because, as Cicero said, "an army in the field is of dubious value unless there are wise counsels at home." He said that England faced a foe whose fury was historic, the *furor Teutonicus* of Lucan, and that this furious foe held that most coveted advantage of war, the initiative. And while he admired the popular belief that one Englishman could beat three Germans, since this deeply ingrained faith would "probably enable him to beat two," the Germans were as like as not to be ten to one against him, and the only defence against superiority in men and the unpleasant surprise that initiative could give was to smash the attack when it came with overwhelming air predominance. And how to achieve that? Mr. Garvin prayed again to God and to Saint George that it was not again too late. Let England have done, he said, with crablike diplomatic manœuvres, so that no man knew any longer whether they were marching on Russia, or Italy, or backing away from them. Let England bend all its energies to get ready for the struggle, which would be sufficiently hard with or without assistance. There was no time to woo or browbeat neutrals, Mr. Garvin said. The British lion must "lash itself with its own tail" into the roaring temper of victory. He was generous in praise of other men who had seen all this even before he did. Bevin and Duff Cooper and Churchill and Herbert Morrison and Sinclair—not to mention, Mr. Garvin said, dozens of unknown subscribers to the *Observer* who had written him "quite uneasy" letters about it. And, above all, Lloyd George had seen it. Then he begged everyone at lunch to help get rid *now* of Mr. Chamberlain. Because this was the great crisis—this was the crisis a nation stands or falls by—the crisis of leadership.

When he paused for breath, a plump, pleasant-faced woman M.P. asked: "Now, why on this particular Sunday morning do you, of all people, feel this way?"

You see, Mr. Garvin had always been a die-hard Conservative, a Munich man—and even afterwards an appeaser. Either they must have thought age had made him "a bit potty," or this was—well, "rather serious."

And then Mr. Garvin quoted Johnson: "When a man knows he is to be hanged in a fortnight, it does concentrate his mind wonderfully." "I see we're going to be hanged at any minute now," he went on. "Hitler has warned us in Norway." Then Mr. Garvin said that, for his part, he wanted his "old enemy" Lloyd George back as P.M. "He's not exactly young," said seventy-two-year-old Mr. Garvin, "but he's a genius. And genius is like radium—it is radium *always*, no matter how little there is of it left! Perhaps Lloyd George can work only six hours a day, but six hours of Lloyd George is worth days of anyone else's month. In the last war Lloyd George knew how to delegate authority. He cared nothing for the political convictions of the men to whom he delegated it, only how they did their war job. That is what Chamberlain," he said, "cannot do: delegate authority to able captains."

And at this point someone, embarrassed that an American should see such a dismal picture of England painted by a Britisher, asked: "Aren't you ashamed to talk this way before an American?"

Mr. Garvin answered: "If she has ears let her hear it and be warned by it. I should not be surprised to learn that her country is in the same position." I said (as you can guess): "Yes, and we also have a leader who is a fine and thoughtful statesman, and just can't delegate authority." He grinned and said then that this *democratic voluntary* delegation of authority must be accomplished or our two democracies, which are the last two strong democracies in the world, would perish.

When he was finished we all talked with sudden enthusiasm about the radium of Lloyd George's genius. And since this was, as I said, a "conservative house," I thought it was wonderful and beautiful and very hopeful to see them, under the knout of Mr. Garvin's eloquence, coming alive to the tragic necessities of the hour. It was perfectly plain that all these important people were stirred. They were, as the under-secretary said, at last forcefully "contemplating doing something."

Two days later the great and now historic debate on the conduct of the Norwegian campaign began in the House of Commons. I remember it was a Tuesday, May 7.

Ever since my talk with Colonel Fuller, I had had a strange desire to see the Low Countries. In fact, faced with the only other alternative, a long Whitsuntide week-end in the English countryside (and here I must mention that Mr. Garvin had not failed to point out that all factories and businesses were closing for four days over Whitsuntide!) playing bridge or golf, and talking politics, I decided on a short trip to Holland and Belgium. "One last look," I told someone, who commented: "You are very brave to go to a *neutral* country." It was a standing joke in both France and England that the only safe places in Europe were the three belligerent countries. In fact, the definition in England of a neutral country was a country both enemies were at war with. So on the sunny May day when Mr. Chamberlain was defending himself, and Mr. Churchill was helping him to, as a military strategist, I went to Heston Airport and took a KLM plane and landed several hours later at the Schiphol Airport at Amsterdam.

I arrived there on the afternoon that began the three-day crisis which culminated in the rape of Holland. Motoring from Amsterdam to The Hague you couldn't have told there was a crisis, except in the wonderful tulip fields, which had reached their maximum bloom and were about to wither.

But when I arrived, in time for a luncheon at our Legation at The Hague, our Minister, Mr. George Gordon, told me at once there was a "nice big juicy crisis" brewing. Mr. Gordon is a gallant, gay, pink-cheeked, dapper little man who looks like *Esquire*. When he smiled, his white moustache seemed to emit little sparks—like a Fourth of July sparkler. But his blue eyes were serious. "You've picked a bad hour for a visit," he said; "our friends on the east may also arrive—unlike yourself, uninvited and unwelcome."

Uninvited, yes. But in the three days I spent in Holland I never quite made up my mind whether or not the Germans would be entirely unwelcome. The Norwegian affair had made me, like everyone else in Europe, terribly fifth-column-conscious. I asked Mr. Gordon about fifth-columnists in Holland. He spread his slim hands helplessly.

"The Dutch don't hate the Germans the way the French and English do," he said. "Most of them even like them. A lot of the Dutch are half-German. Many are even pro-German. Undoubtedly hundreds are paid German agents." He looked very troubled. "All I can tell you," he said, "is that the government itself is scrupulously neutral, and all of the people want to be let alone by *everybody*. The Dutch government does what it can to tread the spider-web tight-rope of neutrality between German and Allied pressure, but everybody in Holland is very unhappy. They're not getting rich out of this war, as they did out of the last one. And they're still dangerously in front, instead of safely behind the Germans as they were in 1914."

"Oh, tell me," I said, "do you think the Germans will come?" (It's amazing, and faintly ludicrous, how many talk-hours everybody spent in Europe in the spring seeking the answers today to tomorrow's inevitable tragedies. "Sufficient unto the day is the evil thereof," was not, in the spring, Europe's motto.)

"As to that," he said, "I'll tell you the theories." (Being a professional diplomat, he never, I remember now, really told me which one he favoured.) "There are those who say no: Holland is Germany's breadbasket, also Germany's hole in the blockade. If it's going to be a long war, Germany will not want to close the hole and destroy the breadbasket. On the other hand, if Germany tries for a short war, she'll need Holland's ports from which to strike her real enemy, England."

"I think she'll come," I said with a sudden dreadful certainty.

"Do you?" Mr. Gordon asked. "How ducky! You must visit us often, you're so bright and optimistic."

Mrs. Gordon, who was also little and gallant and chipper like her husband, said: "Mr. Gordon, pour the lady a glass of champagne, and I won't mention until after she's gone that we good Dutch burghers have no air-raid shelters."

"Haven't you?" I asked, appalled. "Why not?"

"Because," she said, "to build them *outside* would not look neutral, and if you tried to dig one in the cellar, you'd have a salt-water swimming-pool. Lovely?" She pointed straight up in the air. "The North Sea is that way," she said; "the dikes keep it back. We draw fifty feet of water. We live, you might say, in the hold of Europe."

"How awful!" I said. (During the next week it must have been very awful for the people who could not hide anywhere.) I asked: "Are the Dutch good soldiers?"

"That remains to be seen," Mr. Gordon replied. "They haven't fought in several hundred years. They make wonderful spiced fruit and cheese, though, so let's have luncheon."

At a dinner that night I sat next to Herr Snouck Hurgronje, Holland's Permanent Secretary General for Foreign Affairs. Naturally, I asked him about the crisis.

"The Germans are making troop movements," said Mr. Snouck placidly, "which strongly suggest an invasion."

"Oh," I said. "Are you sure?"

"*Ja*," he answered cheerfully. "The same sources have informed our government so which informed it five days before the German invasion of Norway."

I said, aghast: "You knew five days before that the Germans were going to invade Norway?"

"*Ja!*" he affirmed proudly. "Our sources of information are excellent. You see, a good Dutchman often can pass as a real German." (I thought: "And vice versa.")

I asked: "You *knew* five days before? Did you—tell the English and French about it?"

"Certainly not," he said indignantly. "Why should we? They're not our allies."

(Mr. Snouck ten days later was in London, a member of her exiled Majesty's belligerent government.)

I said: "If your sources are so reliable, aren't you—er—uneasy?"

He went on eating his planked beefsteak with gusto. "Well, you can never tell really," he said. "We've had three crises since the war began. This may also pass. One does one's best, one waits, one accepts the inevitable."

I think he noticed the rather amazed expression on my face at so much stolidity or fortitude.

"It's just another agony," he added gently, "to fear what cannot be prevented or conquered."

I said severely: "Mr. Snouck, if you really believe you cannot prevent it, why don't you throw your hand in with the Allies?"

Mr. Snouck smiled patiently. "You Americans don't understand the little neutrals. There is no happy solution to our problem. It is only nice to be neutral if you are strong—like America. You see, while we don't want to be 'protected' like Poland and Norway, still we are in no hurry to be 'assisted,' in the way the Allies assisted them."

The argument seemed unanswerable, so I let it pass. The crisis passed, too, in Holland. By the night of the 8th there was, in fact, what the diplomats in The Hague called a "*détente*."

That night I went to another dinner at The Hague. There I met a lady I shall never forget, the Baroness van Tuyll, lady in-waiting to Queen Wilhelmina. She was apple-cheeked, white-haired, and all that the term "*grande dame*" suggests to you. She had a mind that was gentle, lofty, and philosophical. She spoke flawless English. I asked her, naturally: "Will they come?" She said in a sad remote voice: "It is very possible."

I asked: "How will you feel about it?" (I really thought I was being very clever: I wanted to know how the Queen would feel about it, and I imagined that a lady-in-waiting must unconsciously express her royal mistress's convictions.)

She replied: "Oh, there will be death. There will be destruction. I, and all the people like me, will lose everything. That part of it will be unpleasant."

I said, surprised: "Will any part of it be pleasant?"

She answered: "Oh, it is interesting to be allowed to see in your lifetime a new world trying to be born. For good or for evil, the old, old dream of every wise European may become a reality: the unification of Europe." She sighed. "Pan-Europa. . . . It is a pity it could not have happened without so much bloodshed, and under a better master. But I think I always knew that it would be the Germans. Have you ever read Heine?"

I said I hadn't.

"You should," she told me. "He predicted it a hundred years ago in a book he wrote for and among Frenchmen. He said that the revolutionary doctrines of Kant and Hegel were waiting in the womb of time to be reborn and to fill all of Europe with horror and dismay, and destroy the old European order with shell and flame and sword, so that the very roots of Europe's past would perish. And that this philosophy would breed martyrs and fanatics who, like the old Christian martyrs, would neither care for pleasure nor fear torture. And that it would breed men of science who would chain the very forces of nature and evoke demoniac Germanic Pantheism and the ancient Teutonic fighting spirit, which nothing can destroy in the Germans. And that this revolution based on German philosophy would carry the whole civilized world before it. Heine warned the French not to interfere. Well," the Baroness said, "they interfered and the English interfered once before, and their interfering succeeded. But the German Revolution has only been strengthened by frustration. Now its martyrs and proselyters, after years in the catacombs where the Versailles Treaty drove them, are out and ravaging and pillaging again, as their crusade for German thought sweeps over Europe." She sighed again and played with her great soft gleaming pearls. "I do not see how we shall stop it, unless we have some philosophy, some borning revolution, some crusade of our own to oppose to it. Have you found one in France, in England, in Holland?" she asked.

"Democracy," I said feebly.

She shook her head. "Everybody calls what he has in his own country democracy," she said, "but nobody wants to die for the 'democracy' of his neighbour." She smiled sadly. "Perhaps in its way it is more evil to stand still than to march even if it is in the wrong direction, like the Germans. Hitler and his soldiers know, or think they know, where they are going for the next thousand years. France and England and Holland—*ja*, and even your great country—don't even know where they are going tomorrow. *Ja! Ja!*" she said. "Some good may come of a German Europe. It is a great thing to have vision, and then be willing to die for that vision. They see an enslaved Pan-Europa. We see nothing, because we have not seen in time a *free* Pan-Europa." These were not the Baroness's actual words, but they are the substance of them. I think the Baroness, too, is now in London.

After dinner a nice young Dutch aviator took me for an automobile ride through the dark streets of The Hague, "to see if there are still machine-gun nests on the canals and in front of government buildings—a precaution against fifth-column activities," he explained. We only saw one: a little group of blond young men in grey-green, huddled over a small gun on a bridge, laughing. It was very unexciting. I asked the Dutch aviator how many planes Holland had. He said sadly, "We have about three hundred. How many more than three thousand the Germans have doesn't really matter to us, I'm afraid."

In Amsterdam on May 9 I went to a press luncheon in a big sunny, crowded hotel. All the newspaper men at it were happy the crisis had passed, although, as they all told me, none of them had really believed in it. A prominent news-service man explained it to me neatly: "Just Germany jacking up Holland a bit, so she wouldn't get too friendly tradewise with the Allies." Another correspondent had another explanation. "Created," he said, "by the Dutch government itself as an excuse for its projected round-up of thirty thousand—thirty thousand!—listed fifth-columnists. Yes," he said, "the jails are already bursting with them." A well-known American broadcaster had still another explanation. He said: "The government has a military alliance with the Belgians. They both whipped up this little scare to test out their mobilization power in an emergency." An English newspaper man said: "The Germans started the scare for one of two reasons: either to see where Dutch and Belgian troops would be deployed, if they do get desperate and have to come in next spring, or to distract everybody's attention from their secret troop concentrations in the Balkans. You know, don't you, they're concentrating on the Rumanian and Hungarian borders?" A newsreel man said: "Well, you can't say they don't treat all their neighbours the same way."

A very prominent visiting journalist said that he had had interviews that very morning with young Foreign Minister van Kleffens and old ex-Premier Dr. Colijn. He said that van Kleffens hoped the Allies would make peace overtures, because he believed Germany would gladly accept peace today on a basis of 1914 boundaries minus Alsace-Lorraine, but plus some colonies and with a plebiscite for Austria and a neutralized Czechoslovakia with internationally controlled disarmament. Van Kleffens thought perhaps it would not be wise to insist on equal disarmament, since, dollar for dollar, Germans are better soldiers. He strongly recommended that the Allies make this peace with Hitler. He believed the Rauschning theory of world revolution was true two years ago, but he believed every force spends itself and that the very eruptive force of Nazism had spent itself now. He said, however, that what was most terrifying was that the Germans believed they were fighting with their backs really to the wall, and that if they failed to win they would be eternally destroyed. He thought Allied propaganda had been both stupid and ineffective in that it had not allayed Germany's fears of the worst in the event of defeat. . . .

The main thing I learned from this was that the Foreign Minister of Holland himself, on May 10, thought that peace was possible.

Then the journalist quoted the former Premier Dr. Colijn as saying: "The thing I personally dread most is a peace or an end to the war which settles nothing." Dr. Colijn felt that a new *moral* basis for human society must be re-established, and he said he himself was now working untiringly on postwar plans. He said that after all it was not so easy to judge Germany morally. The case of Poland, he felt, was not entirely clear. The case of Denmark and Norway he also thought was not entirely clear because Denmark did not defend itself at all (indeed, had practically courted invasion politically since September 3), and Norway defended itself very inadequately and permitted treason in high places. But it was easy enough to judge Russia. The case of Finland, he thought, was clear as crystal. He said that it was at that point that the United States might have led a great coalition of all the *right-thinking neutrals* against the aggressor nations.

I thought at the time that if Dr. Colijn was working on peace plans, he too must think peace possible. (I wonder if Dr. Colijn is still working on peace plans, or if the case of Holland is so very clear that he prefers to work on war plans.)

So that was "the crisis."

That afternoon I left Amsterdam for Brussels on the train. As we chugged peacefully over that flat, pretty, flower-painted dinner plate of a country, the land of ditches and dikes and ducks and dimpled babies, I felt very happy that it was safe—until next spring anyway. You see how odd it was. Even I, reasonably objective, and dispassionate, disposed by nature to be cynical and pessimistic, found it very difficult to remember for more than a few hours at a time what the war was all about, and what war had to be like when it came. I began to find out the next morning at 5.20 a.m. in Brussels. That was the first morning of the Blitzkrieg.

NINE

Now storming fury rose,
And clamour such as heard in Heav'n till now
Was never, arms on armour clashing brayed
Horrible discord, and the madding wheels
Of brazen chariots rag'd: dire was the noise
Of conflict; overhead the dismal hiss
Of fiery darts in flaming vollies flew
And, flying, vaulted either host with fire. . . .

Deeds of eternal fame
Were done, but infinite; for wide was spread.
That war, and various: sometimes on firm ground
A standing fight; then, soaring on main wing,
Tormented all the air; all air seemed then
Conflicting fire.

John Milton, in *Paradise Lost*

I REACHED BRUSSELS at eleven o'clock on the night of May 9. The smoky North Station was full of soldiers and jostling crowds of calm-faced men and women who had come to see them off. Although the "crisis" was over, the mobilization was still going on. I took a taxi, through the brightly lighted streets—another proof of the *détente*—to our Embassy on the rue de la Science.

Although it was late, Ambassador Cudahy had waited up, with the second secretary of the Embassy, Miss Willis, a handsome, clever young woman, to receive me. I wanted very much to ask him a hundred questions about Belgium, and what the Belgians thought about the French, and American isolationism, and if he really believed the crisis was over, but I saw at once that he was very, very tired. There were dark rings under his steady blue eyes, and although he offered me a drink and said: "Do sit down," I saw that he was gulping back little yawns.

"You've had a bad time of it these three days, haven't you?" I asked.

And he said: "I've been on the telephone night and day. But now—" his voice sounded strangely dubious, as though he himself did not quite believe it—"it's over, thank God. The King has reinstated all his appointments for the weekend. Miss Willis has arranged for you to see some of the government people you want to see in the afternoon."

Miss Willis suggested I go out to Waterloo, if I hadn't ever seen it, in the morning. "It's only an hour's ride," she said. And I told her I'd seen the Waterloo battlefields before, but I'd very much like to see them again, because the very thought of Waterloo was a comforting one at this moment, in the seventh year of Adolf Hitler.[1]

[1] Non-commissioned officer (Marquis) Henri de la Falaise, one of the "last off the beach at Dunkirk" who had fought the rear-guard action in the Battle of Flanders, told me in June, in London, that he also had been "comforted" by finding himself "at Waterloo again," about May 17 or 18. "As we drew up there behind the Belgians for the second Battle of Waterloo," he said, "I thought, ah, *now* history is going to repeat itself. . . . A few hours later we were ordered to withdraw back into Flanders. . . . On the retreat there was much talk—the Belgian soldiers were using wooden bullets in their guns." "Treachery?" I asked. He

Then Mr. Cudahy asked: "How were they feeling in America when you left about the third term?"

I said: "I better skip that—you need a good night's rest."

And he agreed: "Yes, I'm going to get it now." So he said good-night.

And then Miss Willis said: "Things can't go on like this for ever. Human nervous systems can't stand it," and then she said: "Good-night, my dear," and I went right to bed in a pleasant, wide-windowed room overlooking a little park, on the top floor of the Embassy.

I was sleeping so soundly I did not hear the alarm at dawn, but a maid shook me violently by the shoulder and said: "Wake up! The Germans are coming again!" And then she went quickly away. I heard her little feet racing down the corridor. I got up and went to the tall window, and as I stood there in my nightgown watching a lovely red-gold dawn behind the black trees across the park, about twenty planes, very high up, came over in formation. Their bellies gleamed in the gold and red sunrise. Then I heard a thin long, long whistle and a terrible round *bam!* The whistle was from the bomb that pierced the roof of a three-storeyed house across the square, and the *bam* was the glut and vomit of glass and wood and stone that was hurled into the little green park before me. For a long hour after that there was a terrible noise, of the great anti-aircraft guns

---

shrugged. "Something had gone wrong, we shall never know what, with the expected ammunition supplies. Perhaps the retreat had been too precipitous. The Belgian officers were passing out the wooden bullets, the kind they use for peace-time military manœuvres, which had been sent out from the Brussels arsenals, just to keep up the men's morale—because there's nothing so comforting to a soldier as a loud bang when he is making it! I thought afterwards what strange tricks history plays on you while it is 'repeating.' Waterloo again! But we had wooden bullets against tanks to win it! *C'est une drôle de guerre!*" said the Marquis.

going and bombs falling, though only one of them, which destroyed another house a block away, was anywhere as near as the first one. While this was happening I got dressed. I was very careful to fill my purse with an extra supply of powder, lipstick, and cold-cream and to choose the only flat-heeled shoes in my suitcase. Then I went down into the kitchen in the basement of the Embassy and talked to the servants, who were all very frightened. At least, they were for the first ten minutes. But after that they got used to the noises of the guns and gradually their fear gave way to anger. They were very mad, they said, because the Germans were coming again. They made coffee for me and for themselves, and after we had all drunk it, they said we might as well have toast and eggs, because not eating will not keep the Germans away.

Then the Ambassador came into the kitchen, and said good-morning and gulped down a cup of coffee. He had not had his good night's sleep. In fact he had not slept at all, because he had been told by the Luxemburg Foreign Office at 12.30 a.m. that the Germans were on their way, and at one o'clock he had telephoned this to the President.[2] So he looked tired and grim, but quite prepared to face the awful day, because he had had his shave calmly a few minutes after the bomb in the square broke the windows of his Embassy. Then he smiled encouragingly at us all and told

[2] Ambassador Cudahy "scooped the world" with this news. What his precise information from Luxemburg was he did not, of course, tell me. But in Paris on May 14 I saw the refugee Duchess of Luxemburg, so I believe I know what it was now. "At midnight," the Duchess said, "my ministers informed me that all the borders of Luxemburg were being overrun by an extraordinary number of 'German tourists.' " They were coming in cars, on bicycles, on foot, sneaking, crawling, rushing over the borders. These were the advance guards of the German army—the famous fifth-columnists, whose sudden swarming, and brazen appearance, warned the Luxemburg government that invasion was a matter of hours. At seven a.m. the invasion began.

us we really ought to go into the air-raid shelter in the garden. But he went into the street and got into his car with Miss Willis, and they drove off to the Foreign Office to see what news they could get, or what advice they could give, and what from now on a neutral American Ambassador should or could do.

The servants and I stood around for a little while saying how awful it was, but not really saying how very awful we knew it was going to be. Then there was the banshee wail of the sirens again, signalling *all clear*, and I went into the street and the beautiful morning sunlight. The blue glass from the fanlight over the Embassy door lay shattered all over the sidewalk. Several Red Cross ambulances whipped by, clanging. Across the square people began to gather around the wrecked house. Its front was bellied out like a sail. A postman on his rounds looked at it over his shoulder and said to me: "So this is what we call civilization?"—and shifted his pack and went on. After that there were one or two short alarms. You could hear planes and guns, but you could not see anything except little white puffs from the guns, very high up and, even higher, several strange enormous thin white circles of drifting smoke. "What are those circles?" I asked the gendarme on the corner.

"I didn't know," he said, "but they say the German scout planes make those big circles around an objective below, and then the bombers come along and drop their bombs in the middle of the circle. Those circles are off in the direction of the airport."

"That's very clever of them," I remarked.

A civilian, standing near the gendarme, said: "That's nonsense. Messerschmitt planes, circling, always leave a trail of white smoke. They can't help it. It's an excellent target for our gunners."

The gendarme and the civilian began to argue, so I left them. I walked down the street and round the corner, into the rue Belliard. In the middle of that block was the German Embassy, and at the end of it was the other house that had been blown up. The right block but the wrong house, I thought bitterly.

Then I walked down to the big public square, La Place Charles Rogier, before the North Station. Khaki-coloured troops were sitting at the entrance, smoking and talking, waiting for their trains to the front. At the little kiosks in the middle of the square, people were buying the first editions of the papers. All they told the Belgians was what all Belgians already knew—that the Germans were coming again. The people read the papers in little angry groups and then put them in their pockets and, very mad and very calm, went about their business, to their homes, to their shops, to their offices—not because they did not care, but because it was the sensible thing to do, and because men must earn their daily bread, and women cook the midday meal up to the last possible moment.

Now the sidewalk cafés on La Place were full of those who did have the time to talk about it over coffee and rolls with rich butter, but all they said came to this: "*Le sale Boche!* This time he won't get away with it!" Now that I come to think of it, the only time I ever heard the Nazis repeatedly referred to as Huns or Boches was that first morning in Brussels. Perhaps that's because the word "Germans" is after all a word which time and history has given a more peculiar and embracing meaning of immutable, relentless ferocity.

Then an American newspaper man I had known in New York sat down at a little table beside me. "Hello," I said.

"Well," he asked, "you here?"

I said: "Fancy! Tell me at once, what do you know?"

"Only," he said, "what it says in the papers." He unfolded his copy of *La Nation Belge* with its mammoth headline, " '*L'Allemand Revient!*' What a headline!"

"Nothing more?" I inquired.

"Sure. A hundred planes were over this morning. They got the airport."

"Yes," I said, "I heard them."

"See them?" he asked.

"Yes."

He said: "They sure looked pretty. And of course the German troops went through Luxemburg like a cheese-knife. But the Dutch are giving them the water-works in the north, and Leopold is out with his boys holding them. The English and the French are already on their way. And speaking of the English," he said, "you might be interested to know that Mr. Chamberlain is still holding his own in the House of Commons, and claiming that things are progressing nicely for the Allies—in Norway." [3]

"Please!"

He went on: "Well, we must look on the bright side of things occasionally. . . . Now I've got to get around the town and see who and what actually got hit. See you at the Café Metropole tomorrow morning at eleven, if you're still fool enough to be here, and if we're both alive to keep the appointment."

I walked a long way through the streets. Then I tried to get a taxicab to go back to the Embassy for luncheon but already all the taxis had been taken over by the army.

[3] A few hours later Conservative Charles Emery had risen in Parliament, to clip the mumbling apologia of poor Mr. Chamberlain with the harsh words that Oliver Cromwell used to the Long Parliament: "You have sat here too long for any good you have been doing. Depart, I say. Let us have done with you, I say: in the name of God, go!"

So I got a street car. It was full of women who had been shopping, and children, and a soldier or two, and nobody was looking frightened or excited except a child who had misbehaved somehow and whose mother was cross with him.

Back at the Embassy everybody was busy—the houseman pasting paper strips on the windows, the maids dusting and sweeping. The butler had changed into his frock coat with a black silk stock. The secretaries were thumbing over American passports, but telling the people who brought them they did not know when or how there would be a chance to leave. "The roads and trains are crowded with troops," they said, "and Brussels is in a state of siege; come back tomorrow." Most of the Americans said: "We'll come back again this afternoon."

We had a very good luncheon in the lovely mirrored gallery of the Embassy. The Ambassador served his best wine, not in honour of *Der Tag* but, as he said: "Why not gather its aroma while we may?" We had three more alarms between the eggs Mornay and the dessert, so that while we all ate with studied nonchalance, none of us really enjoyed the good food or the wine's wonderful aroma. And all through lunch we talked about how strong the Dutch army was, and how strong the Belgian Maginot was, and how many planes and tanks and anti-tank guns the Allies had. We did not talk politics any more. And from that day to the day I left France several weeks later to return to London, I never heard anyone really talk politics again—just the calibre of guns, and numbers of men, and communication lines and how to throw pontoons across rivers and the speed and range of Heinkels, Messerschmitts, Defiants, Spitfires, Moranes, Faireys, Hurricanes, Wellingtons. Now everybody talked *war*, not politics.

After luncheon Miss Willis insisted on showing me the

air-raid shelter in the garden. It was a low tin tunnel covered with a few inches of earth. There was no place to sit down, and you couldn't stand erect.

I said: "It is very uncomfortable," and she laughed and replied: "Don't cast aspersions on our summer home. This will be the most popular place in Brussels. We're about the only people who have one."

In the afternoon I listened to the radio. It only said things which everybody in Brussels knew—that the Germans were coming. I felt sure people knew more about the invasion of Holland and Belgium in America right then than we did who were there. Later one of the secretaries told me that from dawn until ten o'clock German broadcasters seemed to be on every station, and after that there had been some broadcasting in every tongue in Europe, repeating endlessly the brief Belgian war communiqués, but most of the stuff coming over now was hunks of "canned" American jazz or recordings of the Tchaikovsky "1812," suggesting Napoleon's retreat from Moscow, which the secretary had heard on six stations during the day. [4]

But I kept listening to the radio, hoping to hear some real

[4] The appalling Allied mismanagement of this most important war instrument continued from the first day of the invasion to the surrender. From Lisbon *Life's* correspondent Ralph D. Paine wrote:

"The headlong evacuation of Paris began on June 9. What was needed was: (1) clear, constant radio directions as to who should go, where to go and how to get there; and (2) efficient road policing. There was neither. When the French radio should have been going constantly in an effort to control this incredible population movement, much of it entirely unnecessary, it was playing dance music or repeating over and over stale communiqués. The result was utterly demoralizing and went on days and days with half of France fleeing, the other half watching fascinated. Finally the virus of flight would infect watchers and they too would pack and take to the road, not really knowing where they were going or why. These hordes stripped the countryside of food and, more important, gasoline. Not until last Thursday did the military finally order all refugees to stay put, ending most of this senseless traffic which, in some areas, had paralyzed military operations."

news. After an hour the jazz music stopped abruptly and a broadcaster said: "We are bringing you the message of Pius XII in response to King Leopold's appeal of this morning to use his high moral authority to support the cause for which the Belgian people are fighting with invincible determination." My heart stood still, and I thought that now the miracle would happen. God was just waiting until the issue was joined. Then the broadcaster said that the Pope, seeing the Belgian people, against its will, exposed for the second time to the cruelties of war, was "profoundly moved." He said that the Belgians had the assurance of his paternal affection and that he was going to pray to Almighty God that everything would turn out the way the Belgians wanted it to—in the end. He sent Leopold and his people his blessings and his love. And that was all; the broadcaster signed off, and the radio went on playing canned swing music. I thought: "Well, Almighty God, how can even You get things done except through the works of man?" and I turned the radio off. Then I walked around the room a little while, smoking, and the air-raid sirens, which had begun to get on my nerves, began again. I went to the bookcase and picked a book from the shelf at random. It was Brand Whitlock's *Belgium*.[4a] I flipped through the first few chapters and then a paragraph caught my eye:

> "I was awakened suddenly out of a sound sleep by a light, apologetic, and yet insistent knock at my door. It was six o'clock on Saturday, the first of August. I got up, opened the door, and there stood Omer, in uniform, the rough blue tunic, the linen pantaloons and

[4a] Brand Whitlock: *Belgium: A Personal Narrative*, quoted by permission of the publishers, D. Appleton-Century Company, New York City.

the little *bonnet de police*. He stood at attention, his hand at the salute.

" 'C'est la guerre, Excellence!' The words, of course, were superfluous. Omer standing there ready to depart was the living symbol of the thing we had feared for a week. . . . I fumbled through my *porte-monnaie*, gave him all the money that I had, while he told me the latest news: 'the Germans had invaded the Grand Duchy of Luxembourg and were throwing down the bridges.' "

Here indeed was history repeating. I read on, fascinated:

"At the Legation there were crowds of Americans in panic. What to do? Well, one thing at a time, and doucement as the French say. And try to comfort, to reassure. . . . How many days, how many nights, it was to be my lot to do that when my own heart was sinking! . . .

"All day the Legation was crowded with frightened Americans, who continued to pour into Brussels and remained there hesitant, undecided, bewildered, loath to brave the Channel-Crossing to England, hoping for some miracle that would arrest the war or spare them its discomforts. . . .

"Herr von Strum was nervous, agitated, and unstrung; I suppose that he, too, had been without sleep for nights on end. Tears were continually welling into his eyes, and suddenly he covered his face with his hands, leaned forward, his elbows on his knees, an attitude of despair. Presently he looked up. 'Oh, these poor, stupid Belgians!' he said. 'Why don't they get out of the way! I know what it will be. I know the

German army. It will be like laying a baby on the track before a locomotive!' . . .

"Then one morning de Laval came in with the news that the French had arrived; cavalry had entered the city the night before. He had seen them from his balcony going down the Avenue de la Toison d'Or—a squadron of weary troopers, nodding over their horses' necks; and Gibson had seen them at the Porte de Namur; they were hailed by shouts of '*Vive la France!*' And the cavalrymen roused themselves to reply 'Vive la Belgique!' . . .

"The Crown Prince withdrew with Lancken into a corner near the window and they talked in low tones for a long time, while I chatted with the affable Count about all sorts of things—trying to avoid the war, for the notes on the *Lusitania* were being exchanged in that moment. But by the irresistible attraction of the subject with which the very atmosphere throbbed, the conversation inevitably veered round to it, as the needle, oscillating an instant, turns unerringly to the magnetic-pole. And the Count introduced the topic by saying:

" '*Si vous autres en Amérique n'aviez pas fourni les munitions aux Alliés, la guerre aurait été finie il y a longtemps. . . .*' "

Would that repeat itself?

Now, while I read, the long afternoon had almost gone. I went into the street again. In the green square where the glass from the bombed house lay like jagged hail, a child was playing. I hoped that he would play there tomorrow. Two children had been killed in that early morning raid. I thought: In this brave new world of Hitler's the sun often sets at dawn.

At seven o'clock the maid came to me and said: "What shall I press for you to wear at the dinner?"

I asked, much surprised: "Are we having the dinner? Are we dressing?"

And she, defiantly: "*Mais pourquoi pas, madame?* The Germans have not yet arrived in Brussels."

Of the eighteen Belgians that Ambassador Cudahy had asked for dinner the week before, ten arrived. One, a Countess de Liederkerke, did not come because one of the children who had been killed in the morning raid was a relative of hers. Others were evacuating their families to Ostend and Dunkirk. But those who did come all arrived very punctually, dressed in evening gowns and dinner coats. I felt that they were secretly proud of this and thought that by behaving very correctly and normally they were showing that they did not really believe the Germans were ever coming as far as Brussels.

We sat down to a very good dinner under an enormous crystal chandelier which only shook very slightly when an anti-aircraft gun went off or a bomb landed in the region of the airport. It was now apparent to everybody that the Germans were not after Brussels, but military objectives outside the town. Of course, they could always "slip" a bomb or two, as they had that morning in the square outside this very house and in the heart of the town, and the air-raid sirens *were* nerve-racking. But on the whole everybody at dinner behaved as though these were things well-bred guests should ignore, as they would have ignored the noise made by a servant dropping a whole tray of the host's precious china in the pantry. Only once, when there was a sudden drone of planes overhead, did everybody stop talking and look a little pale and nervous. After the planes passed by, someone said: "I have discovered I don't like the sound of bombs; they really upset my stomach." [5]

Colonel Brown, the military attaché, said: "In the last war there was a Negro in my regiment. I remember, one day when we were being bombed in the trenches, he said to me: 'Boss, you know wut dem boms is sayin'?' I asked: 'What?' He said: 'Boss, dey sayin': WHEeeeeee-ain't-goin'-back-tuh-Ala-*BAMMM!*'" And everybody laughed really quite heartily.

But the hero of the dinner was a Count X, a secretary of the Belgian Foreign Office, who had been innocently shooting woodcock in the woods on the Belgian border that morning and had come out of his blind at dawn to retrieve a dead bird, only to be greeted by a totally unexpected volley of machine-gun fire from an advance patrol of the invading army. His breath-taking escape in his little automobile, which fortunately he had left parked near the blind, and his *savoir-faire* in showing up at the Embassy for dinner were the occasion for many exclamations of wonder and hearty congratulations. He told and retold the details of his escape until at the end of two hours everybody knew them by heart and was a little tired of them. I think we let him go on as long as he did because in a strange way it was a very comforting story. Perhaps he became a symbol of hope and confidence. If one little middle-aged man in shooting-tweeds could outwit and elude Hitler's terrible army, what couldn't Leopold and all his brave Belgians do to them!

And then everybody talked about the King, and how

[5] "Bomb stomach," or "bomb cramps" was a familiar term to everybody by the end of May. It's really quite simple: for days after an air raid in which bombs have fallen near, you are subject to sudden fits of vomiting. Curiously enough, children and animals are very subject to bomb stomach. Many survivors from Flanders told unpleasant stories of vomiting cows and cats and dogs in bombed villages.

brave his father had been, and how he was just like his father, only more foresighted, because his kingdom was infinitely readier for the ordeal it had to face. Everybody seemed to have always known it would come, but had hoped to the last it wouldn't.

So although we were still being bombed, and there was a total black-out in Brussels that night, everybody said *Bon soir*, *Bonne chance*, *Au revoir*, feeling very brave and very confident that tomorrow's news would be good news. Indeed, some good news had come already.

The Ambassador said: "The Belgians brought down twenty German planes today. The French and the English are here. And the Dutch are holding the Germans along the lines of the Ijssel and Maas Rivers."

The next morning at six o'clock once more the anguished air-raid sirens woke me out of a nightmare sleep. (From May 10 until long after I got back to New York I had nightmares. I found out later that everybody I knew in France had nightmares every night too, horrible, elaborate, scream-torn nightmares about the Germans' coming. That was the terrible mental phenomenon of the war. What price Freudian wish-fulfilment in dreaming now?) It had been quiet through the night; now the Germans were seriously at it again. I thought that as an American, a woman staying in the Embassy of a great neutral country, by all the laws of other wars I should be safe, but no one is safe in Hitler's war. Perhaps the difference now between civilian and soldier is that a soldier has a chance to defend himself. At breakfast they told me that eighty civilians had been killed and hundreds wounded the day before, and that fires were burning in all the suburbs.

I went into Mr. Cudahy's office. A houseman on a stepladder was pasting more paper strips across the great glass window before his desk. Now Ambassador Cudahy was patient but firm. "The news is not good," he said. "It is very bad. I think it's going to be worse, too. You must get out of here while you can."

"How?" I asked. "The trains are not running, the frontiers are closed."

He said: "Mrs. Gibson [6] is leaving for Paris by motor this afternoon to join her husband. She will take you along."

I said: "I'd like to stay another day, if you don't mi–"

He answered: "I do. You are of no use here, and you are in danger, so you will please go."

"Yes," I said, and then, looking him squarely in the eye: "And anyway this is not *our* war, is it?"

He grinned. "Wouldn't you give a million," he asked, "to see the American papers this morning?"

So the maid (who was called Angèle) helped me pack my bags, and I thanked her and gave her all the coins in my purse–English shillings and French francs and Dutch guilders. I had no Belgian coins–I had arrived too late from Holland to change money, and the banks had all closed the morning of the invasion. I hoped Angèle would be able to use those Dutch coins some day. Then I thought again of Holland as I had last seen it, so flat, so small, so flowery, resembling itself so in every part. And I thought how Mrs. Gordon had told me that during a crisis all the Dutch people in the town who could afford it moved to the country for safety, because the cities were so crowded, and all the people who lived in the country moved to town because there were so few woods and no hills in the country to hide in. And I thought again of the blond and beautiful babies and the good stolid burghers and wondered if they would be safe

[6] The Belgian wife of Hugh Gibson, former American Ambassador to Belgium, on Hoover's Polish Relief Commission in Europe.

in the tulip fields. The tulip blooms were almost finished in Holland; only the fields of late-blooming white ones stood tall and proud. I thought the white tulip fields must be very red now with the blood of many good Dutch gardeners. . . .

"Angèle," I said, "I am sorry. I'm afraid those Dutch coins won't be of much use to you."

The Ambassador kept his counsel as always, but during the early morning the people who came to the Embassy were full of unhappy rumours. They said that trainloads of refugees were being machine-gunned . . . that British tanks had been pouring through the streets of Brussels last night, which was a dangerous thing for the High Command to let them do, if they wanted the Germans to believe Brussels was an open town . . . that the great fortress of Eben Emael had fallen—fallen before some terrible secret weapon[7] . . . that the fortress of Liége was falling too . . . that German parachutists were dropping like apple blossoms in a high wind all over the spring countryside. . . . The strangest rumour of all was about the parachutists. Someone had sworn that at dawn the silk of the parachutes was gold and orange, at high noon blue, at night black as coal. . . .

I walked through the streets again to the Hotel Metropole to see the newspaper man I had made the date with. He knew hardly more than I did, but we sat in the bar and swapped our wide and varied misinformation with melancholy excitement. Presently a young man in a sky-blue Royal Air Force uniform came along.

The newspaper man said: "Hello, Trotter. Have a drink?"

[7] The stories of the secret weapons used on Eben Emael were countless—flame-throwers, thermite bombs, secret gases. . . . Washington military authorities have since testified that Eben Emael fell in "old-fashioned hand-to-hand fighting."

Trotter asked: "You mean another?" and sat down. He turned out to be a Virginian who had come to London to enlist in the air force the day war was declared, and he and his bombing crew had crashed in a muddy beet field in neutral Belgium in February. Ever since they had been interned. But now the Belgians were Allies, and the night before, he and his crew had been let out of jail, and covered with flowers and kisses by the Belgian girls in the streets. (Their appearance started a happy rumour: "The R.A.F. is already here.")

The Virginian was a first-family boy, but just the same he had gone on a wonderful bender the night before, he was naturally so glad to be out of jail after a long two months of inactivity. Today he was worried. He didn't know how he could get back to Paris to report to a R.A.F. chief. He didn't want to report to Belgian G.H.Q.

"They'll assign me to a Belgian plane," he said, "and, oh boy, is the Belgian air force *lousé!*"

I said: "Come with us at three o'clock in our car," and he said: "Oh, boy!"

So at three o'clock he met Mrs. Gibson and me at the Embassy. To our surprise and dismay, he brought his "crew" along, two other young men in sky-blue. The Virginian was the gunner; the flight lieutenant was an Englishman; the co-pilot was a sandy-haired Canadian boy. They were all very young and very eager to get back to Paris. We saw it would be terribly crowded in the car, but we said: "Oh, all right. Come along." I said good-bye to everybody at the Embassy, knowing that this time it really was good-bye. The Ambassador waved and smiled his warm Irish smile, and said: "Go right home."

"I wish you were coming," I answered; and he said:

"I'm here for the duration!" He looked slit-eyed and

angrily at the sky and muttered fiercely: "Yes, I am, by God!"

Mrs. Gibson was a lovely grey-haired woman who drove like an inspired taxi-driver. We sailed out of Brussels and took the road for Ghent, which one of our rumour-bringing friends had said was all clear. As we sped through the grey avenues of Brussels lined with flourishing green plane trees, life looked normal enough. The streets were still bustling and the trams still crowded. But I knew the people were very sad and very mad, and as I left the sorrowful and angry people of Brussels I prayed that their sorrow would not be too deep and their anger would be avenged some day.

An hour later we passed through a town called Alost, which had been bombed the night before. The railway bridge was twisted like a dirty giant pretzel against the sky, and the station and the warehouses around it were ruins that still smoked and smouldered.[8] The English boy said: "Got what they aimed for. Good bombing." The heart of the town itself had not been touched, but all the streets, even on the outskirts, were covered with a wanton mosaic of glass. A very few old people stood in the doorways and watched with blank faces as we streamed past. Most of the others had gone to join the great tragic army of refugees that Hitler had swelled every day for seven years. Now we began to pass them on the roads, on foot with little bundles on their tired backs, in old carts, in high hay-wagons, on bicycles, in camions, and in broken-down jaloppies of every sort.

At every little town the military police stopped us, exam-

[8] Back in Paris I read: "Alost was bombed, a few civilians were killed, but no military objectives were attained." Since then I have never believed any accounts, either German or Allied, that I have read about the damage resulting from bombing.

ined our papers, and let us pass. We reached Courtrai at five o'clock and stopped and had tea in a candy shop full of gay, wonderful pastries, the last that were to be baked in Belgium for many bitter days.

The two English flyers ate them greedily, as young boys do. Trotter, the American, asked for a whisky, then said: "Oh, all right, a coke," but settled for beer.

I said: "You look so happy," and he answered with his slow Southern drawl: "Well, I guess my *brother's* happy today, anyway."

"Your brother?" I asked. "Why?"

"Why," he said, "because he's in the Maginot. The big bum came to France with me in September. We made it, you know, on fifteen dollars and a bottle of corn. And now my brother—he's a great big guy—he's going to get the chance he's waited for all his life—to fight as much as he likes without getting thrown in the can!"

The English boy was happy, too, for a different reason. He'd married a pretty English girl the day war was declared, and now he said he was probably going to see her again, if they gave him a few days' leave to go to England.

He said: "I wish you knew my wife; she's rather wonderful, and she takes such good care of me!"

The red-haired Canadian sunk his teeth into his third napoleon. "I wish I could go home," he said. "I get awfully down, thinking how I'll never see Ottawa again."

"Oh," I said, "don't be so pessimistic."

He smiled. "I'm sorry, but, gee, sometimes I wish I were flying a Curtiss-Hawk instead of a lousy bomber—a fellow's got a pretty good chance in one of your American planes."

Trotter said: "Pay no attention to the come-on. He's trying to drag us into the war. I tell him it's none of our damn business!"

"Listen, old Trotsky," the Canadian said. "How many times do I have to tell you we're going to win this war without you!"

The English boy explained apologetically: "Trotsky and he are always quarrelling. I expect that's because Canada and America are such close neighbours."

After tea we walked across the old red square of Courtrai into a sort of grey cloister where the members of the lay sisterhood called Beguines lived in a little walled village of their own. It was so serene there. Two centuries divided the walled village from the square. That day there were no planes in the sky and the little black Beguines were safe and serene behind their wall. A week later all the little secluded Beguines joined the citizens of Courtrai on the road to Paris. . . .

Then we took the route again for the frontier. Now down the road came thundering a long line of evenly spaced great camouflaged trucks followed by rows of little guns mounted on rattling tractors, and shrieking flocks of goggle-eyed motorcycle corps. Trotter said: "Holy Mike, they're pouring in fast." We came to a town where the streets were lined with eager people with armfuls of flowers waiting for the British troops to come through. A few miles out of the town we began to pass the troops coming up the wide glistening road. "Scots Guards and the Queen's Own Westminsters," said the English boy proudly.

I remembered how everybody had remarked that it was funny the soldiers didn't sing in this war. Well, these soldiers were singing—singing because they were marching into battle, the bravest and best and youngest of England, singing as their fathers sang—the old war songs, *Tipperary*, and *So Long, Sally*, and their most popular new song, "Roll out the barrel, We're going to have a barrel of fun!" Mrs.

Gibson and I leaned out of the car and waved and yelled "Hello," and they stuck up their thumbs in the new gesture they had, which meant "O.K., everything's fine," and winked and blew cheerful kisses as soldiers on the march always do when they pass smiling women.

Then we left the troops behind, and soon passed an air field that had been bombed. But except for that, and the fact that nowhere for miles were there men in the fields, only women and boys, there was nothing this far back in Belgium to show that this smiling countryside, this Flanders, was so soon to be the cockpit of hell. We sped down long lanes of green poplars. I suddenly remembered the Chemin des Dames as I had seen it a month after the last war—the trees splintered and fractured and beheaded by the dreadful Black Death—all the land around a hideous, muddy dump-pile. It's almost unimaginable what war can do to the land. It disembowels it, rots it, and makes it look like a giant black man dying fearsomely of leprosy. But the sun makes trees grow again, and rains cure earth of its wounds. Men do not arise.

I thought of what English General Carton de Wiart had said just before he went off on his Norwegian command. (General de Wiart had been wounded many times. He had only one arm and one eye left from the last war. He was a tough soldier out of Kipling, full of shy gallantry and honest chivalry. If you hugged him he'd have blushed and popped bullets.) "War," he said, "does one good thing—it makes you see what a man is made of." I thought if *only* you could see what a man is made of without strewing it all over the ground!

Later we passed the monument at Vimy Ridge that the Duke of Windsor had dedicated, when he was King, to the men who had given up there even more than a throne. Lots of people saw what those men were made of, I thought—blood and bowels and bones, and what good is it now? And I thought: "Behind us another generation of young men are marching again into an inferno that will know no parallel in history, singing as they march, and what will they prove?" How often my French and English friends had said to me: "All we need from America is credit. We don't need men." "Oh, they don't need men now," I thought, "but they'll need them later."

And there on the road to the left was a sign: Armentières—"Oh, Mademoiselle from Armenteer, parlay-voo. . . ." And, seeing it, I knew beyond any shadow of doubt in my own mind that the Yanks would not be coming to see Mademoiselle again in Armentières. . . . Too late or too little or both. . . . In any case the Yanks aren't coming, the Yanks aren't coming, they'll stay where they are till it's over, over here. . . .

So on that beautiful Whitsuntide at last we reached the frontier. The frontier was closed. We had great trouble getting across because we had no military *laissez-passer*, and because we had no papers for our car. Mrs. Gibson, who was a patient, lovely, wise woman, explained to the little French official at the barrier how we just couldn't stop to get them at the last minute.

She said: "Do understand, *c'est la guerre*," and he answered: "*Oui, c'est la guerre*, but I shall be held responsible!" She talked and laughed, and laughed and talked, and asked the official all about his family, and what he thought of the Germans, and said how difficult it must be for him to discriminate between spies and proper people at frontiers in war time. Everything he said she disagreed with at first, and then said: "*Now* I see your point, I do agree with you." So finally he was very charmed and let us across.

After we got over and were well on the way, the Canadian boy said: "I don't like it."

"What don't you like?" I asked.

He said, "Well, damn it, it *is* a war, and our papers *weren't* in order, and—well, if he had been a German official, he would never have let us across. That's what's wrong with the Allies. They still don't know this is a war."

We got to Lille a short while after dark. Lille had been ineffectually bombed that day, and R.A.F. pursuit planes had driven the Germans off and brought down a plane, so everybody in town was in a good mood. In the café of the hotel there were dozens of English officers, and several war correspondents who had already been to Brussels and come back to file their dispatches from the Lille telegraph station. They all said, cheerfully: "We're for it, but, thank God, it's come at last."

The correspondents said: "We've got something to write about now."

We slept in little flower-papered rooms on beds stuffed with ossified rice puddings. I was so very tired I thought I was just having more nightmares, but the next day the aviators said: "Last night we had another ineffectual air raid."

That afternoon we reached Paris. Somehow getting back to Paris was like arriving at a summer resort. The Ritz corridors were buzzing with small groups of tense, excited familiar faces, although I saw at once that the ranks of the Harpies had already been thinned by the news.

It was not that people were happy—how could they be?—but they, too, were glad it had begun, because when a thing's begun, it's that much nearer being finished. Everybody felt that at last the *real* front had been found, and that this real front was much farther from Paris than in their most optimistic dreams they had thought it would be.

That night I went to a dinner party in Versailles with some friends. On the way back we were caught on the boulevard Suchet by the *alerte.* It had hardly begun when there was the savage crack of the anti-aircraft guns, and shells began to burst among the stars, and the pale, thin, greedy fingers of the searchlights threaded the sky. A gendarme with a cross little whistle stopped our car, made us get out and go into the cellar of an apartment house.

"Why should they want to bomb Paris tonight?" I asked. "They've got better things to do with their shells in Belgium."

"Why?" the gendarme replied. "Because the Germans are stupid, that's the sort of stupid thing they do!"

The cellar was full of muttering men and nervous women and sleepy children. One of the women said, "I am very tired of this. I wish it would end. This is not a life for *ordinary* people to lead. Why can't the Germans let our soldiers fight this war? *C'est tout de même insupportable.*"

I thought, uneasily: "Has it then become unbearable so soon?"

An hour later the all-clear came. We went up into the starlit night again. I thought that what made them so mad about an air raid was the indignity it visits on the spirit of ordinary people. They must quietly submit to an evil they cannot combat in any way. Airmen raining death on them —it is so hard for them to believe that man can soar so high and sink so low.

That was May the 12th. Then for six days the ugliest battle and perhaps the one that mattered most in the world convulsed the soil of Belgium and France and multiplied the population of hell. Holland fell, and Brussels. *And the bridges on the Meuse were not blown up. . . . Ah! the bridges on the Meuse were not blown up! And the Ger-*

mans have broken through at Sedan!

But Paris in the spring was still Paris in Maytime. The air was sweet and in the gardens of the Luxembourg and the Bois, the unstartled birds sang. In the Quartier Latin bosomy women with grey hair, plain faces, black aprons, and string bags still ambled to market with long loaves of bread under their arms, and in the gilded corridors of the Ritz although now nearly all of them had gone, one or two bosomy old women with bleached hair and painted faces and less imagination than their sisters still minced along cuddling their pedigreed dogs. Taxis tooted on the boulevards, glasses clinked on the marble tops of the bistro tables, the flower market at the Madeleine was madly colourful, and clocks in the towers calmly struck the hours. On days like this, how could there be a war? It was illusion, of course. It was the insanely beautiful May weather that made Paris *look the same*. Paris had really changed to the core of its being. Paris was at last at war. On May 16 an official proclamation had put Paris in *la zone des armées*. The shrieks of the dying in the burning Ardennes were not heard on the Grands Boulevards and the Champs-Élysées, but the echo had driven the last little rich child out of Paris and called up *all* the young men now.

Now at the Gare du Nord and the Gare de l'Est, where the trains came in from the north, you could very clearly hear the sobs of the refugees. Dutch and Belgians and French all pouring into a country, into a part of a country, that all together was not so big as New York State. They came off the trains with their bewildered faces, white faces, bloody faces, faces beaten out of human shape by the Niagaras of human tears that had flowed down them. The plain and tragic and innocent faces of the people, the people who "must be left nothing but their eyes to weep with," as

Sheridan said. Now you saw that Hitler, if need be, would not even leave them their eyes. With bicycles and bundles and battered suitcases, holding twisted bird-cages, babies, and dogs in stiff arms, or holding one another up, they came and came and came. . . . What Victor Hugo, what Shakespeare, what Dostoevsky could tell the Iliad of their woes? The great stations echoed with the saga of their suffering and numbed your brain and sometimes almost your heart.

Do you know what big guns and incendiary bombs and machine-guns are? Do you know what they can do to houses and to roads and to the people on them? Imagine the worst things you can. They all happened in Holland and Belgium and France, things which, if you heard a part of them, would make you squirm with horror, rage, disgust. Quaking, ill old grandparents, half-mad mothers, starving children, the young, the old, the crippled, all driven like leaves before the horrible furnace on wheels that Flanders was now.

Now here, "safe" in the railroad stations, they still faced a desperate future, full of more bombings and burnings and wanderings, facing it with nothing but those tear-drenched, hastily tied small bundles on their backs. I thought: "If the Germans can keep on giving this to ordinary people, the ordinary people *cannot*, will not, take it long! It is not in the nature of ordinary people to do so."

Everybody in Paris was wonderfully kind to the refugees. The stations were full of volunteers. Tireless, white-faced little French Boy Scouts helped them off the trains and stacked their bicycles and bundles in careful confusion. Red Cross nurses bathed their blistered feet and patched their battered faces, and gave the children oranges and chocolates to suck. Rich American expatriates (I saw now there were many good ones) rushed around saying to the nurses in loud and strident (and blessed) voices: "What do you need? Bandages, alcohol, felt slippers? We'll buy them, we'll buy them!" And the nurses would say: "Today we need nipples for bottles; we can't feed the little babies, they choke out of cups." So the American women in their big long cars drove into the city to buy what the nurses wanted. French volunteer nurses with pearl ear-rings and delicate, manicured hands painted the blistered feet of old peasants with iodine and changed babies' diapers, and wiped up the retch from bomb-shocked stomachs, and boiled coffee and milk and potatoes over smelly stoves. They told you how really awful it was for them when some poor woman discovered that the baby in the bundle in her arms was dead. She had been crying so hard she had not known it, and then she stopped crying and just looked, and said: "Here, he is yours now." And they told you how they both pitied and feared the refugees until after their papers were cleared. The refugees remained in these stations for hurtful, lingering hours. Their papers had to be checked and re-checked by the police because Hitler was so clever he had sent in many fifth-columnists with them. They said: "We fear them, because these wretched cattle are used as his Trojan horse." Ambulances (many of them with the names of American donors painted on their sides) came and went and came and went, carrying away the broken little ones and the weary old ones and the wounded ones. But there were not Scouts enough, volunteers enough, nurses enough, rich Americans enough, iodine and milk and beds and ambulances enough; not enough of anything in the stations for the incalculable tide of misery that flowed into them and that you knew then was going to flow all over France for many, many more days. But I don't think the French really knew it then.

An old, old Frenchwoman said to me: "Three times in my life the Germans have driven me off my land, but always I have gone back." And here in the station, as in the drawing-rooms, everybody asked, desperately but honestly: "Remember the Marne? *On les aura.*"

After their papers were cleared the wide green Paris buses came and the refugees were piled in and driven through the town to big barracks, to huge *casernes*, which the soldiers had evacuated for them. There in thousands, in the hot sun, sitting on bundles, they waited many more hours, to be sorted out in truckloads and sent to quiet parts of France, to little villages which were ordered to take them in and try to care for them.

An American newspaper man said to me: "The terrible thing is that all the villages are full now. Most of them will have to sleep in the fields for the summer. There is not now food enough, beds enough, or shelter enough in all France for the ones who have come already. France still does not realize that Hitler has turned it into a half-starving alien gypsy camp."

I said, "The American Red Cross will send them money."

He answered: "They need material, not money. How can we send that? In our ships? You know the neutrality law."

I said: "A way will be found."

"Yes," he said, "but not in time." That was the first instance I heard anyone in Europe in the spring say: "but *not* in time."

Whenever I came back from the stations, long after my ears had forgotten the noises of trains and baggage trucks and the confused shuffling of blistered feet on the cold cement and the shouts of the old, old porters and the horns of the cars and the ambulance bells and the clattering of tin cups on the wooden buffets—even after I had forgotten the hurt wailing of the babies and the desperate silences of the grown-ups, I could always still hear that newspaper man saying: "Yes, but not in time."

The last day I went to the Gare du Nord was May 18. The Germans had broken through along the French border at Capelle and Rethel. They were hardly seventy miles from Paris. Gamelin had given the order of day: "Conquer or die," he said. And fear, cold fear, gripped every heart. Now there were fewer volunteers with pearl ear-rings in the station, far fewer Americans.

An old Red Cross nurse, a Frenchwoman with a white face and staring eyes, put down the bowl of broth she was ladling out to the refugees and came over to me and took my arm in tense fingers.

"Madame," she said, "you are an American?"

I said: "Yes," and she went on: "Then you must tell me the truth: *qui nous a trahi*? Who has betrayed us?"

I asked: "Why do you say '*betrayed*'?"

She said, weeping: "We have the Maginot—we sacrificed so much for it—and *they* promised the Germans could not pass! And now here they are, at our very door once again!"

"Oh, please remember Verdun!"

She continued bitterly: "How can these poor people go through all that again? No, madame, we have been betrayed!" And she turned to ladle out more broth, suddenly dry-eyed.

That was the first time I heard the word "*trahi*" ("betrayed") in Paris. At first it was no more than a whisper, like the little winds that come in the dim days before the hurricane. In cafés, in bistros, in attics and *conciergeries*, in billets, in the farms: "*Trahi?*" "*Trahi?*" And then the whisper became a great wail that swept through France, a great wail of the damned: "*Trahi . . . trahi . . .*" Now it is the sullen roar that has swept away both the defenders and the betrayers of democracy in France: "*Par vous, les politiciens . . . trahis!*"

I watched the nurse for a moment as she filled a child's tin bowl. I saw with wonder that the child was laughing, banging its bowl happily with its spoon. I walked with a very heavy heart to the entrance of the station. Silhouetted against the outside sunlight there, were a girl and a soldier embracing. She gave him a long, young kiss for good-bye. Even in the middle of all this trampled fruit of hate there was still love in young people's hearts and the desire for kisses on their lips—these things must be served, though the Germans are only sixty miles from Paris. Even though they have been betrayed. . . .

I went back that day through the sparkling sunlight to the Ritz, and although I had been gone only a few hours, I could tell by the expensive luggage piled up in front of its doors that all the rue de la Paix refugees were leaving the hotel, because they too must also be properly served, which might be difficult with the Germans only sixty miles from Paris. What is treachery to them, or they to treachery?

On the doorstep I met Vincent Sheean. He looked very grim. "What is it?" I asked.

"Well, it's the thing they've decided to call the Battle of the Bulge," he answered. "But I call it the Battle for the World."

I said: "Vincent, I have been to the station. Have you been to the station?"

"No," he said. "I know all about *that*. I have seen it in Spain, it's always like that."

"But this is worse."

"Yes," he said, "this is worse."

At the revolving door we stepped aside to let a hurried indignant refugee in silver foxes come whirling through. And then Vincent Sheean told me about a fellow with yellow gloves he'd met in London a few weeks before whose finest feelings were outraged when he heard that the Republicans had once changed the name of the Ritz in Madrid to "Gastronomique Number One."

I said: "Let's have a drink in Gastronomique Number Two while we can."

Now, it wasn't remarkable that the inhabitants of the Ritz knew on May 18 how desperate the situation was. They had "contacts." But it was very interesting and wonderful how the people knew, the people in the streets and in the stations. The collective *mind* of Paris—*tout Paris*—was as sensitive during all the days of the Blitzkrieg as a barometer. Everybody knew from hour to hour just how everything was going. How did they know it? They didn't know it from the daily papers—the papers didn't say anything much except that the Germans were about where they had got to yesterday and that France was such a wonderful country, full of such wonderful soldiers, who were fighting like wildcats and angels, that it should be perfectly obvious to anybody that the Germans couldn't get any farther the next day.

They didn't get it from the refugees, either. The refugees were days on the roads and trains. Today's batch brought only the news of last week's disasters. And *tout Paris* didn't get the news from the politicians. On any given day in May most of the politicians didn't know where the front was, and I'll hazard a guess that on some days plenty of the people at General Headquarters were in the same fix. All through May the front staggered back and forth like a drunkard. It was like a giant apoplectic octopus with tanks for tentacles and nobody, even the generals[9] at "the front," knew where, from hour to hour, its tentacles were flung, nor hardly where its slimy belly lay. And what General Headquarters did know wasn't broadcast to *tout Paris*. So it wasn't from official sources that Paris got what it called its "*renseignements*," which is French for "the dope."

Paris got its information about what France had been doing all day, all night, the way a woman gets hers about what her husband has been up to. You know how a woman says, the split second her husband walks in the door with a carefully arranged smile on his face: "So things have been going badly at the office?" And he says: "My God, how did you know?" And she replies: "Because I know you so well, darling." That is how Paris, the wife, knew what was happening to France, the husband. All the smiles or frowns on the politicians' faces when they left their offices, the way military moustaches drooped or bristled at midnight, the inflections of well-known voices saying nothing or something or anything on the radio, on the telephone; the way important people walked in the street; the way ministry doors were slammed; *by the significant silences of a great race of talkers;* by a thousand little downward percolating uncensorable gestures and indications, the contagious climate of a mood spread from the top of Paris to the bottom—from clerk to doorman, to domestic, to waiter, to policeman, to taxi-driver, to the people—so that the people of Paris knew from hour to hour how the fate of France fared. France was Paris; Paris

[9] The Germans announced in May that General Giraud had been captured, with his entire staff, when returning from a tour of "the front"; he had walked into his own headquarters and found the Germans there! The French version of the story was different. A World War I hero, now brave Giraud, to rally the morale of his shattered troops, got into a tank with his staff and bucked the enemy lines.

was France. This explains the most curious phenomenon of the first few weeks of the Blitzkrieg in Paris: how fear could grip the city in an icy chill at midnight, and then how calm could reign in every cellar and garret by midday—though there had been no new communiqués, and nothing new in the news.

The first few days after Weygand took command Paris breathed confidence again as gently as a child who has fallen asleep exhausted after a nightmare. The people were sure that Weygand had what it took and what Hitler couldn't stop. (In early March nearly everybody was saying: "What we need are *young* leaders. The world needs young men with vision to get us out of this mess." And then when the mess became a panic, they had rushed off and got Churchill and Pétain and Weygand,[10] whose ages, if you put them end to end, would take you back to the time of Louis XIV.) The first few days of the Battle of the Bulge everybody believed that the Germans were monstrous supermen who couldn't be stopped. They hadn't been stopped, but now, simply because the French people had confidence in eighty-four-year-old Pétain and seventy-three-year-old Weygand, they felt the Germans might be stopped. This didn't mean that everybody in Paris was happy. Everybody was desperately miserable. They were merely confident again for a very few days, which is something else. The French realized more than ever that what the Germans meant by a total war was a total war for France, that they wouldn't leave a house or a tree standing, or a woman or child alive, if they could help it. And they had finally realized that the Germans had a new war technique to implement that awful decision—the war of movement.

[10] Churchill was made Prime Minister on May 10; Pétain made technical adviser on military operations May 18; Weygand generalissimo on May 19.

Before the invasion nearly everybody in France who was really thinking about war, was thinking about it in terms of firm battle-lines and forts and trenches and "fronts." Now they knew that the real Front in France was the entire blue sky over it, and that the Germans were already bombing that front from the coast to the Maginot and back, and from the Belgian border to Versailles. They were dropping parachutists with thermite bombs, with flaming torches, in villages defended and undefended. They were sending tanks, like clever gigantic cockroaches scurrying across a kitchen shelf, through all the French lines and back to the dark holes they came from. They were driving civilian populations here and there with bombers, cluttering the roads and machine-gunning them and the troop columns coming up, and ambulance trains, with equal ferocity. This war was total. When the French realized that, although everybody in Paris felt, after Weygand first took command, that the chances of the Germans getting away with it for long were lessened, nobody in Paris was at all cheerful.

When the Germans started in the direction of the sea, everybody in Paris began to try to outguess Mr. Hitler. "Maybe he's going to England first," they said hopefully, and the steady drive of the German armies to the coast even after they passed Laon gave some body to the hope. On May 19, when the Germans were at Rethel, apparently driving toward Paris, Churchill had tried to comfort the terrified French. He said it would be foolish to suppose that "well-trained, well-equipped armies, numbering three or four [11] millions of men, can be overcome in the space of a few weeks, or even months, by a swoop or raid of mechanized vehicles, however formidable." But when, two days later, the Ger-

[11] Three *or* four millions? There's quite a difference!

mans reached Abbeville, the English felt the time had come to stop encouraging the French for a moment and warn the English. Alfred Duff Cooper said that day: "We now may expect invasion at any time." What became the fear of the English became once again the hope of Frenchmen.

But, either way, there was something which kept bothering the French as well as the English. "Why," it was asked, "haven't the Germans really bombed Paris? Or London?" Everybody was quite sure that it was for a logical German reason and not a sentimental one. Paris and London are very big, they said to comfort themselves, and it would take prodigious quantities of explosives to really raze them; and their air defences were good—you knew that when you heard them whamming away every night. And besides, the Germans had other work on their minds at the moment. But everybody in Paris and London knew that if they hadn't been badly bombed by that time it was not because Hitler admired the contents of the Louvre or had a sentimental attachment for 10 Downing Street—anyway not since Chamberlain had left it. So while, even after the Germans had reached Abbeville, Paris was still calm, and the stamp market was flourishing on the avenue Marigny, and the book-stalls were still open on the Left Bank, there was still no dancing in the streets, and the people were heartsick and afraid.

•

From the day when the Germans broke through at Sedan and crossed the Meuse, the drawing-rooms of Paris, the sidewalk cafés, and the bars where the news men gathered became a hotbed of rumours that flew from lip to ear and ear to lip so fast that a few hours later *tout Paris* knew them. *On dit:* Corrap's Ninth Army was responsible—a cowardly, ill-equipped, sullen gang of Communists. They threw down their arms and made the sign of the hammer and sickle and fled. *On dit:* they were being picked up in the streets of Paris and shot. Corrap was about to be court-martialed. Corrap had been shot.[12] Corrap had committed suicide. *On dit:* the bridges on the Meuse were not blown up because fifth-columnists disguised as priests and farmers entered the switch-control huts where loyal French soldiers stood waiting for the signal to blow them up, and shot them in the back. *On dit:* Reynaud and Churchill (who had flown to Paris the first day of the invasion) had ordered Gamelin to send all the Allied shock troops and heavy artillery and tanks up into Flanders, and Gamelin had refused. He insisted that France's whole strategy had been based on *defence*, and he wished to let the Belgians and Dutch bear the brunt while he dug in on the Belgian frontier. Churchill and Reynaud had prevailed,[13] Gamelin was dismissed, and Weygand, advocate of the strong attack, had been sent for, to implement a new strategy of attack. *On dit:* It was all Gamelin's fault. He had been warned of the inefficiency of the Ninth Army and had refused to do anything about it. He and General George had long been at loggerheads about that and everything else. If they didn't shoot him he ought to commit suicide. *On dit:* in the ministries they were already burning their papers; they were moving secretly to Tours. . . . Reynaud was refusing to move the government; he felt it would

[12] Everybody quoted Voltaire: "In this country they shoot a general from time to time to encourage the others."

[13] A few days after the invasion Churchill said: "I have invincible confidence in the French army and its leaders . . . [but] the armies must cast away the idea of resisting attack behind concrete lines or natural obstacles, and must realize that mastery can only be regained by furious and unrelenting assault. . . ." It does seem that the first casualty of the blitzkrieg was Liddell Hart's theory of defence. After the surrender Paul Baudouin, Foreign Minister, said: "The first serious strategic error of the manœuvre occurred on May 10 when the French army left its trenches at England's demand and rushed into the Lowlands and the fatal Battle of the Meuse."

have a terrible psychological effect on the people.[14] The English were insisting that the government move so Paris could be defended. . . . *On dit:* They were quarrelling night and day whether or not to defend Paris. If the Germans destroyed Paris, they would have destroyed France. If the French government refused to defend Paris, it was refusing to defend France. . . . But everywhere rumour, riding frightened, unleashed tongues like a mad jockey, told of counsels divided in the highest places. The French were distraught; only the English in Paris were calm. I think now that only the Americans really knew what the end had to be.

The British colonel said to me: "Don't be such an alarmist. Remember the last war, how in the spring of 1917 when General Nivelle was placed in supreme command of the French armies for the defence of Verdun, he made quite disastrous blunders . . . but we survived them. We will survive these. Naturally the French are a bit hysterical, telling all these tall tales, which quite possibly are true. No matter what our goodwill, we all do inevitably tend to look at things from a rather national point of view. But, as I say, just remember the last war." You see? . . .

St. George he was for England;
St. Denis was for France;
Sing Honi Soit . . .

And all the while the Bulge was lengthening quickly, like a long sausage balloon blown from the powerful lungs of the Teuton, everybody asked: "Why don't we prick it at this point, or at that? Why don't the Flanders troops fall back behind it?" And Rumour, swifter even than Hitler's tanks, gaining strength through terror, answered: Weygand

[14] The government moved to Tours on June 10, to Bordeaux on June 14.

ordered the English and French to retreat into France, but Churchill insisted that the English fall back to the coast to defend the Channel ports.[15]. . . And all the while the balloon bulge grew fatter and longer, until desperate hope counselled it must burst of its own pressure, and when finally it reached to Abbeville across France, everybody, groaning, asked: "Why, oh, why don't the French attack it from the south, and the English from the north? Then the balloon will burst and our armies be joined and the Germans trapped, as they have trapped us." Rumour cried aloud: The English, *God damn the English! They insist, they still insist on defending those ports!* . . .

But the English in Paris said calmly: "Don't you see?—we can't attack from the north: the Allied guns and tanks that Gamelin ordered to steam up into Flanders so recklessly are all turned the *wrong way* now, and our lines of communications and reinforcement are cut!"

And now the Battle of the Bulge was over, and the Battle of Flanders began. *On dit:* Weygand is making an attack from the south. He'll get through to them. If he can't get through to them, they are lost . . . lost! And as the attack never came, rumour grew: *On dit:* We haven't really got tanks enough, or planes enough. The English won't send enough planes; they are afraid for their own island now. Now they say they need them for "home defence." Oh, God damn the English! Oh, God, we can't win if we can't *dig in soon somewhere.* Weygand must see that! Everybody in France can *feel* it!

[15] After the surrender Baudouin said: "Weygand . . . tried to close the Artois gap . . . asked the British to strike south . . . while the French drove north. . . . The British delayed for two days . . . raced northwards to the [Channel] ports. . . . German divisions poured through the gap. . . . If the British army had obeyed [Weygand's] orders, the gap could have been closed."

Little by little Paris, and all of France, had begun to feel in its bones that the "reasonable expectation of victory" was hourly becoming an "unreasonable hope of just holding on." Then morale began slowly but surely to crumble.

Everybody desperately tried to hold it together a little while longer with small sticking-plasters of quotations from history. They quoted Napoleon, that "most battles are won by General Luck." They quoted Joffre, that "a battle won is a battle in which you won't admit defeat." They quoted Foch: "My right has been rolled up, my left has been driven back, my centre is smashed. I have ordered an advance from all directions." And Marshal MacMahon: "Here I am, here I stay."

Captain Brousse, his dark brave eyes very sombre, quoted Homer. "Remember," he said, "when bold Hector into battle went against the Greeks, he saw before him in the sky a soaring eagle bearing in his claws a dragon, which the eagle dropped, and Hector's councillors advised him that it was an evil omen for the Trojan cause. But Hector marched right on and said: 'The best of omens is our country's cause.' " And then, because he thought it would please me, he said: "Your fort is firing hard today. You will see—the Maginot Line is where we will win after all." That is what every Frenchman tried to feel at that zero hour.

Nobody quoted Voltaire, that "God is always on the side of the big battalions."

Now Paris began to talk about the Germans with a strange and awful respect. They said: "They are religious maniacs, you know. They don't care if they die, if their Führer is pleased." And they all told you the story about the dying German pilot who refused a blood transfusion because he would rather die than have "unclean French blood" in his veins. And about the parachutist who landed in a field guarded by French soldiers, and did not surrender, but emptied his pistol into them, taking careful aim, and then fired the last bullet into his own brain. And about the German infantryman who said: "Please don't say anything about my Führer," and then, smiling, died. . . .

And even on the days when the people of Paris went to Notre-Dame and the Madeleine and prayed in anguished voices: "Our Lady of France, save us! Our Lady of France, save us!" they rushed home and turned on their radios to hear the German broadcast of the news.

My good Catholic French maid said: "*Et pourquoi pas, madame?* The Germans have not yet died of the 'lies' *they* tell on the radio. Our government tells us nothing but lies."

Then the terror of the "fifth-columnists" began. The German radios broadcast to the "home front" the names of people working beside them on factory benches, the rich and delicious menus that ministers had had at some public function the night before, the movements of their own troops a few hours before they were made. . . .

A typical story was the one told to me by Bertrand de Jouvenel, a young French journalist, who said that when he had been in Germany several years before, he had been fond of reading a small technical German magazine. "Today," he said, "I received a recent copy of it in the mail, and on the cover was scribbled: 'From an old German acquaintance who just wants you to know *he* is in Paris, too!' That's terrifying," he said. "That's going on everywhere."

At the end of May there were very few Americans left in Paris. I realized with a sinking heart that most of the familiar faces I saw now belonged to what Vincent Sheean called the Vultures of the Press—the newspaper boys who had been in Madrid, in Warsaw, in Prague, in Helsinki, in Oslo, when "it happened." [16] H. R. Knickerbocker and Virginia Cowles and Arthur Mencken and many others sat late in bars or, when they closed, in hotel rooms, where they weighed all these rumours and sifted these mottoes of faith and found very dark answers indeed.

I remember one such night. It was the night, I believe, the Germans reached Rethel, and everybody believed they were then heading straight for Paris. Vincent Sheean, Knickerbocker, Louis Huot (of Press Wireless) and I sat in my brightly lit, pretty little blue and white salon in the Ritz. The satin curtains were drawn against the beautiful spring night. In the distance you could hear the bark of anti-aircraft guns. We felt the war now in the pits of our stomachs. And while we talked about what the three liquid-air bombs the Germans had dropped in Madrid had done to the city (everything was laid flat for a quarter of a mile, Sheean said, and a half-mile away the repercussion sucked out your eardrums so they bled for an hour), we tried not to think about how it was out there now in the cold moonlight where the awful racket of the unwearied guns and bombs fell on the forever deaf ears of those who were sleeping the iron sleep of death. It was no use, that is all we could think of or talk about on that lovely, lovely night of the blitzkrieg.

I said: "I went out with an ambulance today. You know, evacuating refugees. The driver told me that she had been at Vouziers several days before, to get the wounded out of the base hospital that had just been bombed there. She said the doctors and nurses had gone right on operating, because the operating-room hadn't been touched. She said when the doctors and nurses came out of the operating-room, she

[16] With very few exceptions, the foreign correspondents never got to the front. The invariable answer from the Bureau d'Information and G.H.Q. was: "Later, later, when the picture has cleared."

thought at first: 'How funny! They're all wearing *high red shoes*.' "

Louis Huot said: "All right, that's enough. Let's have a drink. Let's talk about America for a change."

Red-haired, ardent Knickerbocker said bitterly: "Well, New York is only three thousand miles away, but Ohio is forty-five hundred and California is six thousand. And *sure* it's nice to be able to say that even at six thousand miles away everybody at home is highly indignant. But will that righteous indignation stop Mr. Hitler? Not by a damn sight! Is it important for America to keep Hitler out of Paris? Is it? *Is it?* Why don't people in America please stop being 'sorry for refugees' and 'ninety-eight per cent sympathetic to the Allies,' and answer that question God-damn quick?"

"You think it is our war?" I asked, and he said:

"Hell, yes."

I said: "Write them that," and he retorted violently: "That's not what my editors want, it's not what my readers want. They want 'local colour' from Paris! They want to read how all the taxicabs have been requisitioned to send troops to the front, followed by a short biography of long dead and gone Gallieni! They want to hear how people are examined by armed police in the cafés to find fifth-columnists. How crowded but calm the subway shelters are in an air raid. How the grass in the gardens of the Tuileries hasn't been cut this spring, owing to more important operations and pressing amputations. Local colour from the press at any price! But the colour of men's souls on both sides of what is not a one-way ocean they're not interested in. No, by God! They're interested in hearing nothing that will arouse anything in them but 'pity' and 'righteous indignation.' Above all, don't make them think what America will have to face if France and England fall; don't make them think—not in an election year, anyway! So what are we American journalists doing here? I'll tell you: writing thrilling little Baedekers for Armageddon! And God, the whole time most of us would like to throw all these palpitating details of dirty and gallant deeds into the ash-can and ask our editors and readers one question: 'Look, folks back home, if we let France fall, can we say that what we call Democracy is good enough *anywhere*?'" Those are not Knickerbocker's exact words, but they are the gist of them.

Ah, the poor American journalists in France! They knew, they saw the defeat that was coming, but gagged by the violence of incredibly stupid French censorship, hamstrung by criminal American indifference to the real issues at stake, in the end they all wrote—little Baedekers to Europe's Armageddon.

By the end of May it had begun to be a painful thing to be an American in Paris. Although all the important French people still went on saying: "*On les aura*" ("We'll get them yet"), they were not at all sure of it, and as they became daily, hourly, less sure, they grew violently interested in what America was going to do about it. "Will America send us planes, quick?" they all asked with agonized eagerness, and I replied: "Of course—if we have them." When I admitted unhappily that I wasn't really sure we had them, they said: "Go home! Go home now, and tell everybody, anybody, we've got to have them! [17] In God's name, can democracies never learn? Won't you profit in time by the

[17] They wanted me to *go home* and tell everybody because, incredible as it may seem, you could not cable or broadcast from Paris, owing to censorship, the tragic direness of the need. And when Eve Curie and Vincent Sheean finally prevailed on the censors to allow them to broadcast "modified appeals," their appeals were censored by the broadcasting companies from the New York end!

lesson Hitler is teaching us?"

Now had come the end of the Battle of Flanders, and the beginning of the evacuation. I watched with fear the hatred of the French for the English growing by giant leaps and bounds. Many people now quite openly blamed the whole horrible fiasco on the English High Command, or on some rumoured counter-order of Churchill's, which had marred Weygand's last attempt to get through. Still, my sympathies and admiration were all with the French. They were tough and sentimental and ferocious all at once in that incredible zero hour. And there was so much individual gallantry and decency among them.[18] It was splendid the way nearly all Paris still turned out to help the refugees, the way the soldiers smiled and waved to you as they rumbled rapidly through the streets in great truckloads going off to the front, which was rumbling as rapidly to meet them. The stoicism and cheerfulness of wounded soldiers in hospitals, and the gentleness of the good weary Sisters that cared for them there, were doubly magnificent because they knew they, too, were doomed. And you liked them so for the decent way most of them still behaved in air raids, which were coming more frequently now. I got a bird's-eye view of the way *tout Paris* behaved when one day I bummed a ride on an ambulance which was evacuat-

18 Most people were never too busy, never too sad, to do something, anything, for France which might help. M. Gillet, an old friend of mine, a silk-manufacturer from Lyon, telephoned me one day: "I have heard that you are having trouble with the authorities in getting permission for that photographer friend of yours to photograph the refugees. I have this morning made it my business to call a few influential friends on your behalf." "Thank you so much," I said, and then: "How is it going with you, M. Gillet?" "Oh," he said in a colourless voice, "all of my factories at Lille have been destroyed. And I have heard nothing from my three sons who are in Flanders. But one hopes for the best. Take care of yourself. Don't stay too long. Au revoir." It was very often like that in May in Paris.

ing convalescent soldiers from the big hospitals to the small ones because the big ones were expecting a very special rush clientele from "out there."

Now, ambulances don't stop during air raids, so we whizzed through the streets of Paris although all the other cars parked, and their drivers headed for the nearest shelters. Then you could see how differently people act in an air raid—some sauntered to the shelters, some ran, some just stood in doorways looking curiously at the sky. But none were panicky. In the end the gendarmes made everyone go to shelter. One little Frenchman on the street I shall never forget. He had a spade-shaped white beard, and a cane and spats, and as he sauntered along doggedly, his beard pointed at the sixteen planes which were crossing the blue sky in formations of three. Suddenly he sidled a bit and sort of sidestepped gingerly, as though by suddenly drawing in his slim waist and jumping nimbly back he could cleverly avoid a bomb if it fell at his very feet. The planes were French pursuit planes, sweeping the sky of the invaders. (I wished with all my heart that the nimble old gentleman had known that.) In a way that little old gentleman typified France. He was old and tired and gallant, but he was living in another age, and he still hoped by sheer last-minute resourcefulness to avoid death and destruction. By his actions you could tell he at least had a reasonable expectation of that victory.

On May 28 the King of the Belgians surrendered. It was a very bitter day in Paris. Enraged Parisians began to throw Belgian refugees out of their houses, and to burn their poor carts in the streets, and heckle and buffet them in the stations and on the highroads, until this tragic scandal was stopped by the government, which threatened to imprison anyone who molested a Belgian. Overnight the "brave Belgians, our allies," changed colour in the eyes of Paris as they seemed to reflect the yellow of "noble Leopold's" action. Now everybody said: "We always knew he was pro-German! We always felt he was a traitor."

A gendarme said to me bitterly: "His father was killed in an accident, mountain-climbing. His wife was killed in an automobile accident while he was driving!" He put a sly finger to his nose. "Accidents? I wonder now if they were accidents." [19]

But Leopold's surrender had the dubious merit of briefly healing the growing breach in Anglo-French relations, which, badly strained by the Bulge disaster, had been about to snap when it became apparent that the English were going to get most of the benefit of any evacuation, and the French would be left to fight their way back to France alone.[20] The surrender of Leopold drew a shortlived red herring across the military bungling of the whole campaign and offered a convenient explanation of the inevitable evacuation to both the French and the English people. Now everybody said the whole disastrous course of the war, from the very day of the invasion, was "engineered" by Belgian treachery. That's why the bridges on the Meuse weren't blown up, that's why Eben Emael and Liége fell so quickly, that's why . . . But you are not stronger for having one *less* ally, even if you like the one you have left the better for it. The French knew that. So while they were happier in one way because they could now blame the Belgians, in

[19] That's what I'm wondering now about the automobile accident of Reynaud and Hélène de Portes, and the strange accident which killed General Billotte, group commander of all the Armies of the North, an hour after his secret meeting with Weygand in Flanders on May 25 to tell the new generalissimo what had gone wrong in Flanders.

[20] Paul Baudouin said in July: "The British furnished only 14,000 troops for rear-guard action . . . the remainder of the 200,000 were French. . . . They saved four-fifths of their troops . . . we lost half of ours."

another way they were infinitely more despairful than they had been (even than when they had thought the week before that the Germans were headed straight for Paris). They knew now that they had irrevocably lost the aid of the whole British army, and that on France's soil there would soon be only Frenchmen, tired and doubting Frenchmen, left to defend it.

Ever since my return from Brussels I had been trying—perhaps not desperately, but nevertheless trying—to get back to New York. In the middle of May I had bogged down in official red tape over my Spanish and Portuguese visas, which I needed to get to Lisbon to take the Clipper I had reserved passage on.

In spite of the pressure put on me by good friends, in spite of a firmly worded letter from Ambassador Bullitt, I quite as firmly refused to go to Bordeaux and "wait for an American ship" to call for me. I knew by this time, with a certainty that was too deep for argument, that the Germans would soon be in Paris, and that when they came to Paris, they wouldn't be long in reaching Bordeaux. (Paris was France.) Finally I decided to go by plane to London. (Besides, I wanted to see what the English thought about the war now.) That was a very strange and difficult business to arrange (almost as difficult and involved as the Maginot trip), but it has no bearing on this tale except as it illuminates a comment made to me by Louis Huot. When I told him of the infinite pieces of stamped paper some twenty officials and military men had made me sign and the hours and hours spent in getting them—by wheedling, cajolery, and flattery, by friendly pressure applied in high places, and gentle bribery in low ones—he said: "When this war is over, you will see that what defeated France was Communism, defence psychology, and *papier timbré*, but most of all *papier timbré*"—which is to say, red tape and rotten bureaucracy.[21]

At last, on May 31, my papers and passport were in order. I went, as ordered, to Le Bourget airport at seven o'clock in the morning. A French plane was on the ground waiting to go. At eleven o'clock the sailing was cancelled without explanation.

"What do we do now?" I asked the airport official.

He shrugged. "Go back to Paris if you wish. Or wait; who knows? Perhaps an English plane will come in. If it goes back with an empty seat you can have it. If it doesn't—" He shrugged again. "*C'est la guerre, madame!*"

I waited—until six o'clock that night. An English plane did come in, and I was lucky to get an empty seat. By nine o'clock, flying by a southern route, I reached Heston and went to London.

While I was sitting in the great barren airport waiting-room, a very beautiful and heartening thing was said to me.

A calm little Frenchman sat down in a chair near me, opened up a copy of *Paris Soir*, and began to read it thoroughly. He had grey hair, grey suède gloves and grey spats, a black Homburg hat, and a black brief-case, so I knew right away he was a diplomat. When he had finished every word of the paper, I asked him in English if I might borrow it. Naturally that started a conversation. We talked about the chances of an English plane coming in, and I told him I hoped I was on my way back to America. Then he said:

[21] Captain Hoffman Nickerson, writing in *Harper's* in August about "The New German Military Theory," said: "The jungle of written orders which was cited everywhere during the trench warfare of 1914 to 1918 was wholly swept away. Even division commanders were taught to issue them seldom and then very briefly. Every subordinate commander was constantly thrown on his own initiative, both as to how he should execute the directions which his immediate chief outlined to him in a handful of words and as to how he should act when wholly on his own."

"I am a French diplomat attached to our Embassy in London." And as we talked, and as he realized I was truly unhappy and despairful for France, he said: "Do not despair, madame, I do not despair. Something good must come of all this. This is a world revolution, and when we peoples of the democracies see what we have lost in money and life and human dignity by not sticking together, we will start our own counter-revolution to unite the world—to unite the world under some free system."

I smiled (because he reminded me so much of the Baroness in Holland) and said: "But if France is beaten—if England is lost—where will this revolution start?"

And he answered: "*You* would like me to say in America. I don't think so. I think America must first learn her lesson in sacrifice and bloodshed. America will betray herself to her enemies at home and abroad, as we have. No," he went on, "the counter-revolution will begin in my country, in France. I believe," he said, smiling, "that the history of nations' souls repeats itself!" I smiled back at him and said: "You are perhaps the only truly confident man in France today."

"*Oui*," he replied. "Let me tell you a story." He was, he said, a captain at Verdun in the last war. The first day he was in the trenches, the barrage was so frightful it made the heavens tremble, and the next dawn it began again, and the following dawn it was the same. And the death that the Germans' cannon belched was quite prodigious. The third night, he said, "of my regiment thirty men were left, and that night I said to myself: 'The battle is surely lost. Tomorrow at dawn—because, after all, life is the thing most precious—I will crawl out of my trench and I will do as soldiers have done time without number—surrender to the enemy.' " All night he thought happily how he would do that, and he couldn't sleep, watching the star rockets and the red flames from the guns, and saying: "Tomorrow I live." Then as the fourth dreadful dawn began to break, he suddenly said to himself: "Ah, but tomorrow not even tomorrow can I live *for ever!* And those short years I live, I shall not be happy. I shall always know that I am the man who surrendered." So, he said, although it was not easy to do, he decided when the sun hit the summer horizon to rise from the trench, his rifle turned to the sound of the guns, saying: "Good morning, Death. I believe what I believe in." And that is what he did. Of course he was not killed (because there he was talking to me), and the next day the German barrage was not so heavy, and the next not so heavy as the day before, and everybody knows who in the end won the Battle of Verdun. "Since that day," the little grey-haired diplomat said, "I have had my motto: *Il n'y a pas de situations désespérées, il y a seulement des hommes désespérés* (There are no hopeless situations; there are only men who have grown hopeless about them)."

May his sons be many!

TEN

MESSENGER: *My honourable lords, health to you all!*
Sad tidings bring I to you out of France,
Of loss, of slaughter and discomfiture:
Guienne, Champagne, Reims, Orléans,
Paris, Guysors, Poictiers, are all quite lost. . . .
GLOUCESTER: *Is Paris lost? Is Rouen yielded up? . . .*
EXETER: *How were they lost? What treachery was used?*
MESSENGER: *No treachery; but want of men and money.*
Amongst the soldiers this is muttered,
That here you maintain several factions,
And whilst a field should be dispatch'd and fought,
You are disputing of your generals:
One would have lingering wars with little cost;
Another would fly swift, but wanteth wings;
A third thinks, without expense at all,
By guileful fair words peace may be obtain'd.
Awake, awake, English nobility!

Shakespeare, *in King Henry VI*

THE FIRST THING I found out in London the first of June was that everybody was enormously proud of their second splendid evacuation. Indeed, they were so full of the glory of what the London *Times* called "one of the most magnificent Naval and Military feats of all time" it was with actual displeasure that they heard Mr. Churchill say rather fiercely: "An evacuation is *not* a victory." The second thing I found out was that everybody was still saying: "England loses every battle but the last one." To be sure, it was no longer said so lightly and casually. People were really disquieted by the loss of all their best equipment in Flanders, and more than a little concerned as to whether or not they could replace it in time to send back a few properly equipped divisions to France, whose reproachfulness in the matter had begun rather to get under their skins. The English were, with very good reason, deeply proud of the heroic role the R.A.F. had played in the battle. If all was not lost when the Artois gap was not closed and in Flanders, it was because of the R.A.F., and not Gamelin's disorganized armies, they said. And besides, the French ought to realize that without the British navy nobody, including quite a number of Frenchmen, would ever have got back alive out of that Inferno. ("After all, it's our navy that's really going to win this war for us!")

While the drive to the Channel ports and the Battle of Flanders had been going on, there had been a few days of "real uneasiness" when the English thought the Germans might after all be headed toward Dover. This had resulted in a rash of sudden, unfamiliar activities in England. A quarter of a million people had volunteered as "parashooters," more trenches were dug in the London parks, gasmasks came once more off kitchen shelves and out of panelled closets, the government had agitated and continued to agitate (rather uselessly) for Londoners again to evacuate their children, who had been drifting back to London all winter and spring.[1] The A.R.P. got on its toes and called for more volunteers, and got them; and, most marvellous and incredible to behold, there were sandbagged machine-gun emplacements in front of the Admiralty and Buckingham Palace.

But in the first days of June the battle-lines had momentarily settled along the Aisne, facing France again, and there was a lull in German activity. Weygand was preparing for the battle which he later called, with such tragic prescience, "the Battle of France." (That the French instinctively knew that this was to be the last battle of the war is proved by the fact they so willingly accepted the title that Weygand gave it. There was no "Battle for France" in the last war.) So the English, I discovered, still felt they had time.

A British general himself said to me: "It took the Germans all winter and spring to prepare for the invasion of the Lowlands. The break-through at Sedan, and the surrender of Leopold, were just lucky breaks that carried them farther than they had planned, even in their optimistic moments. But that too rapid advance has this merit: it has undoubtedly exhausted them, militarily. For the big attack on France they will have to wait for their reinforcements and supplies to catch up with them. No matter how powerful they are, they'll have to *mount* their next attack properly. It takes two or three weeks to mount a major attack in modern warfare." The implication, I suppose, was that the last attack had been "mounted" improperly. (In the time it took a modern army "to mount an attack," France, over-

[1] This problem of "evacuated children" was the saddest and thorniest the government had to face. The English people had begun to realize that if "total war" hit England, the children would really be "safe" nowhere; and, this being true, their instincts told parents to keep the children by their side no matter what the government ordered. The sky over England is so small that there "ain't no hidin'-place down there. . . ."

run to its heart, had surrendered.)

So the English in early June, insensibly, once again relaxed their efforts, drawing much comfort from the fact that the Germans were headed definitely toward Paris. All that they had seen in Flanders had still not given the English any reason to believe that France's great army could be overwhelmed before winter. This left them free to consider domestic matters. The airplane-production scandal had never really "broken," but there had been enough suspicion and rumour about it to cause a complete turnover of personnel in that governmental department. Further, the English had begun as quickly as possible to abandon the stingy war principle and were now buying all they could lay their hands on at any price from America. If not so terrified, they were at least quite as shocked as the French at the discovery that the United States, as a grab-bag for the many things they now wanted quickly, was in a pretty flabby condition. This gave point to the old amused taunt, which had now become almost a bitter accusation, that America was going through her Munich. As the cry for planes, planes, and more planes had come from France, and as the heroic R.A.F. had answered as best it could (without leaving England too undefended), English entreaties to America also had become more sharp and insistent. One morning in early June I was collared by a lady Member of Parliament, a titled socialite, and a bell-boy, who all asked me in accents of varied culture but unvarying urgency: "When are you Americans going to send us enough aeroplanes?"

But one thing was certain in England in June. The average Englishman, while worried, was not, like the average Frenchman, despairful, although he, too, from time to time was shaken by unpleasant rumour. . . . "Have you heard?

The French are already negotiating a separate peace. . . . Have you heard? We haven't got those shadow factories. . . . The government hasn't called the '28's up yet because they have no guns to give them. . . . Have you heard? Our losses in Flanders were much greater than Churchill says they were. . . . Eire has a secret alliance with Germany. . . . Have you heard? When they caught that German agent, Tyler Kent, the code-man, in the American Embassy, they got fifteen hundred spies . . . and three members of Parliament. How many more are there walking the streets? We've simply got to do something more drastic about our fifth-columnists." And so on and so forth.

But although most of the English were stiffening themselves for the coming battle, they were still in no wise in the war the way the French people were. People still dressed for dinner. Their theatres were still open. There were flat racing,[2] and cricket and tennis and golf and bicycling and week-ending going on, nearly the same as in any other summer. People still lounged in the parks and went unconcernedly to the movies. Even Churchill's totalitarian decrees had not visibly affected the daily life of the average Englishman. But the thing that was most disturbing of all to me was that everybody still talked politics.

Now, there being so very few neutrals left, people concentrated mostly on Russia, Italy, Spain, and America. Having called Russia a "bloody bore" in September and a "bloody bane" in January, they now found many hopeful and pleasant things to think about Russia, and they were much excited about the appointment of Sir Stafford Cripps as Ambassador Extraordinary to Moscow.

[2] Not until the middle of June was flat racing abandoned, and as this book went to press, an anti-Nazi play called *Margin for Error,* by Clare Boothe was scheduled to open at the Apollo Theatre in London on August the 1st.

"You will see," they said, "he will bring something off. Russia has a pretty fine army and a good air force. (Not as good as it ought to be, because in the days after Munich we rather stupidly refused to sell them planes.) But now if Germany makes much more progress, especially if we egg the Soviets on or do something or other diplomatic, Russia is sure to strike at Germany, and she will be a very formidable enemy." But if you suggested that Russia might not strike, that she might stay "neutral," they said, quite philosophically: "Well, Russia is really a half-broken reed as an ally for Germany, you know. For instance, there is great hunger and want and political unrest in Russia now, and her wholly inadequate railroad system cannot transport grain and oil and supplies to Germany much longer without breaking down completely."

Why Russia's railroad system and domestic economy wouldn't suffer a worse strain, and collapse even more rapidly, if she went to war *against* Germany instead of peacefully aiding her, nobody ever explained to me.

And the first week in June the English still did not quite believe that Mussolini would come into the war. "He is waiting to see how the next battle turns out," they said. On the whole they tried to forget about Italy. "A watched pot never boils," they said—only this one finally did. Spain, they said, is a miserable, weak country, and would not move unless France were completely conquered, and that was not, as everyone knew, an immediate eventuality.

Mostly they talked about America. America, they had all begun to feel, as a war ally was pretty hopeless. All that they wanted from "hopelessly myopic" America now was credits and planes and guns and destroyers, and possibly some pilots (who could come in via the Canadian route) rather quickly. This, everybody said, would help enormously. Not that it would really change anything in the end, but it would tide them over a "rather difficult period," you know. Most Englishmen felt that when Churchill said in the House of Commons, on June 5: "We will carry on the struggle until in God's good time the New World, with all its power and might, sets forth to the liberation of the Old," he was not envisaging a situation which he really believed could come about, but merely trying to shame American democracy and frighten the blind adherents of the Monroe Doctrine into more rapid and "enlightened" action. Even Englishmen who seriously thought that England just might not win were themselves ashamed to be caught expressing such thoughts.

On May 6 Mr. B–, a well-known London banker, came to have tea with me. He said: "Look here, I've written down a few questions I'd rather like you to ask Americans when you get home." He read them aloud in a calm, clear English voice:

1. Would it be dangerous to the United States if the British fleet should disappear and there should be a German fleet supreme in the European and African waters of the Atlantic Ocean and a Japanese fleet supreme in the Far East and the Indian Ocean?
2. Do you wish to see Hitler Führer of Europe and thus able to use the German, British, French, Dutch, Danish, Norwegian, and Swedish shipyards to build such a navy against the United States?
3. Would it be dangerous to the United States if the Dutch East Indies, Singapore, Malaya, French Indo-China and Hong Kong should fall, if not to Germany, then to Japan, thus forming, with her control over China, a vast Japanese Empire in the Far East?

4. Would it be dangerous to the United States if Germany, in possession of British, French, and Belgian colonies in Africa, should have military, naval, and air bases much closer to South America than similar bases of the United States?
5. Would the United States refuse to abandon isolation rather than help to defend, in case of need, the white communities of Australia and New Zealand if they were left without protection in the Far Pacific?
6. Might not another World War be kindled if India, with its 350,000,000 people, were deprived of British control merely to lapse into anarchy and fall a prey to competition between two or more other great powers?
7. Is isolation
   (a) the best way to prevent the danger of these developments?
   (b) a possible way of dealing with them if Germany wins and they do arise?

   If your answer is no, can they be prevented in any way except by readiness to fight Germany either (a) now with England and France or (b) alone later?
8. Is the entry of the United States into the war and the provision of all possible aeroplanes, tanks, and ships, together with their pilots, to the Allied cause a high price to pay to save the United States from the danger of a German victory?

I asked: "May I keep these questions, Mr. B—? I'd really like to hear the answers myself, when I get home."

He answered: "Do, that's what I brought them for. You

do realize I should never have asked them if I didn't feel that the matters were—well, rather serious?"

But the next day Mr. B— telephoned to me. "I say," he said, "those questions I gave you—"

"Yes?" I said.

"I'd rather you never quoted me as asking them, you know. Would seem, almost, as though *I* doubted that this thing were going to turn out all right in the end. And, I do assure you, I haven't the faintest doubt we'll pull through. Not the *faintest*." His cold English voice was now very warm.

"Oh, Mr. B—" I assured him, "of course I realized, even while you were asking, that it was a purely academic questionnaire!"

He said, very relieved: "Quite. But I do feel it's time that the United States were educated a bit to think of the world in larger terms. If I may say so, they do rather need a lesson in geography, and such questions will train their minds." He sounded very hurried now on the telephone. "It can't possibly hurt them to *speculate* a bit, you know. But if you feel all that sounds too much like British propaganda, just throw the wretched piece of paper away."

For one split second Mr. B—, one of the wisest and shrewdest bankers in England, had caught himself denying the immemorial credo of Englishmen, that the English always lose every battle but the last. I'm afraid that, no matter how it turns out in the end, Mr. B— will never again be a really happy man. Mr. B—, with his belated "propaganda" and his sad doubts, which he so quickly denied, was an exception in London in early June. By then most of the British spokesmen who had begun in early May to turn a sympathetic ear to pleas for "more American propaganda" were saying rather tartly to American journalists: "My

God, if America doesn't see what this thing is all about now, nothing we say or let you say will change you!" I had begun very strongly to agree with them.

But this attitude of "Figure it out for yourself; why should we humble ourselves before you?" was very hard on American journalists in London. They wanted to co-operate, but between British pride and British news censorship, and—a minor inconvenience—the aliens' curfew law which kept "foreigners" off the street after 10.30 p.m. and curtailed all movements during the day, American journalists in London, like those in Paris, were having a hard time sending home the real picture of England and its danger.

In early June these journalists had a very particular grievance against the British Information Bureau. The night that the "last survivors" began to reach Dover, none of the American journalists were informed in time; in fact, most of them were not informed at all, so that they did not get to Dover to report this biggest and best and most significant story of the war until after the English journalists had written the cream of it off.

On the other hand, British war correspondents themselves had had a pretty thin war. A British war correspondent, Captain D— W—, told me the story, which I merely repeat here to show how the Allies (unlike the Germans) had organized their own "army publicity" so badly that even the British public never really got the true story of the Flanders campaign.

During the "long phony war" the B.E.F. correspondents had been attached to various sectors, with headquarters at Arras. Nominally civilians, they carried no weapons, though they wore uniforms and were subject to military orders. When the invasion finally broke, as I have told you, they streamed up happily with the B.E.F. into Belgium. A few days later, when the front became what the French communiqués called so significantly "*un état de confusion,*" and the English "an indescribable mêlée," they, either because they were "nuisances," or because they were in too much danger, or simply because the Military Intelligence had lost its head, were ordered back again to Arras. There they were all put under military guard in a small hotel and left to rewrite the short, cryptic communiqués that were brought to them by dispatch from G.H.Q. Sometimes they were allowed to make an organized trip to a nearby bombed village where they were shown a pile of smouldering ruins, or a stream of refugees coming down the roads. For a week they sat poring over their machines like children doing "a hundred-word thesis on war," pounding out "phony" eyewitness stories of what was no longer a "phony war" for eager home consumption. At the end of this week of civilian immolation, Arras was bombed a bit and they were all piled hastily into cars and camions and taken to Boulogne. There in the big hotel of Boulogne, again under military guard, and now minus their typewriters and kit, which had been abandoned in their own "indescribable mêlée" in Arras, they were left to write out still more "phony" stories—in *long hand.* Anyone who knows a newspaper man knows that this is the punishment he dreads most in the place he expects to go hereafter.

At last, by threatening to expose their plight to the public, they prevailed upon a liaison officer to drive to Hasbrouck, where General Gort's headquarters were, to plead that they either be allowed to go to "some front," or be given information a little more detailed and colourful than the daily "state of confusion" out of which they had been writing their fanciful (and often conflicting) tales of "massed tank and air battles." The officer got in his car and left for Hasbrouck. An hour or so later he reported to G.H.Q. "I represent," he began, "a group of starving newshounds who demand some news."

The general cut him short. "It's rather more quiet here today," he said. "Here is the communiqué. Take them that." The officer began to plead again for the poor deceived fourth-estaters. The general snorted impatiently. "If they must have hot news," he said, "here is a report that came in this minute: 'The Germans have just bombed the hell out of *Boulogne*'!"

From Boulogne the twice-bombed newshounds were evacuated, well ahead of the B.E.F., back to London.

I told Captain W— about Bertrand de Jouvenel, the talented young French writer and journalist whom I had seen in Paris the week before in a private's uniform, and how he had said to me: "The only way for a journalist to see the war is to join the army and pray to God he'll be alive to write about it after."

The British war correspondent said bitterly: "I've already tried, but they won't take me; I'm over forty. I fought four years of the last war as a captain of artillery. I suppose I'll finish out this one whamming away with an ancient fowling-piece at parachutists armed with bombs, revolvers, and sawed-off shotguns!" [3]

So while American journalists in London had some cause for complaint, the English ones had even more.

Perhaps it was because they had so long been starved for stories, that all the British correspondents "went to town" in such a big and glorious way on The Evacuation. I don't

[3] Captain W— cabled me last week: "Joining my old regiment in two days. . . ." Now he is going to see the war.

know. But I do know that one day some wise historian will show that what is now called the Maginot Madness was a contagion you could call in England "Evacuation Ecstasy."

The evacuation absorbed every mind, inflamed every heart, monopolized every conversation, in every home and pub and restaurant all over that green and happy land. No conquering heroes returning heavy-laden with the loot of a rowdy and plunderous war ever received a more royal welcome than England gave her two hundred thousand troops who, driven out of Flanders, returned with nothing but their bare hands. These same English, who so bitterly condemned the French a month later for not "standing and dying" to the last man (as the French, in turn, had condemned the Belgians), welcomed their whole army in precipitous flight as victors of deathless fame. I think I know now why they were so glad to see their army come—even in defeat—home. I think the English also knew, deeper than anything they said or even thought, that France was doomed. And they were very happy to gather this brave brood of their blood under the wings of the English sky on their own soil. They knew England would be England then, with Englishmen defending her, if need be against the whole world.

A strange picture, which no journalist seems to have commented on, was the one presented by some of the "last survivors from the beach at Dunkirk," unshaven, still covered with mud and soaked in salt sea-water, who came right off the Dover train to pop into lunch or dinner at Claridge's or Quaglino's or the Ritz. It was difficult for the mind to comprehend that these men had been a few hours before in the hell of Flanders, as they sat down smiling and waving to friends, among gaily dressed, perfumed ladies in flower toques, in rooms filled with sweet music and sweet voices and the clink of fine glasses.

Major T– said to me: "Just like old times. In the last war I used to sleep at the Ritz in Paris every night, and barge out to the front right after breakfast." He laughed. And then a shadow crossed his grey eyes. He said: "Queer though, I should now be coming back from the front to Claridge's. . . ."

These men (all, of course, officers) were gallant and gay and very confident, and they had few complaints to make of anything that had happened to them in Flanders. The note they struck was reflected in the most popular story told in London in the first week in June about the British tommy who said: "Oh, we'd have licked those Germans right enough if we hadn't been himpeded by the Belgians and the Frenchies!"

The French survivors felt differently. They felt "*quelqu'un*" (they meant the English) had managed the withdrawal, as far as the beach anyway, with criminal stupidity.

Lieutenant de la C– said to me: "*Nous, nous autres Français*, we fought the rear-guard action! Every morning we were left to face the German tanks and heavy guns with nothing but our rifles and machine-guns . . . The anti-tank guns of the British were always ordered back six hours before we were ordered to withdraw. They should have stayed back with us," he said. "*Zut!* they couldn't hope to take their anti-tank guns back to England!" And then he asked: "Do you know why Leopold surrendered? Now the English are saying he didn't give the Allies any warning, so they could withdraw. They were withdrawing for an evacuation two days before he surrendered without giving any warning to him! *Bien!* When he found that out, when he discovered that an evacuation from the coast was already prepared by the English, it made him so furious he surrendered. The British will not face the truth: this was the most idiotic, humiliating campaign in the histories of our two countries. And what do they do, these unimaginative oxen? They make a hero of Lord Gort. The King covers him with medals." He looked very bitter, and then he smiled rather unpleasantly. "I have no doubt that when he successfully evacuates the army to Canada, the King will greet him there and make him a duke of the realm. But I," he said, "I shall not have to witness this, because tomorrow I go back to France, and I go on fighting. This time it will not be as it was when I fought at the Marne; this time I fight for a country that is lost–lost." And then he said: "Let us have another bottle of champagne," and he smiled and sniffed, and said: "You smell so sweet. I never thought I should ever again smell a woman's perfume. Are you wearing a Chanel perfume? Will you be able to make perfumes like that in America, when France is gone?"

There was also between the French and English survivors considerable disagreement as to the morale of the German soldier. The French I saw said it was magnificent. They said that the personal initiative and the courage of the Germans was so great it was almost insanity, and that their discipline was almost inhuman; that their command and soldiers were both highly trained, since otherwise their speedy and daring operations must have failed. They told of tanks and armoured cars breaking through the Allied ranks, apparently oblivious of the fact they courted sure death because they had no bases to fall back on.

Captain de R– said: "These men were no robots or automatons–they had to think for themselves, think fast." He thought they were heroes in any man's language. With the infantry it was the same. "I saw them come into a little village, at a dog-trot, their rifles slung on their backs, four abreast. They did not look to left or to right, or break ranks. And the whole time we were machine-gunning them from the head of the street in our armoured car."

But English Major T— said: "Every time we got them at the point of a bayonet, they squealed like pigs for mercy!"

Captain de R—, when I told him that, remarked: "The English didn't often get close to them with cold steel, you know!"

St. George he was for England,
St. Denis was for France,
Sing Honi soit qui mal y pense. . . .

In the end the High Commands of both sides were blamed for the long series of stupidities, both at home and in the field, of which that evacuation was the tragic fruit. (Until the full and documented history of that campaign is written, years hence, it is equally stupid to try to assess the blame. I tell these stories here, not because I believed them, but because the French did, and that belief played an important part in the French conduct of the last days of the war in France.) But in the end there were and there are no words to describe the courage of the plain soldiers, British and French, who took part in it. The drama of Dunkirk will perhaps never be completely written, although all its horrors and heroisms will provide the material for a thousand memoirs and histories still to be written. And yet, and yet —the English were (to me) the more endearing of the two bands of warriors, perhaps because they complained less, and criticized less, and hated less, and fought I know quite as well as their allies.[4]

[4] Even at the end, facing the Battle of Britain alone, the English were generous in their judgments of their former allies. Sane and without rancour, Mr. Churchill was the first to acknowledge the gallantry of the

I happened to be motoring in Gloucestershire on a beautiful sunny day shortly after the "last survivors" had got home. I stopped in a small wayside inn for a late luncheon and there I overheard two Englishmen who had been at Dunkirk tell the tale to each other.

The scene was a little mullioned-windowed dining-room, and the smell of late lilacs came in very heavy from the air outside. I was sitting alone at a table in a corner when they met in the doorway. They were both very young British non-commissioned officers, healthy, rangy, and red-faced. One of them was a redhead, the other a curly-haired blond. They shook hands stiffly, smiled awkwardly, mumbled first names at each other. You saw that they were meeting for the first time in quite a while. They proceeded at once to a table near me, and ordered lunch thoughtfully. Then this conversation followed:

REDHEAD: H-um-er-er-when did you get back?

BLOND: Yesterday. You?

REDHEAD: Day before. [*Pause for eating.*] Did you have a party?

BLOND: Oh, quite.

REDHEAD: Rum business.

BLOND: Quite. See many Jerries?

REDHEAD: Oh, yes. They kept it up all the time. Noisy bastards.

BLOND [*very embarrassed*]: I–er–I–er–well, I was just wondering what became of old Vyvian.

French people. The London *Economist* said in July: "There will never be a word of recrimination from this side of the Channel against the people of France, who have fought and laboured and died for the cause we share. . . . [The fundamental fault lay] in the characters of the ruling men." This was the "treachery" note, a useful one to strike in explaining the French débâcle at home and abroad, but that does not make the British attitude any less generous and sincere.

REDHEAD [*equally embarrassed*]: They got him.
[*Pause for eating.*]

BLOND: Well–what–er–happened to him?

REDHEAD [*with an awkward, painful, inclusive gesture*]: Oh, everything.
[*They both looked gloomy for an instant. Then the blond officer changed the subject brightly.*]

BLOND: Lose your kit?

REDHEAD: Oh, rather!

BLOND: A nuisance, what? [*No answer.*] Er–er– Glad to be back?

REDHEAD [*quietly*]: Oh, yes. [*Radiant.*] Wonderful weather!
[*Another pause for eating.*]

BLOND [*very apologetic at changing the subject back to a more distressing topic*]:
U-mm–er– By the way, I–er–had a further distinction–was *torpedoed* on the way back.

REDHEAD [*coolly*]: Oh, I say.
[*Another pause for the happy arrival of beef pudding.*]

BLOND [*doggedly*]: But the whole thing proves one thing–we've got them licked.

REDHEAD [*coldly*]: Obviously. [*Pointing to pudding.*] Not bad, for a change?

That ended the conversation of two British soldiers who had participated in the most historical and deadly campaign in modern history.

May their sons be many!

I reported this conversation to a friend when I returned to London. He said: "Yes, that doggedness and courage and faith combined with a lack of imagination does give you hope. But sometimes it gives you equal cause for fear." And then he told me of a conversation he had overheard in the lobby of a similar little inn near his country home. It disturbed him as much as that of the Dunkirk lads had encouraged me. A raw-boned, healthy-looking Englishwoman said to a plump little friend who was knitting thick brown socks: "I'm rather afraid the Sunday-school festival is off for next month." Her friend, appalled, asked: "Oh, why?" "Well," she replied, "somebody came down from London and told the rector they wanted the meadow for a tank-trap or something." And her friend said, reproachfully: "Oh, not really?" "Yes, but the rector thinks he can stave them off until after we've had our picnic." And the sock-knitter said: "Oh, I do hope so!"

I should like to have got the two officers from Dunkirk and the two ladies together—with a French interpreter, of course.

On June 8 I finally got passage on the plane from London to Lisbon which made connections with the Clipper. As I left the Consul's office, where I had gone to see if all my papers were in order (in London, too, you had to have dozens of papers in order: ration books, police cards, identification papers, passports, censors' seals), I ran into an English friend. He asked me to give his regards to his American friends in New York. Then he spoke with faint disdain of certain titled English friends who had—well, rather "ratted," he thought, by "going abroad."

I said: "Yes, I suppose they could have gone to the country." Then I added: "I hope your wife has gone to the country."

"No," he said, "my wife has always come down to London in June every year for thirty years—and besides," he said, with a smile so bland I shall never know whether he was serious or, as the English say "pulling my leg," "besides, you see, my wife doesn't *believe* in the Germans.". . .

I told this story to the oil man, who drove me to the Heston airport. (He was now very busy with some more shenanigans, about Dutch and Belgian oil cargoes, putting them, too, I suppose, under the American flag.) I said: "I don't understand the British at all, at all. It just makes me so ill and so mad! Don't they, for God's sake, know what they're in for?"

"How would it help them if they did?" he asked.

I answered miserably: "I don't know."

He said: "Exactly. Do you think they'll take it when it comes?

I replied impatiently: "Why yes, of course."

"I mean *really* take it, from John o' Groat's to Land's End, until there's hardly an English home standing or an Englishman left alive."

I said: "You know I think they will."

He said: "Then you've found out the only fact worth knowing here."

As I got into the plane I said: "Good-bye. I'm glad to go home. It's really awful here."

The oil man said: "No. All over the world, *these* are the good old days now. . . ."

ELEVEN

Languages are the pedigrees of nations.

Samuel Johnson, in Boswell's *Life*

THE PLANE TRIP from London to Portugal (with a short stop at Bordeaux) was steady and swift enough, but we did not fly to Lisbon, which was our objective. At about four o'clock in the afternoon we suddenly began to lose altitude as we circled over a field by the sea that looked like a postage stamp, and then levelled out behind it and came down and almost overshot it, and then rose again, circled, levelled out again, and landed in a series of kangaroo bumps at a small military airport outside of Oporto, three hundred and fifty miles from Lisbon.

The pilot said: "We get out," and we did. Right away we were surrounded by a smiling group of squat dark ugly men in spotty, unbuttoned olive-grey uniforms, covered with patent-leather trimmings and gold buttons. We looked at them and they looked at us. I said something and discovered instantly that conversation was impossible. No one on the plane spoke Portuguese, and the men on the field spoke nothing else.

The pilot said: "We'll have to wait for the customs officer to come from Oporto. He speaks a little English." Then he told us we had landed here because there was a thick fog over Lisbon, and we had the choice of proceeding to Lisbon by a midnight train or spending the night in Oporto's one hotel and leaving (if the fog lifted) by plane at dawn. Never having been in Portugal before in my life—indeed, remembering it only as the country of Vasco da Gama and Dias and Henry the Navigator and Magellan (and I was afraid one of them might be Spanish), and more especially (I blush) as the country whose last King, Manuel, once loved a certain lush French lady called Gaby Deslys, who always referred to her ransom in pearls as "my little beads" —I thought that here was a good opportunity to see what it appeared would be a fair-sized slice of Portugal's coast. So when the customs official arrived, and after my bags were cleared, with a speed and nonchalance that reminded me of the almost forgotten blessing of a country's being at peace, I used his good offices and bad English to get an automobile down from Oporto to drive the road to Lisbon.

The air pilot, with the disdain of the insular Briton for any country as near Africa as this one, said: "Oh, I wouldn't, you know. You'll have a very long rough ride. I'm told most of the country out there is just bush."

When the car I had hired arrived, it turned out to be a Buick of boom-time vintage. The driver was a great smiling, unshaven, bull-necked man with a gnawed straw hat, who looked vaguely like a very dirty Oliver Hardy, an impression that was strengthened by his companion "on the box," who looked like an even dirtier Stan Laurel. He wore a very flashy torn tweed jacket and a pair of ancient white duck pants.

I asked: "Are they both driving me?"

The customs official said: "It is a long trip. One does not like to come home alone."

"How long is it?"

"You will be there in a very short time."

I thought: "Well, I now know two things about the Portuguese. They are sociable people, and they have no sense of time."

Then, while they dumped my baggage cheerfully and roughly into the back of the car, the customs official gave them instructions to take me to the Hotel Avis in Lisbon. I don't know what other instructions he gave them in Portuguese (I now strongly suspect sabotage), but this drive to Lisbon was the worst mistake and the most dangerous adventure I had during four months in war-torn Europe.

Hardy (who was driving) at once left the airport by a bumpy sandy road at breakneck speed. From then on, for six agonizing hours, I saw really nothing more of Portugal. I said: "Please," I said: "Don't," I said: "Hey!" But neither he nor Laurel paid the smallest attention to my squeals of terror. I think they thought I was just encouraging them to further efforts, or that really I was enjoying it and that my screams were like the ecstatic yells people emit on a roller-coaster. As I did not know one word of Portuguese, I could not correct this unfortunate impression. I tried French, then German, then a little pig-Latin. Finally I yelled a phrase I was sure they must be familiar with: "*Dolce!*" I screamed: "*Dolce far niente*,[1] for the love of mud!" But after the first hour I gave up and closed my

[1] The right term, for anyone who intends to go to Portugal, is "*devagar*" (slow down).

eyes and clutched the hand-strap on the side of the car to keep from being hurled from one window or another, or into the seat ahead, as we rounded mountains and hairpin curves, or jammed on the screeching brakes when we came upon great ox-carts which would not instantly make way for us on the narrow roads. When I did peek from between my dusty, wind-tossed eyelashes, I had a fleeting impression of a very poor but rather pretty countryside, of windmills screaming as we screamed past them, of homely, dark little people in bright aprons and blouses with high loads on their heads, of umbrella pines and dark oaks and cork trees, peeled of their bark so their trunks looked like the trunks of glistening Negroes as we flashed by, of little buildings with Moorish arches, and rambler roses growing over them, of gondola-shaped boats on ponds, of mules and donkeys and pigs and goats and chickens and children flying for their very lives as we hurtled through the narrow streets of small villages. And it all might have been in Majorca or Italy or Spain for all that I now remember of it.

And then quite suddenly it was dark. And with the dark came no light from the car. I gathered from the way the Laurel fellow fiddled and banged at things on the dashboard that there must be a short circuit in the headlights. Now, being trapped alone in the dark like this, with a foreigner in the back seat, encouraged Hardy to a fresh burst of speed, and for another hour we tore along the thin white thread of the bumpy road by the thin white light of a thin new moon. Sometimes when we whizzed through the black streets of a little town, past a red gasoline pump, and I shouted: "Garage! Oh, please, *garage!*" Hardy just drew in his neck so the roll of fat at the back looked as though it would burst in my face, and stepped harder on the gas. About one hour out of Lisbon I heard the sweet familiar chug of fast motorcycles behind us, and I thought: "Thank heavens, we've picked up a traffic cop!" But when the two motorcycles came alongside, Hardy did not stop. He yelled something to the cyclists (who turned out to be soldiers) and they yelled something back; then they got 'way ahead, and from then on, Hardy really gave his all to the business of keeping up with their distant headlights.

When I finally arrived at the Avis Hotel, safe but shattered, I was too weak to offer more than a sad protest that my "reservation" had not been made. The limpid-eyed receptionist said he was sorry, but "all Lisbon was jammed" because of the *festa.*

"What is Portugal celebrating?" I asked, incredulously.

The manager answered: "Eight hundred years of Portuguese independence."

"That's a record of some kind," I said, "but where do I sleep?"

"That is indeed a question I ask myself," and he began to make a horrible clucking, sorrowful noise.

At last I telephoned our Legation, where the Minister was Mr. Herbert Pell, an old friend of my dear dead Newport days—those days in the twenties when the worst disaster of any year was an oil tanker's going aground on Bailey's Beach and you swallowed even more oil.

Bertie Pell said: "My wife and I insist you come right here."

"Oh, darlings," I said, "you don't have to insist; I'll be right up."

They met me in the hall. Bertie is as big and lumbering as a white polar bear, and he was all in white duck. Olive looked as lovely as anyone in Newport ever did in trailing beige chiffon and pearls.

She said: "Oh, my! You look tired. You were very brave to stay in France so long."

"I was in the Maginot when it was firing," I said, "I was in Brussels when it was bombed, and in Lille and in Paris, but I never thought until tonight I was really going to die." And I was so cross and tired maybe I cried.

"Oh, you must have had one of those faster Portuguese drivers," the Pells said. "Nobody in his right mind ever hires one of those."

"If I were in my right mind what would I be doing in Europe at all?" I asked. And then they gave me some scrambled eggs and beer and told me that my Clipper sailing had been delayed a day, but Portugal really was a lovely country, and I must profit by the delay of the Clipper to see it tomorrow.

Rallying a little, I asked: "Now what's the news?"

And they said, "You know, you've just come from London."

"But that was at seven o'clock this morning. Haven't you heard anything since on the radio?"

Bertie Pell said: "I won't have a radio in the house. I prefer to get my bad news from the papers every morning in one slug instead of having it shot into me all day long in hydrophobic hypodermic doses. But here's yesterday morning's *New York Times*."

I almost wept at the miracle of that, and took the paper quickly and sat on it while I ate. Bertie told how everybody in Portugal was sure Italy was coming into the war now, because the Italian boats in the harbour had just been ordered to dump cargoes and go home; and how nervous Portugal was, because if Germany penetrated farther into France, Italy would certainly go into France, and Spain would probably come into Portugal. Very tired, I said: "Well, everything goes into everything, so I'll go into bed, if you don't mind." I went up the stairs of this great old Portuguese house to a great big lovely bedroom, which was almost as far from the bathroom as Oporto, so for the first time in Europe in the spring I didn't brush my teeth, saying: "Well, *c'est la guerre*." Then in bed I tried for a few minutes to read the *New York Times* of June 7. But all that it said was that the front was "an immense hell," and that Paul Reynaud now had "reasons to hope" the Germans would be stopped, although the "danger was immense," and that he was making another conciliatory offer to Italy to settle their differences. The English were *still* trying to eliminate Chamberlain from the government. And nowhere in the *Times* of New York was there any reflecton of that certainty in the heart of thirty million Frenchmen that now it *was* going to be finished—but by the Germans. It was very depressing. Even in well-informed America, I thought, people are going on believing that what they don't want to happen can't possibly happen. Maginot Madness, Evacuation Ecstasy, Isolation Idiocy. . . .

The next morning I was awakened out of my usual running nightmare by very loud gunfire. I jumped out of bed, saying: "Viva caramba! Now Spain's in!"

I wondered if the Legation had an air-raid shelter. And as I walked to the window (very cautiously, crabwise, because I had had my lesson in flying glass in Brussels) I thought: "Before I die I must leave in my will some money to found a home for Unemployed Bombed American Ambassadors." But the gunfire was just coming from some American warships [2] lying in the harbour at the foot of the hill. I found out later they were firing courtesy salutes for

[2] The cruiser *Trenton* and the destroyers *Dickinson* and *Herbert*.

the eight-hundred-year *festa*.

When the maid brought me my breakfast and a morning Lisbon paper, I found to my surprise and pleasure that I could read the Portuguese in the paper because Portuguese seems to be a strange mixture of French, Latin, Spanish, and Italian, and I can read a little of those four languages.

I said to someone at luncheon: "Why, if I can read it, can't I understand it? Is it an inflected language?"

And he answered: "No, it's a vomited language. They just swallow the whole thing and spit it out at you. But what really makes it tough is that everyone spits a little differently."

I read enough in my breakfast paper to learn that the Portuguese seemed to be much more interested in the details of the *festa*, which occupied almost the whole two sides of the one-sheet newspaper, than they were in the war.

A man at luncheon said: "That is not altogether true. To be sure, they *are* interested in the *festa*. Eight hundred years of independence is certainly worth celebrating. And a people that has once been so great, that once owned one of the greatest empires on earth" (it's still the fifth largest), "and whose prestige has dwindled over the years, until now they are everywhere considered as a mere British satellite, bolsters its ego mightily by remembering its past glories." [3]

I thought: "Is Portugal going to be the Killeyoo bird of Iberia in 2040?"

"But," he said, "the fact that they don't talk about the war more in their papers has other, not so pleasant explanations."

He said that the Portuguese, like all the other neutrals, wished to be neither "protected" by the Axis powers nor

[3] He thought that the mania for fast driving, a well-known Portuguese trait, might well be a frustrated Magellan or Henry the Navigator complex.

"assisted" by the Allies. They wouldn't in any case be able to defend themselves, because they had only 165,000 soldiers and 35 small warships, so that if the Allies really wanted to "assist" them, they'd have to "get thar fustest" with a terrible lot of boats and men, which they obviously couldn't do, the way things were shaping up in Europe now. And anyway (he thought) the Portuguese *secretly preferred* the protection of the Axis. Then he said that, first, Portugal was really totalitarian under Dictator Oliveira Salazar, and they like being totalitarian, because between 1910 and 1926 they'd had forty governments and eighteen "democratic" revolutions, and they were pretty sick of change; second, the people felt the *logic* of Peninsular solidarity (as Gibraltar goes, he said, so would go Portugal); third, the Portuguese, like the Spanish, were a Catholic people and dreaded Communism more than they dreaded anything else, including the smallpox plague that was raging in Portugal; fourth, in view of all the above, the alliance with Britain was every day growing more embarrassing; and for all of these reasons the dictator censored newspapers and found it convenient to wax very, very dithyrambic about the *festa*, and play down the war.

All I discovered further was that Portugal was absolutely bursting with Nazi agents and "tourists" and fifth-columnists, and with refugees of all nations and stations from the wrath of totalitarianism—kings without crowns, and duchesses without duchies, and writers without books, and bankers without banks, and industrialists without factories, and politicians without jobs, and just plain people without anything at all, who were waiting for boats, waiting for Clippers, and—just waiting. They would have no place to go if Hitler or Franco came here, except to sail across to America, or jump into the Atlantic. And the

Portuguese wouldn't care which they did, so long as, after their escudos gave out, they were rid of them. I learned that the Portuguese were a very melancholy, gentle people who liked to think about death, but really weren't bloodthirsty, since they didn't kill the bulls in their bull-fights, but only tortured them a little.

That afternoon I didn't go out walking by myself in the streets of Lisbon, because I had looked for my vaccination mark and couldn't find it anywhere.[4] (All I could find was a very old bullet-hole in the calf of my right leg, but that is another story.) So I was sitting quietly in the Legation reading a booklet about the *festa* (entitled, rather satirically, in view of the refugee situation: *Portugal Expects You!*) when the telephone rang. It was René de Chambrun, who, as I told you, had left Paris in late May with a message for the President; he had been hanging around Lisbon for almost a week waiting for a Clipper.

"There's something wrong with democracy," de Chambrun said, "when I have to give priority to zipper-salesmen and throneless royalty, and me with a message to the President in my pocket!"

Then he said: "Hello, I have just spoken to our Embassy here, and Italy's in now."

I said: "Poor France."

"Yes, poor France: 1915 and 1940 are tragic extremes. Between those two dates, in 1935, Laval and Mussolini chose to build the Stresa front, because they remembered 1915 and feared 1940. It was not their fault that that front crumbled," he said bitterly.

I thought: I do not envy those who truly believe that any single act or policy of a statesman in the past twenty years

[4] The Clipper people vaccinated me, when I landed at North Beach.

might have averted this great war of mass ideologies. They must drink deep indeed of the stale and bitter cup of misanthropy.

At five o'clock the Pells came back from the Cathedral where they had gone for a *festa* church celebration. I rushed to the head of the stairs and said:

"Italy's in now!"

Bertie Pell answered: "We heard that from the diplomats just as we went into the Cathedral. So the service was not a great success."

Mrs. Pell said: "The Italian and French diplomats glared horribly at one another all during the service. I was afraid something might happen."

I thought: "If Christ came back now, and God ought to know there never was a time His Son was more needed, it's the war-mongers and diplomats and politicians He'd have to drive from the Temple. . . ."

That night the Clipper from Horta got in. On it were Madeleine Carroll and Noel Coward and Simon Elwes, the famous English portrait-painter, on their way back to dear old London.

At midnight we all met in a little Portuguese café and they told me about America, and how America still didn't know what the war was about and thought any attempt to explain it was rank British propaganda.

Noel said: "It's really frightening. America is so smug and complacent, in a way, and everybody says: 'Oh, we have plenty of time'!"

Then I saw right away that everything Americans were thinking about England, the English were thinking about Americans, and that both were probably right. I said: "Nobody has time." I told them some of the sad things that I have told you here.

Noel Coward looked very white and said: "So you really believe now the French are going to surrender!"

"Yes, they are," I answered.

And he said: "England will never, never surrender!"

Then he began to make speeches about England, dear England, and they were so fine and so heartfelt and so really and grimly determined that Madeleine Carroll wept copiously, and her beautiful face looked smeary and pulled apart and honest, not at all like the neat, dishonest, glycerine-teared face she uses to cry with in the movies. Even Simon Elwes, who is not an actor, and is therefore an average Englishman, looked very wretched and said some emotional and patriotic things, though of course he didn't say them as beautifully as Noel.

Finally Noel said, very embarrassed: "I'm afraid that everything I say sounds rather like lines from *Cavalcade*, doesn't it?"

And I answered: "Yes, a little. But it was a very fine play and a very true one. You won't be jealous if I quote Shakespeare, will you, who once said the same things even better than you do?"

And I quoted a passage from *Henry V*, which I had learned in school in English II, when I was a very little girl and believed that all European wars were just a silly but rather exciting game that kings played in order to get an extra throne or two into the family:

> *Once more unto the breach, dear friends, once more;*
> *Or close the wall up with our English dead. . . .*
> *Now set the teeth and stretch the nostril wide,*
> *Hold hard the breath and bend up every spirit*
> *To his full height. On, on, you noblest English! . . .*

After that we all drank more red wine, and talked about

Hollywood, which was in a terrible state because the movie magnates didn't know whether to make war pictures or not, though the general feeling out there was that the safest thing to do was to make pleasant "escapist" pictures, strongly directed at the South American market, which was the only foreign market they could count on until the war in Europe blew over.

"Blows over what," I asked—"the Atlantic?"

Then we all laughed a little more, and wept a little more, but *they* felt much better. They knew in their sad hearts England would fight to the last man, and that in a way settled the question for them.

Then, drinking red Portuguese wine with them, laughing and talking with them *in English*, not thinking about politics, not thinking about war or the "political objectives" which they sought to achieve, I suddenly knew then that the English not only feel the same things about Justice and Liberty we do, but say them in a language I love and know, a language which has as much reality and importance and nearness to me as the face of my own mother. I knew that if England were going to die, a large part of American me would die with her. Because (I thought) we are the children of the Mother England. Perhaps children must stand alone one day, since mothers generally do die before them. But only when mothers die do children suddenly realize they have with death grown up—they are no longer *children*, they are that most painful thing, adults in an enemy world. I thought, that's why everybody cries even over the loss of a hard or capricious or neglectful or even cruel mother. When your mother goes, you know at last you are no longer "somebody's child"; you are an adult. This is a bitter and frightening moment for a man, or a colony, or even "an independent nation." And they never know how bitter it is until it really comes to pass.

You see what an emotional moment that was for me, there in that little Portuguese restaurant, talking with my English friends, who were all going back so cheerfully to the hard thing.

I said:

"Good-bye and God bless you all, from John o' Groat's to Land's End."

And they said: "Good-bye. Don't worry so much about Great Britain. We'll muddle through. You'd better start worrying about America."

"I read a copy of the *New York Times* yesterday," I said. "It seems we are a nation without arms, without an army, and without a warlike spirit. How can we fail?"

"Darling," Noel answered, "I can't possibly imagine."

The next morning I went down to the Tagus River, where the Yankee Clipper was lying like a great lazy flying fish. And I thought: "Now I am leaving Europe by the last open door—the door from a land where the people, like the people in Italy, where I arrived in Europe, are also afraid to talk. A land where the people, seeing no hope in the future of democracy, are turning for comfort and inspiration and guidance to the long-forgotten patterns of the world of a thousand years ago." And I suddenly knew that unless Uncle Sam wedged his toe in the door, or, better still, God performed some miracle in men's hearts, that door, too, would soon be closed.

At 9.20 we took off, over Lisbon, over Cape Roca, crowned by the castle of Cintra, and then we headed up into the great endless blue sky over the world, and after a day and a few hours we landed at a place called North Beach, on a field called LaGuardia, which is in the Land of the Free, called the United States of America.

TWELVE

Sail, sail thy best, ship of Democracy,
Of value is thy freight, 'tis not the Present only,
The Past is also stored in thee,
Thou holdest not the venture of thyself alone,
not of the Western continent alone.
Earth's résumé *entire floats on thy keel O ship,*
is steadied by thy spars . . .
With all their ancient struggles, martyrs, heroes,
epics, wars, thou bear'st the other continents.

Walt Whitman, in
"Thou Mother with Thy Equal Brood"

NOW I HAVE TOLD you many of the things I saw and felt, and how people were and what they were saying in Europe in the spring of that first Blitzkrieg, and although you feel very sorry for the Allies and the neutrals, you probably feel on the whole a little disgusted with them. You think in many ways they deserved what they got, because they weren't smart enough to see it coming. That ought to finish this book, but it isn't finished until I tell you what the first thing was that I found out when I returned to America.

After two weeks at home I found out that nearly all the things that people felt and many of the things which happened in Europe just before and during the "phony war" are happening here today. What England and France have been and were until the invasion of the Low Countries, America is. We are on the same road they took to disaster.

Do you doubt it? Do you really doubt that this picture which you have seen is just a mirror held up to America? Then please ask yourself the questions I have been asking myself in this hot July in this peaceful country.

What "fundamental principles" of democracy do we give lip service to that they also did not give lip service to? What "fundamental principles" of democracy do we really practise that England now and France almost to the end did not also practise? Freedom of expression, freedom of religion, trial by jury, asylum to the politically and religiously oppressed? They harboured five million European refugees as a proof of their sincerity in this. (Oh, you say, in France they had already begun to go in for Jew-baiting. And do you really doubt that anti-Semitism is growing in this country?)

Faced with a crisis, did the Allies waste precious hours quarrelling interminably about "what democracy really is" besides freedom of expression and religion? How many parts free competition, how many parts monopoly, wage hours, undistributed profits, social security, vested interests, unearned increment, or just a decent *quid pro quo* on the franc? Isn't this the quarrel that absorbs many good minds in America?

With the enemy at the door, did they spend valuable time in the peace-time pursuit of social objectives, in trying to perfect their democracy before they stopped to think how best to defend it? Aren't our politicians dedicated to the principles that we must lose none of the social gains we have made during the past seven years and must even make more? Haven't the C.I.O. and the A.F.L. and the W.P.A.-'ers and all the current beneficiaries of those gains and all the stop-the-war groups, and many another group gone on record as saying that a big defence program will strike at the roots of social progress and democracy in this country?

Threatened by Nazism, were the labour-unionists and the New Dealers like Blum in France, who it is claimed gummed up industrial production after Munich with a forty-hour week, stupid not to realize that all weeks are one-hundred-and-sixty-eight-hour weeks in a concentration camp? Were the people (oh, the people) who fought at every last economic ditch for the proposition that "the world owes a man a living" pathetically blind not to see that in certain circumstances it doesn't even owe him life?

But the French didn't think it would work out that way in France, and we don't really think it will work out that way here either, do we?

Faced with a crisis that struck at the very existence of their state, was there no real "national unity" in high places? Did the politicians quarrel bitterly among themselves and call names and each impugn the motives and character and past records of the others? What about Roosevelt versus Willkie? What about the names each of their partisans call the other candidate? Did many Allied politicians care more for their jobs than they did for their country's welfare?

How many third-term politicians who feel that the re-election of Roosevelt is "vital in this crisis" would vote for him if they individually lost their jobs by it? Or how many for Willkie in the same case?

Was the fault not in the politicians but in the people who elected or re-elected them? Did the people distrust their leaders but fear to change them? Or did they change them too often? How do you feel about re-electing Roosevelt or ousting him in the middle of a crisis for Mr. Willkie? Do you really trust the mayor or the governor or the senators you've got? Do you think everything will be all right if we just get rid of New Dealism, or do you think everything will be all wrong then?

Was the trouble that in their crisis the French and the English people couldn't see straight or think straight because they were so bedevilled by Communist propaganda, Nazi propaganda, peace propaganda, war propaganda, all propaganda, so that often they didn't know what was falsehood and what was truth? Don't you often feel cynicism and doubt concerning many a public statement and wonder: "What propaganda group was behind that one?" Aren't our newspapers and our politicians full of timely warnings against other American individuals and groups who are the "perhaps unconscious" instruments of an alien or dangerous propaganda? Did not President Roosevelt himself in his third-term acceptance speech imply that everyone who didn't agree with him was a fifth-columnist? Is he not dedicated now, and all of America with him, to a fifth-column hunt? Aren't Red-baiting and Jew-baiting, and alien-baiting of all sorts growing in this country? Are we not also bedevilled and a little frightened?

Was France just "ripe for Communism or Fascism anyway"? Haven't you heard even wise people tell you in magazines and newspapers that we are also? And don't you sometimes secretly think so yourself?

Or were the Allied peoples not really at fault? Was the real trouble that their leaders did not tell them the truth long before the war broke so that they were not really ready for it? What truth? The need, if the menace were to be met, for drastic taxation, for the curtailment of labour privileges, for sacrifice in every station and walk of life, the truth about armaments? Who in a position of authority, knowing a year ago, two years ago, what we faced, dared risk his job by telling it to us? Who dares risk it now? Do you really believe we have been told the truth about armaments yet?

Would the Allied people perhaps not have believed the truth if it had been told to them? Churchill told the English, Eden told them. Did we believe Lindbergh when he told us about the strength of the German air force two years ago? Do you believe Major Elliott, the military expert, when he says we may very well be invaded by the Germans next summer? Would you even believe Roosevelt or Willkie if they told you that? Wouldn't you think it was a scarehead political statement meant to secure his place in office? Do you believe politicians should abide by or buck (when their information warrants it) the mandates of the people? Do you believe in government by the Gallup and *Fortune* polls?

Was the real trouble that even after the Allies knew what they had to face they didn't get ready in time? Do you think that even if we are not ready now, of course we will be in plenty of time? Isn't that what they were saying?

Was the real trouble that the Allied armament program bogged down in bureaucracy, in military and political and industrial red tape? Do we fully realize that appropriations are not armaments; that "on hand" and "on order" are two quite different things; that a "contract cleared" is not a "contract signed"; that if we scrap what armament-manufacturers and industrialists consider to be reasonable profits for reasonable risks we can't get armed quickly or efficiently; that if we want arms but no profits for manufacturers we must scrap our present economic system? Are we prepared, faced with the threat of war, to have in the name of social justice an economic revolution at home? Or are we committed to the economic compromises the Allies made, which resulted in neither sufficient armament nor social justice?

Was the real trouble that the Allies didn't know what the enemy had to fight them with? Do we really know what Hitler has, or do we just guess that by this time it can't be much?

Was one of the troubles that the Allied government Intelligence Services couldn't get by the Gestapo to find out? How many agents do you think we will get past the Gestapo? Did the Allies both underestimate the enemy and rely too heavily on the Maginot? Can you find many people who really believe the Germans could get here in less than five years? Who doesn't think of the two oceans as the French thought of the Maginot, and the English are still thinking of the Channel?

Was the real trouble, not that they relied on the Maginot too much, but that they didn't build defences on neutral borders for fear their neutral neighbours might think that would look too aggressive? During the next six years we are building our two-ocean navy, shall we also build defences on the Canadian and Mexican borders, or will that look too aggressive to these neighbours? Will they insist on being behind instead of in front of these defences? Shall we build forts on Canadian and Mexican coasts? What shall we do about defending Alaska, separated from us by Canada, and one and one-half miles across the Bering Strait from Russian air bases which are rapidly being built there?

Was their great strategical error that they didn't jump on Hitler while he was busy fighting Poland, and therefore weaker than at any other time? Are we willing to jump on Hitler while he is occupied with Great Britain? Or do we prefer to wait until he can give his undivided attention to us?

Was the real trouble that the Allies took the advice, not of generals, but of politicians in military matters? Do you realize that the problems of total hemisphere defence are headaches that all our generals claim they would not wish on Keitel or Brauchitsch? Do you realize that most of our military men believe with General Pershing that the best way to defend the U.S.A. against Nazi aggression is to stop it now in Europe? Do you know that they are hamstrung hopelessly in all plans for hemisphere defence until the American people and their politicians form a clear-cut foreign policy in South America and the Pacific? Do you realize that they can make few intelligent plans for any kind of defence until the people and the politicians decide what they want to defend and whom they are prepared to attack? Do you realize that most of our military men believe that an army and an air force of less than a million highly trained men are inadequate for any real hemisphere defence?

Was France really defeated, and Great Britain if she is to be, by defence psychology? What do you call American psychology at the moment? Was the real trouble that the Allies did not see that the security of Austria, Czechoslovakia, Republican Spain, and Finland was important to their vital interests? Does the fall of France, the defeat of England, menace our vital interests? If they do, are we going even now to the assistance of Great Britain?

Was the real trouble that although they saw the loss of these countries menaced their vital interests, they were in the end unable to send assistance, and that the road to disaster was "too little or too late or both"? Could we go to Great Britain's assistance with a proper army now if we wanted to?

Was the real trouble that they did not really send all the aid they could, even short of men, for fear of weakening their own defences? Aren't many of us thinking and saying we'd better not send any more planes, any destroyers at all, and very little material to Great Britain now because the time may soon come when we shall need everything we have to defend ourselves?

Was the real trouble that they had no realistic war aims with which to rally their own people or appeal to neutrals? What would be our post-war aims if tomorrow we found ourselves attacked by the Fascist countries of Europe? Would you put Czechoslovakia back, guarantee Poland and France for ever? Would you demand democratic régimes in Germany, Spain, and Italy? Would you federate central Europe? Would you *now* join a League of Nations? On the whole, wouldn't your idea be, like the idea which so many of the English had and which you deplored so, just to lick this fellow Hitler? And if you licked him would you retire once again from Europe's family squabbles and leave anybody who was strong enough to do so in Europe to pick up the pieces? Suppose that person was Stalin. Would you stand for it or would you then fight Russia?

Was the worst error of judgment of the Allies that they thought Hitler would be satisfied with Austria, then with Czechoslovakia? (Some people were quite sure he would be satisfied with Poland if they had let him alone.) Are you one of the many people who feel Hitler will be satisfied with Europe if we let him alone after he has got it?

Was the real trouble that they wanted nothing but peace and security? What else are we willing to fight for?

Or do you think the real trouble with the Allies was their post-war diplomatic ineptitudes, and that France fell and Great Britain faces a defeat as a result of their failures in foreign policy? Did they fail to win military allies soon enough? Should they have lured Fascist Italy long ago away from the Axis or beaten Germany to a deal with Communist Russia? Or did they, two strong democracies, simply not act effectively together soon enough? What strong military alliances have we got? Should we try to lure Japan away from the Fascist bloc? Should we beat Russia to a deal with Japan by making one with her ourselves? Or should we make the deal with Russia? Have we, the third and strongest democracy, now or in the past acted effectively with France and Great Britain?

Were they wrong in counting on the little European nations to swing into their orbit on the strength of trade agreements and offers of "military assistance" which, when the time came, they were unable to deliver? Are we not counting on the little South American neutrals and Caribbean neutrals to do likewise? What kind of assistance could we send to Brazil or the Argentine this year if she were to be attacked?

Shall we appease Japan? Having aided Japan to conquer China, shall we now recognize her puppet government in Nanking? Or shall we make an alliance with Russia and/or China against her? Or should we enter into a joint deal with Russia and Japan against China? If we make a deal with Japan, shall we abandon the Philippines by withdrawing our guarantee, which runs until 1946? Nearer home, what shall we do about Mexico? Does it make any difference to us how many revolutions they have down there, or how any of them turn out? Have we decided how many Nazi or Communist agents we will permit to operate in Mexico? Fifty? Five hundred? Five thousand? Fifty thousand? Five hundred thousand? At what point shall we interfere with the sovereignty of Mexico—long before or just before or after she goes Nazi or Communist, or not at all? And what about the Panama Canal? Do we intend to defend it or do we not? If we intend to defend it, would we follow the advice of our military experts, who claim that in order to do so we must have adequate air and naval bases in the Caribbean and Central America? What diplomatic procedure short of war shall we follow to get them? If diplomacy fails, shall we make war on Caribbean neutrals, on South American neutrals, to secure them? Shall we scrap our good-neighbour policy in order to do this? At what point should we scrap it? As to the whole of South America, what are we trying to accomplish? Preserve democracy in South America, force democracy on South America, or simply militarily defend ourselves? If the Argentine or Brazil or any of the South American governments goes Nazi or Communist, do we propose to stop it? How do we propose to stop it? Do we subsidize counter-revolutions, or do we land the marines and mop them up, or do we withdraw economically and respect their sovereignty so long as they do not threaten to attack us? And in Europe—if Hitler wins a clear victory over Great Britain this year, shall we, as the Lindbergh school thinks we ought, respect the Nazi sovereignty in Europe and try to do business with Hitler, providing he shows no inclination to attack us, or should we refuse to recognize his conquest, or should we seek to promote a quarrel between Germany and Russia or between

Italy and Germany? So they had no foreign policy, and what sort of foreign policy have we got? Our foreign policy is what?

So how are we any different from the Allies?

No, you will say (you must say), we are not different, only we are bigger and richer and stronger and farther away than the Allies were. These Germans are not, after all, supermen; they are simply efficient, and that's not a word on which Nazis have any patent. Not so many years ago—as recently as 1918, in fact—the word seemed to be made in America. We believe (you say) that the American production machine, once it gets going again, will make that of the Nazis and all their combined vassals and slaves look like a child's gadget. Naturally this machine doesn't run very well in the hands of tinkerers, soothsayers, and men whose counsels are hopelessly divided even if they are well-meaning, honourable fellows, but we'll get all those wrinkles ironed out. We'll survive our domestic squabbles over conscription and social legislation and everything else. We are not rotted internally. We know what we want: we want to get ready, and we will get ready. We may go a little totalitarian in the process; that's inevitable, of course, in any realistic defence effort; but fundamentally we will, like the British, still stay democratic.

Now (you say) all these questions you have asked are paralysing and frightening for only one reason. We are not ready yet, but we are going to be in spite of every difficulty which besets a democracy trying to prepare for war in time of peace. Oh, do believe us, we are going to get armed—armed to the teeth, so that, in the words of Paul Reynaud, we shall be prepared "for all eventualities." We believe we can do it in time. Yes, that's what the Allies were saying, but we really will do it.

Very well, I believe you: let us choose between the extremely optimistic view of experts that we will be "ready by 1941" and the pessimistic one that we can't be ready until 1944. Let us say we are ready by 1942. Let us even admit that by that time we have the mightiest military machine on earth, adequate to meet the physical forces of the whole world (which will then be aligned against us), a machine impregnable in our continental domain, and run and assembled, if you can imagine such a thing, democratically under our present economic system. In short, we are ready.

Ready for what?

Shall we continue to appease Japan if by that time Japan has conquered Asia, or shall we then attack? Or shall we then attack Hitler? Shall we land an expeditionary force in Europe? To fight for what? To fight whom? The French if they have accepted a Hitler peace and gone totalitarian? The British in the same case? The Belgians, the Dutch, the Spanish if they have also accepted Hitler? If we win what shall we do with Europe? Or shall we attack Mexico or South America?

Why? To accomplish what?

Or shall we wait for Hitler to attack us? How long shall we wait? One year? Two? Three? Four? Five? Ten? Twenty years? How will the farm group, the factory group, the business people, and the taxpayers feel about staying armed to the teeth? How long can a democracy remain an armed camp without going totalitarian, or without breeding Communism on the home front?

Shall we try to do business with Hitler while we are waiting for him to attack? Shall we say that our policy is going to be Armed Appeasement? If it looks as though we could do business with him, if it looks as though he were satisfied with what he had got, if he swears he has no more territorial demands on the world, that the Monroe Doctrine is the thing he believes in most, next to *Mein Kampf*, shall we believe him? Shall we begin to demobilize? How soon? How fast? How much?

Perhaps you think that if we are really armed and stay armed and "ready for all eventualities" in either ocean, time will play on our side and pestilence, famine, and revolution in Europe will bring Hitler to his knees. The Balkans will come aflame, Stalin and Hitler will "finish each other off." That is of course what the Allies were hoping. But supposing it does happen, how will it help us? Do we prefer pestilence, famine, revolution, a Europe aflame for years, to the peace of Hitler? Is this your cheerful thought for the future? Or do you think somebody will take over and bring order out of chaos? Stalin, perhaps? How would a totally Communist Europe help us? Another dictator? How would that help? A beneficent democratic dictator? Then why not we?

Isn't it the truth that even if we had tomorrow fifty thousand airplanes, one hundred Panzer divisions, five million trained men under arms, and a navy twice as big as it is, we still shouldn't know what to do with our force except sit home year after year and wait? Or do you on the face of it feel that is an absurd supposition? Do you feel we would use it, would do something with it?

What?

Why?

Quo vadis?

The problem which faces us does not therefore seem to be simply one of acquiring armed might. It is also a question of what to do with armed might if in time we do acquire it.

The real question would seem to be to what use, to what spiritual or ideological use, shall we put this physical force? What spiritual ideals or ideas have we?

To return to the trouble with the Allies:

Was the real trouble that they hated all their neighbours and even one another? Whom do we love now in this world except ourselves, we Americans? Do we even love one another? Was the real trouble that by letting republican Spain down, by letting down Austria, Czechoslovakia, Finland, they let down the ideal of democracy in the world? In this sense have we not also let down France and England?

Are we more patriotic than they were? There are hundreds of thousands of men dead in France and England now who died to prove the answer is No.

Does America, do you as an individual, care any less for pleasure, for comfort, for material success than the average Frenchman did?

Then here is the simplest and perhaps the most fundamental question of all: Are we a more Christian nation than France and England now?

Allied spokesmen have sometimes said that they fought to destroy the "pagan" dictator. Do you really believe the Allies fought for Christ, or the Christian way of life? Do you think they were really Christian soldiers marching onward to the foe? Would it occur to you to call yourself a "Christian soldier" if tomorrow we were attacked? Weren't you rather disgusted when they poured into Notre-Dame and Westminster Abbey after the invasion? Didn't you think they were rather late in contacting their "Christian God"? How many of us have yet discussed on our knees with God this crisis we are facing? Wasn't part of the freedom they wanted from Hitler, and the freedom we want, the freedom *not* to worship God as we please? If they were fighting for God and Christian civilization, why didn't they fight the first day Hitler began to pursue his policy of religious persecution? Did it occur to any of us to do so? Were we not all, all the Christian nations, simply content to deplore and denounce but not to act about it? Did they then simply think of God, when they thought of Him at all, as a Super-Economist who only operated on the gold standard or whose emissaries on earth were all labour leaders and unionists? Are we not in the habit of confusing Christian civilization with private monopoly, with a forty-hour week, with a socialization of utilities? Have we perhaps not come to believe, as they did, that "Christianity" is just another word for anti-totalitarian economics? In that sense we may say we are willing to "defend Christianity," but in what other?

In the end wasn't the real trouble that the Allies never saw in time anything worth dying for except their shirts or the land they were standing on? And didn't they discover that those who hold this belief paramount often find it easier in the end to save their shirts and their land and their property by surrender?

What were the real questions for which the Allies had no answer?

What is the meaning of man?

Why is he on earth?

Where is he going?

The Allies had no plan, no dreams, no ideal of a future, no standard to which the wise and honourable in every country could repair. They forgot the world was all of a piece. They might have survived that geographical myopia, but what they could not survive and what we cannot survive is spiritual blindness to the fact that the spiritual world too is all of a piece. Or isn't it?

In the world of men's souls are there Monroe Doctrines?

This is the unhappy truth: like the Allies we have no counter-revolutionary ideals, no dynamic ideals at all to set up against that of the Nazis.

Is it possible that what we need most now is not a program for a party, not a plan for national defence, but a redefining of a Way of Life for Christian and Democratic people?

A new way of life is what the Nazi revolutionaries gave their people. And what in our secret hearts alarms us most, or ought to alarm us most, is not the economic aspects of that life but the fact that it is fundamentally pagan and undemocratic.

But because we all are ourselves (and by "we" I mean all the professed enemies of Nazism everywhere) not really democratic or Christian, we concentrate our fire on Nazism's economic aspects. These will greatly damage but they will not destroy our civilization in the end.

The best defence against a powerful and positive dynamic ideology is neither verbal attack nor criticism, which are useful, but to set up an equally powerful and dynamic ideology against it.

So today we Americans are standing at a great crossroad in the evolution of civilization. There are three signs at that crossroad. One sign says: "Road for Victims." That road is for the people who close their eyes or turn their backs or plug their ears, for the people who quarrel among themselves far more bitterly than they are willing to quarrel with Hitler, for the people who by and large don't care who worships God or how He is worshipped providing they are not obliged to worship anybody themselves, for the people who think "Democracy is probably a failure," and for the people who wait "prepared and armed to the teeth" for the thing to happen to them.

You will find this road cluttered with Czechs and Belgians and Poles and Dutch and Norwegians and French and perhaps tomorrow the English.

The second signpost says: "Road for Fellow Travellers." These two roads meet eventually. On it you will find all the Balkans and Russians and Japs and some South Americans and Spaniards and all the peace-at-any-pricers and the armed or unarmed appeasers, and a wonderful crew of cynical or opportunistic or terrified folk who set out down that road armed with a little lie or a little hope and the habit of mentally cheating. The great thing they have in common is that they are all spiritually and morally bankrupt. This is above all the main highway for people who think: "Maybe we can do business with Hitler." But in the end they all die or are enslaved, or they all raise their right arms and cry: "*Heil Hitler!*"

There is of course the third road. It is narrow and straight and hard for the feet, and perhaps bloody (but not nearly so bloody as the first one). No one in Europe took it. At this time it looks as though no one here intends to take it. That is the road of a new democratic and Christian revolution. Perhaps you do not like the word "revolution"? Will you like it better if I say this is the road of Christian and democratic imperialism? Its plan is simple: to march forward and conquer the world again, piece by piece, for all free and Christian people; to battle the flag of Nazism on every border wherever it flies in whatever hemisphere. Does the program seem to you over-ambitious? And does throwing the word "Christian" in make you vaguely uneasy?

Well, we are the only nation of so-called Christians and so-called Democrats strong enough to take that road now. And do you doubt for a moment if we took that road in the name of God that we would come to the end of it victorious?

If "poor Germany" with eight million unemployed, ringed around with a wall of steel, could physically conquer half of Europe and rot the other half with her pagan, immoral, revolutionary ideas (or don't you believe them to be entirely pagan and immoral?—does totalitarianism in many of its aspects intrigue you?—do you see its merits?—does it offer an easy solution?—then don't bother to read this, you are already beginning to cheat, you are already a Nazi fellow traveller) what could we not do with our greater brains and greater initiative and all the raw materials and the greatest productive plants in the world out of which, as you have already announced, we are determined to create the greatest army on earth?

I ask again what shall we do with that army?

Quo vadis?

The situation as it stands in America is just about as it stood in the spring in Europe. You see few people here in America who really care very much about living a Christian life in a democratic world. But I am glad that I went to Europe in the spring, because there I found out what I went to find out: I found out what I, anyway, mean by Democracy. I mean what the Declaration of Independence meant by it: "Liberty and justice for all." And when the Declaration of Independence said "for all," it did not mean merely for United States citizens; it was written before there was a United States of America, before there were Americans. Then we were a people who had left the Old World in order to redefine and live a Christian way of life, and who found that one of the principles of a Christian way of life was "Liberty and justice for all." So we fought for it, and that is what made us Americans. And out of that revolutionary belief, by the grace of God, we made of ourselves a great and mighty nation, so mighty that we could if we would, again by the grace of God, set out on a program for a thousand years of world democracy and world Christianity.

But I think if we no longer believe what we believed then and are no longer willing to fight for it, it is very likely that our "Christian Democracy," like this book, is at last finished.

These are the good old days now.

A NOTE ON THE *Type*

IN WHICH THIS BOOK IS SET

This book was set on the Linotype in Janson, a recutting made direct from the type cast from matrices made by Anton Janson some time between 1660 and 1687.

Of Janson's origin nothing is known. He may have been a relative of Justus Janson, a printer of Danish birth who practised in Leipzig from 1614 to 1635. Some time between 1657 and 1668 Anton Janson, a punch-cutter and type-founder, bought from the Leipzig printer Johann Erich Hahn the type-foundry which had formerly been a part of the printing house of M. Friedrich Lankisch. Janson's types were first shown in a specimen sheet issued at Leipzig about 1675. Janson's successor, and perhaps his son-in-law, Johann Karl Edling, issued a specimen sheet of Janson types in 1689.

COMPOSED, PRINTED, AND BOUND
BY H. WOLFF, NEW YORK.
PAPER MADE
BY S. D. WARREN CO., BOSTON